LUTHERAN AND CATHOLIC
RECONCILIATION
ON JUSTIFICATION

To: Paul and Mary
With gratitude for many years
of friendship and common cause
in promoting Christian unity,

Jack Radano

Lutheran and Catholic Reconciliation on Justification

*A Chronology of the Holy See's Contributions, 1961-1999,
to a New Relationship Between Lutherans and Catholics
and to Steps Leading to the* Joint Declaration
on the Doctrine of Justification

John A. Radano

WILLIAM B. EERDMANS PUBLISHING COMPANY
GRAND RAPIDS, MICHIGAN / CAMBRIDGE, U.K.

Published 2009 by

Wm. B. Eerdmans Publishing Co.

2140 Oak Industrial Drive N.E., Grand Rapids, Michigan 49505 /
P.O. Box 163, Cambridge CB3 9PU U.K.

Printed in the United States of America

15 14 13 12 11 10 09   7 6 5 4 3 2 1

Library of Congress Cataloging-in-Publication Data

Radano, John A.

Lutheran and Catholic reconciliation on justification: a chronology of the
Holy See's contributions, 1961-1999, to a new relationship between
Lutherans and Catholics and to steps leading to the Joint Declaration
on the Doctrine of Justification / John A. Radano.

p.   cm.

ISBN 978-0-8028-4860-4 (pbk.: alk. paper)

1. Lutheran Church — Relations — Catholic Church. 2. Catholic Church —
Relations — Lutheran Church. 3. Joint Declaration on the
Doctrine of Justification.   I. Title.

BX8063.7.C3R33   2009

234'.7 — dc22

2009019366

www.eerdmans.com

Dedicated with Gratitude to
Archbishop Peter L. Gerety
Archbishop Emeritus of Newark

and to

the Memory of Johannes Cardinal Willebrands (1909-2006)
Second President of the
Pontifical Council for Promoting Christian Unity

Contents

Part II
From Centuries of Isolation to Dialogue and Mutual Respect
The Immediate Post-Conciliar Period, During the Pontificate of Pope Paul VI, 1966-1978

Contents

Part IV
From Acknowledging Common Bonds
of Faith and Friendship to Mutual Commitment

Developments During the Pontificate of Pope John Paul II, 1988-1999, Leading to the Joint Declaration

CONTENTS

Foreword

Edward Idris Cardinal Cassidy
President Emeritus,
Pontifical Council for Promoting Christian Unity

As we celebrate forty years of official Catholic involvement in the modern ecumenical movement, there is undoubtedly good reason to be satisfied with the progress made. At the same time, those involved in the search for restoring Christian unity are well aware that the road still to be covered is long and not without difficulty. The new relationships that have been forged since the Second Vatican Council by the Catholic Church with other churches and ecclesial communions provide the Catholic ecumenist with solid hope for the future journey under the powerful guidance of the Holy Spirit.

As Pope John Paul II pointed out in the encyclical letter *Ut Unum Sint* (On Commitment to Ecumenism), the ecumenical movement is built on three pillars: prayer, to which His Holiness assigns the priority; cooperation and common witness, seen as a school of ecumenism; and theological dialogue as an essential means of overcoming the doctrinal misunderstandings and divisions of the past.

It is in dialogue especially that the way is cleared for Christian communions to enter into full communion. All the dialogues in which the Catholic Church is involved with churches coming from the Reformation period have reported good progress in their attempts to clarify and seek consensus on the doctrinal disputes that were at the heart of the separations within Western Christianity at that time. The dialogue has not only led the various partners involved to a new appreciation of each other's faith understanding, but in fact each partner readily admits to having been enriched in its own faith understanding as a result of the discussions.

Moreover, there have been particular achievements of the dialogues that have brought all concerned great joy and given the dialogue partners reason to hope more firmly in the future development of their relationship. Within the ecumenical movement in general, certain official agreements come at once to mind: the Christological declarations between the Catholic Church and the Ancient Oriental Churches, together with the ARCIC I report on eucharist and ministry, and more recently, the *Joint Declaration on the Doctrine of Justification* between the Catholic Church and the Lutheran World Federation, which forms the subject of this work by Monsignor John Radano.

The *Joint Declaration on the Doctrine of Justification* was the fruit of dedicated dialogue between the LWF and the Catholic Church from almost immediately after the Second Vatican Council. It was the first official dialogue between the Catholic Church and a church coming from the Reformation period. Beginning already with the Lutheran observers to the Council, a gradual realization between Lutherans and Catholics that they were "all under one Christ," and that more actually united them than divided them, encouraged the dialogue members to move forward in hope to a new common understanding of questions that for centuries had kept them apart.

By 1985, substantial convergences were being seen in areas of justification, baptism, eucharist, and ministry. A decision to concentrate on reaching an accord on justification led to the signing of the *Joint Declaration on the Doctrine of Justification* between the Catholic Church and the LWF in Augsburg, Germany, on October 31, 1999.

In many ways, the *Joint Declaration* is unique even among other official dialogue agreements. For it goes to the very heart of a division within the Roman Catholic Church at the time of the Reformation and is the only such accord so far officially approved by the Catholic Church and churches coming from the Reformation.

The signing of the *Joint Declaration* not only gave those involved in dialogue renewed courage and hope, but sent out a clear message to a divided Christianity that even such divergences can be resolved in sincere dialogue which "seeks the truth in love." The 1999 signing also provided them with a fine example of how such dialogue can be conducted in order to reach the desired goal.

Such examples become all the more important as time passes, and new members take over in the dialogues from the pioneers of the first forty years. They will need to look back and learn from the early dialogue efforts that have produced lasting results, and find there information that will guide their ongoing search for still greater unity.

It is for this reason in particular that Monsignor John Radano's exceptionally thorough and detailed account of the development of the consensus between the LWF and the Catholic Church on justification, from the days of the Second Vatican Council itself up to the signing of the *Joint Declaration* in 1999, will be valuable guidance and assistance to those responsible for future Lutheran-Catholic dialogue, and indeed to the ecumenical movement in general.

The story of the way in which the seed sown during the Second Vatican Council developed into a plant that developed over thirty years and produced lasting fruit in the form of the *Joint Declaration* is truly fascinating. Surely it was an example of one planting, another watering, but God giving the growth (cf. 1 Cor. 3:6).

Foreword

REVEREND DR. ISHMAEL NOKO
General Secretary,
Lutheran World Federation

As ecumenists today engage in discussions about the reconfiguration of the ecumenical movement one cannot help but ask the question: Why now? There are many answers to this question, but it is important to realize that they are rooted partially in what has happened ecumenically during the last fifty to sixty years. During this period ecumenical dialogues have resulted in the achievement of several theological agreements that have laid a strong foundation for church fellowship.

During this same period we have also witnessed church fellowship coming into being in the regions of Europe and North America and in a limited way in other parts of the world. These ecumenical achievements include the signing of the *Joint Declaration on the Doctrine of Justification* (JD) on October 31, 1999, in Augsburg, Germany.

The *Joint Declaration* was a result of conscientious and meticulous joint work by theologians from the Lutheran World Federation and the Roman Catholic Church. We are grateful to God for these "lettered" women and men who took part in that dialogue and who sought patiently to listen to one another; allowing themselves to be led by God's Spirit in finding new language to communicate the gospel of Jesus Christ. In this demanding journey, which required great patience, they rediscovered new ways of talking to each other without undermining the integrity of the gospel's message.

Lutherans and Catholics learned a lot about each other's position during the various studies leading up to the JD itself. We learned that it is too simplistic to claim that the Roman Catholic Church teaches that human beings are saved by works alone and/or that Lutheran churches teach that works are irrelevant in the life of faith.

Bringing peace between our churches on the fundamentals of a doctrine that has for centuries been the lightning rod for conflict between us confers on the *Joint Declaration* the status of a document contributing to peace in society as a whole. It should be recalled that the conflict at the time of the Reformation not only affected the church, but society at large. It manifested itself in wars and political and economic tensions with implications that continue. These theological, ecclesial, and social divisions created in Europe during the Reformation were exported to the rest of the world through colonization, immigration, and missionary activities.

In this light the signing of the *Joint Declaration* has helped to close a chapter of conflict and division in Europe and the world. One of the most important messages of the *Joint Declaration* is that, wherever in the world they may live, Lutherans and Roman Catholics are not enemies anymore but sisters and brothers in Christ.

Martin Luther has often been described as a pessimist regarding human nature and therefore Lutheran anthropology has unfortunately often been considered "negative." However, when Martin Luther preached about human inability to contribute to salvation through works, the main thrust of his teaching was not negative in relation to the human being, but awesomely positive in relation to God and to our salvation in Christ. He sought to make it clear that even the noblest intentions and strivings are subject to sin. Therefore, his purpose was not to discourage, but rather to encourage believers in his own time by pointing to the sufficiency of God's grace.

The *Joint Declaration,* supported by the Annex, makes it very clear that for Lutherans a life in faith is necessarily also a life with good works. Lutherans should see that the main concern of the Decree on Justification promulgated by the Council of Trent goes in the same direction. If, on these points, the *Joint Declaration* can bring a corrected picture into the Christian education material for confirmants, seminary textbooks, etc., all our efforts will have been worthwhile.

I hope that the *Joint Declaration* will be an important contribution to creating understanding between the Roman Catholic and the Reformation churches. Insofar as it addresses and clarifies key aspects of the pivotal issue of dispute at the time of the Reformation, the *Joint Declaration* may help build a bridge between the Roman Catholic and the Reformation churches. The success of the *Joint Declaration* process, especially on a doctrinal issue of such centrality, is an important encouragement to the whole ecumenical movement as it strives towards visible unity in Christ.

Moreover, I would suggest that the positive experience of the process and outcome of the *Joint Declaration* affirms the ecumenical value of bilateral dialogues. Bilateral dialogues, in my view, are not inconsistent with a broad ecumenical commitment. Certain issues specifically relevant to particular church relationships are best addressed bilaterally, and the deeper understanding created between partners in such bilateral dialogues helps to promote ecumenical openness.

The *Joint Declaration* process has also helped the Lutheran churches involved to deepen their understanding and practice of communion. Historically, the Lutheran churches have had differently nuanced understandings of the doctrine of justification. The opportunity to consult widely among themselves during the course of the JD process helped them, for the first time, to reach a solid consensus on this fundamental article of faith. At the same time, this process has strengthened the Lutheran communion as well as its instrument, the Lutheran World Federation. A wide communion of churches needs such an instrument precisely for common ecumenical purposes such as the *Joint Declaration* and for a common witness in our increasingly global society.

Lutherans and Catholics can now face remaining difficult questions with courage and mutual trust. This *Declaration* succeeds in demonstrating precisely this point. We are grateful to Monsignor John Radano for this meticulous piece of work which is an important gift to the church today and the church in the future.

Acknowledgments

With gratitude I acknowledge the generosity of those Catholics and Lutherans who took the time to read all or part of this manuscript while it was in preparation, providing valuable suggestions and information. These include, in alphabetical order, Dr. Eugene Brand, Edward Idris Cardinal Cassidy, Revd. Norman A. Hjelm, Walter Cardinal Kasper (chapter 11), Dr. George Lindbeck, Revd. Dr. Ishmael Noko, Revd. Sven Oppegaard, Dr. William Rusch, Revd. Dr. Matthias Türk (chapter 12), Fr. Jared Wicks, SJ. All of them have participated at one stage or another, and some now, in fostering the new relationships between Lutherans and Catholics that began to evolve at the Second Vatican Council, as guided especially by the Secretariat (later Pontifical Council) for Promoting Christian Unity and the Lutheran World Federation. Most of them have been or continue to be participants in official Lutheran-Catholic dialogue. I offer a special word of thanks to Dr. William Rusch, with whom I have been in contact for more than twenty-five years concerning matters of Lutheran-Catholic relations. The suggestions of all of these friends and colleagues about the text itself or about bibliographical materials related to it have helped improve the text.

I want to express appreciation to Edward Cardinal Cassidy, President Emeritus (since 2001) of the Pontifical Council for Promoting Christian Unity, and to Revd. Dr. Ishmael Noko, General Secretary of the Lutheran World Federation, for writing forewords to the volume. They were in close contact during the 1990s when the *Joint Declaration* was being drafted, together fostering its development. When a crisis developed in 1998-99 that threatened to delay or even prevent the official signing of the *Joint Declaration,* many persons contributed in different ways to resolving it. But it was they who had particular responsibility to see that the obstacles were removed, and remained in close contact with each other as steps were taken to resolve the crisis. Both Cardinal Cassidy and Dr. Noko were then among the official signatories of the *Joint Declaration* on October 31, 1999.

I want to thank Catholic News Service, copyright holder of *Council Daybook Vatican II* (3 volumes), for permission to use excerpts from that source, which was originally published 1965-66 by the National Catholic Welfare Conference.

Gratitude is offered as well to the leaders and staff of the Centro Pro Unione in Rome, especially to its Director, Fr. James Puglisi, SA, and to Fr. Brian Terry, SA, who opened its library to the author even during some off-hours, and to its research assistant Dr. Teresa Francesca Rossi for help in finding some particular bibliographical resources. Helen Putsman Penet, Photo Archivist of the Lutheran World Federation, provided several photos of the first meeting in 1965 of the Lutheran-Catholic "joint working group" that made preparations for the international dialogue which began in 1967. The author expresses deep gratitude to Silvana Salvati of the Pontifical Council for Promoting Christian Unity for her generous editorial assistance. The author is indebted to the assistance of many persons. Whatever shortcomings may be found in this account are the responsibility of the author.

Introduction

The Second Vatican Council had, as a primary concern, the promoting of "the restoration of unity among all Christians" (Decree on Ecumenism, *Unitatis redintegratio* [= UR] 1). The Council's mandate on ecumenism was reflected in its various documents, and spelled out in detail in its Decree on Ecumenism. Among many efforts to bring an ecumenical spirit into the Catholic Church, and to promote new attitudes towards other Christians, and new contacts with them, the Council called for dialogue "between competent experts from different Churches and Communities" through which everyone could gain "a truer knowledge and more just appreciation of the teaching and religious life of both Communions." It envisioned that, through dialogue and other ecumenical activities, "little by little . . . the obstacles to perfect ecclesiastical communion" could be overcome (cf. UR 4).

The *Joint Declaration on the Doctrine of Justification* (= JD) is one of the best results of such dialogue. Its achievement was to overcome one of the significant obstacles to perfect ecclesiastical communion between Lutherans and Catholics. The understanding of justification, which concerns how God brings persons into a right relation with himself, overcoming their sin and its effects, was highly disputed at the time of the Reformation. But the *Joint Declaration,* officially signed by representatives of the Catholic Church and the Lutheran World Federation [= LWF] on October 31, 1999, in Augsburg, Germany, states that Lutherans and Catholics have achieved a consensus in basic truths of the doctrine of justification (*JD* 40).[1] It states that the teaching of the Lutheran churches and of the Roman Catholic Church found therein does not fall under the condemnations formulated in the sixteenth century by the Council of Trent and the Lutheran Confessions towards the other's view of this doctrine (cf. *JD* 41). This result is historic since both Lutherans and Catholics understand that the doctrine of justification was decisively important for the Reformation.[2] When Edward Idris Cardinal Cassidy, President of the Pontifical Council for Promoting Christian Unity, made public the Catholic Church's formal approval of the *JD* on June 25, 1998, he stated the achievement that the *JD* represents in relation to sixteenth-century divisions in this way: "the consensus reached on the doctrine of justification, despite its limitations, virtually resolves a long disputed question at the close of the twentieth century. . . ."[3]

This essay seeks to trace the path of this significant ecumenical development over more than three decades, from Vatican II and the mandate for ecumenism it gave to the Catholic Church, to the successful achievement of the signing of the *JD* in 1999.

A Broader Chronology

The specific development of the *JD*, which took place during the 1990s, was made possible by a new relationship that developed over several de-

1. *Joint Declaration on the Doctrine of Justification*, Official Common Statement by the Lutheran World Federation and the Catholic Church, Annex to the Official Common Statement, Augsburg, 31 October 1999 (Geneva: Lutheran World Federation, 1999). The *Joint Declaration* and the official responses to it in 1998 by the Lutheran World Federation and the Catholic Church are found in Pontifical Council for Promoting Christian Unity, Vatican City, *Information Service* (= *IS*) 98 (1998): 81-100. Documentation relating to the official signing of the *JD* on October 31, 1999, is found in *IS* 103 (2000): 3-35. The original language of the *Joint Declaration* was German. The English translation was prepared in parallel to the German original by English-speaking members of the drafting committee that developed the *Joint Declaration*.

2. *All Under One Christ, 1980: Statement on the Augsburg Confession by the Roman Catholic/Lutheran Joint Commission*, no. 14, in *Growth in Agreement: Reports and Agreed Statements of Ecumenical Conversations on a World Level* (= *GA*), ed. Harding Meyer and Lukas Vischer (New York/Ramsey: Paulist Press; Geneva: World Council of Churches, 1984), p. 243.

3. "Presentation of the Roman Catholic Response to the Vatican *Sala Stampa* of His Eminence Edward Idris Cardinal Cassidy, President of the Pontifical Council for Promoting Christian Unity, 25 June 1998," *IS* 98 (1998): 97.

cades after Vatican II between Catholics and Lutherans, especially those represented by the Lutheran World Federation. This essay presents a broader chronology illustrating the evolution of that new relationship, and in that context, traces the dialogue on the specific issue of justification, and the specific steps leading to the *Joint Declaration*.

The new relationship between Lutherans and Catholics, of course, contrasted sharply with previous centuries of virtual mutual isolation. This change involved decisions taken at the highest levels within the Catholic Church, and in relationship with the Lutheran World Federation[4] and with some LWF member churches, which fostered closer bonds and fellowship, including the theological dialogue that made the *JD*'s development and signing possible. This new context was necessary for agreement on justification to develop. "Stating a consensus in questions of doctrine is not only a matter of theological inquiry and judgment, but also a matter of trust developed in many and manifold encounters, common engagement, and in the experience of believing together in Christ."[5] Therefore, this essay traces important contacts that fostered the fellowship and common trust between Lutherans and Catholics required for the mutual commitment the official signing of the *Joint Declaration* represents.

Contributions of the Holy See

While this process leading to the *JD* was obviously a joint venture with the LWF, the role of the Catholic Church is the primary focus of this study. At the same time, this narrative shows that there was a full and equal partnership between the Catholic Church and the LWF in this ecumenical event, and that in the decades of Lutheran and Catholic ecumenical engagement described here, it was often the Lutheran side that took key initiatives. While this process involved not only international Lutheran-Catholic con-

4. The Lutheran World Federation, with headquarters in Geneva, Switzerland, is a communion of 138 churches, found in 77 countries around the world, comprising approximately 66 million persons. Most of the member churches are Lutheran churches, although a few are the result of church unions in which a Lutheran church has joined with another or other churches. For these statistics see *Lutheran World Information* (= *LWI*) 01, 2005.

5. From the discussion on the *JD* at the 9th Assembly of the LWF. See "Reports and Commitments," *Official Report of the Ninth Assembly of the Lutheran World Federation, Hong Kong, 8-16 July 1997* (Geneva: Lutheran World Federation), p. 46.

tacts and dialogue, but also significant contacts and dialogue between them in various countries,[6] the emphasis here is on the decisions and activities of the Holy See. There are other sides of this story that can therefore be taken up. Since they are not taken up here, this project cannot be a full history of events leading to the *Joint Declaration*.

This account is limited in other ways. It does not trace the evolution of theological issues treated and formulated in the *Joint Declaration,* a task that has been done elsewhere.[7] Nor does it discuss extensively those Lutheran-Catholic dialogue reports, international or national, or the theological issues treated in them, which are listed in the *Joint Declaration* as "resources" used in the formulation of some of its paragraphs. It refers to them, showing their importance within the developments leading to the *JD,* but does not discuss their findings at length. Theological analysis of these reports has been done elsewhere. Furthermore, this account refers to (cf. Chapter 11) but does not discuss at length the intensive theological debate and disputes over the *JD* as it was being completed, and which even carried over after the *JD* was signed in October 1999.

This presentation is mainly a chronology of the contributions of the Holy See,[8] in contact and dialogue with Lutherans, to steps leading to the *Joint Declaration* over almost four decades. It highlights in particular the ecumenical commitment to the new relationship with Lutheran churches, and to the *Joint Declaration* that resulted, of three Popes, and of offices and

6. Cf. *Justification by Faith* (1985) of the Lutheran-Catholic dialogue in the USA, and *The Condemnations of the Reformation Era: Do They Still Divide?* 1990 (original German 1986), produced by the Catholic, Lutheran, Reformed Study Commission in Germany, both of which were important resources used in the process of formulation of the *JD* (see Chapter 5 below).

7. See, for example, Pawel Holc, *Un ampio consenso sulla dottrina della giustificazione: Studio sul dialogo teologico cattolico-luterano* (Roma: Editrice Pontificia Università Gregoriana, 1999, Tesi Gregoriana. Serie teologia; 053); André Birmelé, *La Communion Ecclésiale. Progrès oecuméniques et enjeux méthodologiques* (Paris: Editions du Cerf; Genève: Labor et Fides, 2000), Chapter 3, "La Déclaration Commune"; Cardinal Walter Kasper, "The Joint Declaration on the Doctrine of Justification," *IS* 117 (2004): 155-60.

8. The Holy See is distinguished from Vatican City State, which is a country in its own right. The Holy See, which has its headquarters in Vatican City State, refers to the central administration of the Catholic Church, which includes the Roman Pontiff, who is the Bishop of Rome (the successor of St. Peter), but also the Secretariat of State and the other dicasteries (Congregations, Pontifical Councils, and other offices) of the Roman Curia. These dicasteries act both in the name and with the authority of the Roman Pontiff. Cf. *The Code of Canon Law* (1983), canon 361.

leading officials of the Roman Curia, especially the Secretariat (from 1988, the Pontifical Council) for Promoting Christian Unity. Events are traced from 1961 to 1999. It is hoped that this chronology will provide a helpful and broad perspective for appreciating the range of ecumenical contacts and developments that led to the *Joint Declaration.*

Earlier Studies

Even though the Second Vatican Council was decisive for a new beginning in Lutheran-Catholic relations, theological discussion and research took place before and during the Council in which "the former Catholic polemics against Luther and the Protestant polemics against any kind of Catholic thinking had receded and a new way of listening to each other began."[9] These included, in the 1960s, numerous appreciative studies of Luther's thought by Catholics and appreciative studies by Lutherans of the thought of Thomas Aquinas.[10] The theme of justification was a major subject of Catholic research on Luther and of Protestant research into Thomas Aquinas. The results suggested that "Thomas and Luther do not exclude each other in this field."[11] Diversity remains, not because Luther and Thomas held opposed dogmatic convictions, but because their conceptual tools and theological aims differ.[12] Recent Catholic study of the Augsburg Confession (1530) and the response to it then by Catholic apologists has shown that "on the doctrines of sin, justification by faith, and sacramental mediation of divine grace an agreement was reached on August 16, 1530 . . . ," but this did not flower into reconciliation because of insuperable differences over other significant issues.[13] At the same time Lutheran studies of the

9. Ulrich Kühn, "The Joint Declaration on the Doctrine of Justification: Opportunities, Problems, Hopes," *Gregorianum* 80, no. 4 (1999): 610-11, quote 611.

10. Jared Wicks offers a concise summary and overview of some key studies in "The Lutheran-Catholic Joint Declaration on the Doctrine of Justification," *Ecumenical Trends,* June 1998, 5/85-6/86. Also, Kühn, "The Joint Declaration on the Doctrine of Justification," p. 611.

11. Kühn, "The Joint Declaration on the Doctrine of Justification," p. 611.

12. Wicks, "The Lutheran-Catholic Joint Declaration on the Doctrine of Justification," referring to the findings of H. Otto Pesch.

13. Wicks, "The Lutheran-Catholic Joint Declaration on the Doctrine of Justification," after referring to a study of Vinzenz Pfnür.

Council of Trent's decree on justification brought out that what Trent condemned did not correspond to Lutheran teaching, e.g., on "faith alone," and the forensic declaration of righteousness.[14]

The Decisive Role of the Council

But while such convergence, even agreement, was emerging before and during the Second Vatican Council, it was this Council that enabled the Catholic Church to commit itself to the one ecumenical movement, and to formal dialogue with the Lutheran World Federation. In this new context, these new discoveries could be explored further toward bringing reconciliation between Lutherans and Catholics, and eventually, in 1999, to the *Joint Declaration*. From the perspective of the Catholic Church's participation, the *Joint Declaration* was, in a particular way, the fruit of the Second Vatican Council.

In light of the focus just described, this work is organized in four parts, with each part representing a period of time corresponding to that of the Second Vatican Council and the pontificates of the subsequent decades. At the same time one finds appropriate transition points from one of these periods to the next, which also warrants this arrangement. Part I, "Conciliar Foundations of Dialogue," covers events before and during the Second Vatican Council, 1961-65, when the seeds of a new relationship between the Catholic Church and the Lutheran World Federation were planted, and first steps toward dialogue were taken. Part II, "From Centuries of Isolation to Dialogue and Mutual Respect," covers the immediate post-conciliar period, and the rest of the pontificate of Pope Paul VI, 1966-78. In this period, a variety of contacts between the Holy See and the Lutheran World Federation developed, the formal theological dialogue between Lutherans and Catholics began, and the initial acknowledgment was expressed, at high levels, of a growing convergence on the doctrine of justification. Part III, "From Dialogue and Mutual Respect to Acknowledging Common Bonds of Faith and Friendship," covers the first decade of the pontificate of Pope John Paul II, 1978-87. Contacts between the Holy See and the LWF deepened, but contacts between the Pope and the wider Lutheran family in different countries also developed. More than once John

14. Wicks, "The Lutheran-Catholic Joint Declaration on the Doctrine of Justification."

Paul II acknowledged that Lutherans and Catholics share common bonds of faith. In the theological dialogue, a far-reaching consensus on justification was deepened and affirmed. Part IV, "From Acknowledging Common Bonds of Faith and Friendship to Mutual Commitment," corresponds to the second decade of the pontificate of John Paul II, 1988-99, when the Holy See and the LWF began to cooperate in new ways, turned decisively toward the official response and reception of dialogue results, focused specifically on justification, worked together to develop the *Joint Declaration on the Doctrine of Justification,* and made a formal mutual commitment by officially signing it in 1999.

PART I

Conciliar Foundations of Dialogue

*Events Before and During the
Second Vatican Council, 1961-1965*

CHAPTER 1

Initial Contacts Between the Catholic Church and the Lutheran World Federation Through Observers at Vatican II

The initial contact between the Holy See and the Lutheran World Federation that would lead to a continuing relationship and official dialogue concerned the invitation to the LWF to send observers to the Second Vatican Council.

Pope John XXIII had announced his decision to call a Council on January 25, 1959. Intending that the Council would also be concerned with the question of Christian unity, the Pope established the Secretariat for Promoting Christian Unity in June 1960 to assist the Council in this area, naming Jesuit biblical scholar Augustin Cardinal Bea its president, and Monsignor Johannes Willebrands, who already had more than a decade of ecumenical experience, including contacts with the World Council of Churches, its secretary.

Pope John XXIII and the Decision to Invite Observers, 1961

The Central Preparatory Commission for the Council took a crucial step in November 1961, when, at its second session, it approved the decision to invite observers from other Christian communities to the Council.[1] Pope

1. A concise presentation of the role of Cardinal Bea in this decision, the motivations for it, the preparatory role of the SPCU, and the decisive contribution of Pope John XXIII in this decision, is found in Stjepan Schmidt, SJ, *Augustin Bea. The Cardinal of Unity* (New

3

John XXIII attended the meeting in which this was taken up. In his opening address the Pope listed many reasons for hope, highlighting the respectful interest other Christians had shown in regard to the Council: "This attention . . . is the very reason for anxious exultation, and cannot leave any member of the Catholic family unmoved."[2] The resulting vote was mostly positive "largely due to the influence of Pope John and his orientations. . . ."[3] The Commission's vote was consultative, and needed a formal decision by the Pope. This came with the publication, at Christmas 1961, of the papal bull *Humanae salutis* convening the Council. It also mentioned other churches:

> We also know that the announcement of the Council was not only welcomed joyfully by them, but that many have already promised to offer prayers for its success, and that they hope to send representatives of their communities to observe its work at first hand. All this is a source of comfort and hope for us, and in order to facilitate such contacts we set up a Secretariat for Christian Unity some time ago.[4]

Through this general statement John XXIII had created the possibility of inviting observers,[5] and a very cordial atmosphere from which to reach out to them. The fact that the Pope sent official observers to the 1961 World Council of Churches Assembly in New Delhi[6] made it easier for the other Christian communions to send observers to Vatican II when invited.[7] The SPCU had the task of organizing this process by which churches and con-

---

York: New City Press, 1992), pp. 357-59. This Central Preparatory Commission consisted of 75 members including 44 Cardinals, two Eastern Catholic patriarchs, 21 archbishops, four bishops, and four major superiors of religious orders (p. 359). The possibility of inviting non-Catholic representatives to the Council seems to have been raised as early as 1959. See *History of Vatican II. Vol. I. Announcing and Preparing Vatican Council II Toward a New Era in Catholicism,* ed. Giuseppe Alberigo; English version ed. Joseph A. Komonchak (Maryknoll, NY: Orbis; Leuven: Peeters, 1995), pp. 318-19.

2. Schmidt, *Augustin Bea,* pp. 357, 358. Quote on p. 358.

3. Schmidt, *Augustin Bea,* p. 359.

4. Quoted by Schmidt, *Augustin Bea.*

5. Schmidt, *Augustin Bea,* referring to a report of the president of the SPCU.

6. In light of long-standing Holy Office policy to the contrary, this first required negotiation between the SPCU and the Holy Office. *History of Vatican II. Vol. I,* p. 319.

7. Cf. Edmund Schlink, "The Decree on Ecumenism," in George A. Lindbeck, ed., *Dialogue on the Way: Protestants Report from Rome on the Vatican Council* (Minneapolis: Augsburg Publishing House, 1965), p. 188.

fessional bodies would be invited to delegate observers to Vatican II, and the major responsibility for exploratory contacts fell to its secretary, Monsignor (later bishop and Cardinal) Johannes Willebrands. During 1962 he traveled to various Orthodox and Western church headquarters, including that of the Lutheran World Federation.[8] The task was not easy because there had been "a total absence of relations" between the Catholic Church and other communions at the onset, but the SPCU "in two years . . . had successfully established contacts on all sides," so that from the beginning of the Council there were representatives from most Christian communions, "except for Orthodoxy and the Baptist Convention."[9]

The Popes, the SPCU, and the Observers

The Official Lutheran Observers

While the Vatican Council would have an impact on the observers, the observers would have an impact on the Council as well.[10]

Official Lutheran observers were among the most consistent in their actual presence at the Council. There were 152 observers, officially delegated by the various communions, present at one or more sessions over the four years of its life (1962-65) as well as twenty-two "guests" of the SPCU.[11] Ten of the observers were from the LWF,[12] and two from the Evangelical Church of Germany.[13] Twenty-four of the 152 observers participated in all four sessions, and fifteen of these twenty-four participated during the entire period of the four sessions, including two LWF observers: Dr. Kristen Skydsgaard and Dr. Vilmos Vajta, and also Professor

8. Schmidt, *Augustin Bea*, pp. 360, 361.

9. Schmidt, *Augustin Bea*, p. 363.

10. Schmidt, *Augustin Bea*, pp. 456-59.

11. *Observateurs-Délégués et Hôtes du Secrétariat pour L'Unité des Chrétiens au Deuxième Concile Œcuménique du Vatican* (Civitas Vaticana: Typis Polyglottis Vaticanis, 1965), pp. 85-93.

12. Revd. Dr. Jerald C. Brauer, Revd. Dr. Friedrich Kantzenbach, Revd. Dr. Walter Leibrecht, Dr. George Lindbeck, Revd. Dr. Warren A. Quanbeck, Very Revd. Dr. Sven Silén, Revd. Dr. Kristen Skydsgaard, Revd. Dr. Hagen A. K. Staack, Revd. Dr. Seppo Antero Teinonen, Revd. Dr. Vilmos Vajta, *Observateurs-Délégués*, p. 89, cf. pp. 13, 77.

13. Revd. Dr. Edmund Schlink and Revd. Dr. Wolfgang Dietzfelbinger, *Observateurs-Délégués*, p. 90, cf. p. 78.

Edmund Schlink representing the Evangelical Lutheran Church of Germany.[14] Among the guests of the SPCU there were also three members of the Lutheran Church–Missouri Synod.[15]

John XXIII and the Observers at the First Session, 1962

The observers were warmly welcomed at each annual session of the Council, especially by the Popes and the SPCU. John XXIII met the observers in private audience on October 13, 1962, shortly after the beginning of the first session. This was a "completely new experience," marking "the first collective meeting of non-Catholic representatives with the pope of Rome."[16] The Pope assured them of their "welcome presence here" and spoke of the intention that "burns in my heart" to hasten the hour when "for all men the prayer of Jesus at the last supper will have reached its fulfillment." This is a result of ". . . the emotion of our priestly heart . . . the emotion of my beloved fellow workers," and, he presumed to say with certainty, "your own emotion too."[17] Edmund Schlink recalled that "Pope John created an atmosphere of fraternal openness in which a cordial and fruitful exchange of ideas could take place between observers and Roman Catholic theologians who had gathered for the council."[18] The observers could feel "that they were leading actors in a transition."[19]

14. Thomas F. Stransky, "Paul VI and the Delegated Observers/Guests to Vatican Council II," in *Paolo VI e ecumenismo* (Rome: Istituto Paolo VI, Brescia/Edizione Studium, 2001), p. 124, note 25.

15. Revd. Dr. Oswald C. J. Hoffmann, Revd. Dr. Carl S. Meyer, and Revd. Dr. Walter F. Wolbrecht, *Observateurs-Délégués*, p. 82.

16. *History of Vatican II, Vol. II. The Formation of the Council's Identity First Period and Intersession October 1962–September 1963*, ed. Giuseppe Alberigo; English version ed. Joseph A. Komonchak (Maryknoll, NY: Orbis; Leuven: Peeters, 1997), p. 22.

17. *Acta Apostolicae Sedis (= AAS)* (Civitas Vaticana: Typis Polyglottis Vaticanis, Vol. LIV, 1962), pp. 814-16, here p. 816. The names of the observer-delegates and SPCU guests at the first session were also published (pp. 810-14). English in "Pope Intends to Work, Suffer to Hasten Unity," in *Council Daybook* Vatican II, Sessions 1 and 2, ed. Floyd Anderson (Washington, DC: National Catholic Welfare Conference, 1965), pp. 36-37. The *Council Daybook* comprises three volumes. The second covers Session 3 (published 1965), and the third, Session 4 (published 1966). Hereafter references will be to *Council Daybook* session(s) and page.

18. Schlink, "Decree on Ecumenism," p. 188.

19. *History of Vatican II, Vol. II*, p. 23.

Cardinal Bea, the SPCU, and the Observers

The observers were invited, within the necessary limits, to enter into the life of the Second Vatican Council, and found ways of doing so. Cardinal Bea, meeting them at a reception during the first session, October 15, 1962, addressed them as "My brothers in Christ," and described their meeting as a "family gathering."[20] He assured them that "[a]ll of the members of the Secretariat will always be most willingly at your disposal and I myself shall be the same, in every measure allowed by my work within the council."[21] Thus, he said,

> This is the reason why I ask you to grant us complete confidence and thus to tell us very frankly — above all during the sessions specially organized for you by the secretariat — everything you dislike, to share with us your positive criticisms, your suggestions and your desires.[22]

He assured them that the SPCU would try to do "as far as we are permitted, everything that can be done now and in the future."[23] The "official observers and guests," as George Lindbeck reported, "were admitted to the closed sessions of the council and had the same access to its secret documents as did the council fathers."[24] They had excellent places in the Council's meeting place, St. Peter's Basilica, near the Council's leadership, enabling them to follow events closely. The SPCU provided persons to help in the translation or interpretation of speeches of the Council fathers, or events.[25] Being present at all the general congregations, they were able to follow the work of the Council as it developed.[26] As Bea recalled: "Both they and the Council fathers had complete freedom to establish contact

20. Remarks of Cardinal Bea to non-Catholic delegated observers, October 15, 1962, *Council Daybook,* Sessions 1 and 2, p. 39.
21. *Council Daybook,* Sessions 1 and 2, p. 39.
22. *Council Daybook,* Sessions 1 and 2, p. 39.
23. *Council Daybook,* Sessions 1 and 2, p. 39.
24. George Lindbeck, Preface to *Dialogue on the Way,* p. vi.
25. Stransky, "Paul VI and the Delegated Observers," p. 128.
26. According to Stransky, three dominant sets of issues which the observers were especially interested in following were related to (1) Scripture-Tradition, e.g., the role of Scripture in the church vis-à-vis Tradition, (2) Roman Catholic attitudes towards other Christians and their churches, (3) questions of religious freedom and church-state relations. "Paul VI and the Delegated Observers," pp. 124-28.

with each other, and they soon began to make use of this."[27] The observers, according to Schlink, "were even asked to offer suggestions and to make contributions."[28]

Responding on behalf of the observers to Bea's address at the reception, Professor Schlink acknowledged this generosity offered to them:

> We see the fact that our meetings at the Council now have an official character as a major step forward, and we realize that it was by no means a matter of course that we should be given the same schemata as are given to the Council fathers, and the opportunity to express our thoughts on these schemata. We know that we owe these opportunities to His Holiness himself, who has followed the promptings of his heart and brought about a new atmosphere of openness toward the non-Roman churches.[29]

At the beginning of the second session and of the fourth, since new observers came in, Bea repeated his plea to the observer-delegates to "grant us complete confidence. . . ."[30] His statement to them at the second session, October 17, 1963, also included an expression of satisfaction for the collaboration of the observers during the first session, acknowledging that "with the help of the Lord . . . our work has had satisfactory results."[31] They were getting involved.

According to Thomas Stransky, an SPCU staff person who worked closely with the observers, by the second period of the Council, the observers had begun to find other channels, besides directly to the SPCU, by which to make their views known:

> [T]he observers were learning other various ways to transmit their oral or written *opiniones et suggestiones* besides directly to the SPCU: directly to a SPCU *Pater* or another friendly bishop; the *Pater* would incorporate it as his own in his intervention *in aula*; or directly to a SPCU consultor or a *peritus* who had his own ways of finding a benevolent *Pater*. The

27. Cited in Schmidt, *Augustin Bea*, p. 457.

28. Schlink, "Decree on Ecumenism," p. 188.

29. Cited in Schmidt, *Augustin Bea*, p. 456.

30. Cardinal Bea's address to observers at the second session, October 17, 1963, *Council Daybook*, Sessions 1 and 2, pp. 195-96, here p. 196. Bea again repeated this plea to observers at the fourth session, September 18, 1965, *Council Daybook*, Session 4, p. 28.

31. Address to observers, October 17, 1963, *Council Daybook*, Sessions 1 and 2, p. 195.

SPCU also had its own ways of transmitting the observations either to a commission or through a commission member.[32]

One result is that "the Observers did influence the contents and word-ings of several constitutions and decrees," but "most specifics seem impos-sible to trace."[33]

Paul VI and the Observers at the Second Session, 1963

Pope Paul VI addressed the observers both at the Council itself, and also on meeting them in private audience at the beginning of the three sessions at which he presided. The first time that he addressed them, at the opening assembly of the second session, on September 29, 1963, Paul VI dedicated ten paragraphs of his discourse to the observers. He spoke with emotion, and made clear the impact of their presence. "Our voice trembles," he said, "and our heart beats the faster both because of the inexpressible consola-tion and reasonable hope that their presence stirs up within us, as well as because of the deep sadness we feel at their prolonged separation."[34]

In an important gesture, the Pope called for mutual forgiveness for events leading to division in the past:

> If we are in any way to blame for that separation we humbly beg God's forgiveness and ask pardon too of our brethren who feel themselves to have been injured by us. For our part we willingly forgive the injuries which the Catholic Church has suffered, and forget the grief endured during the long series of dissentions and separations.[35]

This address also had a positive impact on the observers. What made the biggest impact on them, according to Stransky, was that "for the first time since Adrian VI (1522-1523), a Pope acknowledges *Nostra culpa* for the separations and pleas for forgiveness of past Catholic sins against unity."[36]

---

32. Stransky, "Paul VI and the Delegated Observers," pp. 138-39 (emphasis original).

33. Stransky, "Paul VI and the Delegated Observers," p. 139.

34. Address by Pope Paul VI at the opening of the second session, September 29, 1963, *AAS*, LV, 1963, pp. 841-59, here p. 853. English translation in *Council Daybook*, Sessions 1 and 2, p. 148.

35. *Council Daybook*, Sessions 1 and 2, p. 148.

36. Stransky, "Paul VI and the Delegated Observers," p. 137 (emphasis original).

In their private audience with the Pope at the beginning of each of the last three Council sessions, a different observer-delegate addressed the Pope on behalf of the others. At the first, October 17, 1963, LWF observer Dr. Kristen Skydsgaard addressed the Pope. His address was memorable, as it started a dialogue on a question to which the Pope would later come back, and which, some years later, would have concrete results. Bea later described this as an example of how open and attentive Paul VI was to the suggestions and proposals of other Christians, in this case the observers.[37]

Skydsgaard, stating that the doctrine of the Church is the point at which all our divisions culminate, and precisely where they seem insurmountable, pointed to an area of study that he thought was extremely important:

> I am thinking of the role of Biblical theology which concentrates on the study of the history of salvation in the Old as well as the New Testament. The more we progress in understanding the hidden and paradoxical history of the people of God, the more we shall begin truly to understand the Church of Jesus Christ in its mystery, in its historical existence, and in its unity.[38]

Paul VI responded that he would willingly subscribe to the developments expressed for "a concrete and historical theology centered on the history of salvation." The suggestion "seems to us wholly worthy of being studied and worked out in detail." Going further, the Pope said that while there were Catholic institutions that would not be prevented from specializing in this kind of research, if circumstances demanded it, "the establishment of a new institution for this purpose would not be excluded."[39] In this exchange a seed was planted for the birth of the institute built in 1972 in Jerusalem and called the Tantur Ecumenical Institute.[40]

Paul VI came back to this idea the following year. In January 1964 he had traveled to the Holy Land, having there a historic encounter with the

37. Schmidt, *Augustin Bea*, p. 465.

38. French original in *Observateurs-Délégués*, pp. 27-30, here pp. 28-29. English translation in "Dr Kristen E. Skydsgaard," *Council Daybook,* Sessions 1 and 2, pp. 197-98, here p. 198.

39. French original in *AAS*, LV, 1963, pp. 878-81, here p. 880; English translation in "Pope Paul," *Council Daybook,* Sessions 1 and 2, pp. 198-99, here p. 199.

40. Thomas F. Stransky, CSP, "Tantur Ecumenical Institute," in *Dictionary of the Ecumenical Movement,* ed. Nicholas Lossky et al. (Geneva: WCC Publications, 2nd ed., 2002), p. 1092.

Ecumenical Patriarch, Athenagoras I. Just after the beginning of the Council's third session, the Pope received the observers in private audience on September 29, 1964, and in his address to them, showing that the Catholic Church is disposed to dialogue, he illustrated some development in the idea discussed the previous year:

> We still cherish the memory of the proposal made to us last year on an occasion similar to this; that of founding an institute of studies on the history of salvation, to be carried on in a common collaboration; and we hope to bring this initiative to reality, as a memorial of our journey to the Holy Land last January; we are now studying the possibility of this.[41]

The Pope would recall this proposal made by Skydsgaard still again after the Council, in 1969, when meeting a visiting delegation from the Lutheran World Federation (cf. below, chapter 4).

The Third (1964) and Fourth (1965) Sessions: New Attitudes and Relationships Begin to Emerge

The observers' presence helped to foster new attitudes among the Council fathers towards other Christians. Pope Paul VI's statements to the observers during the third and fourth sessions suggest that these new attitudes confronted deep historical conflicts. His statements indicate at least three important points.

First, the observer delegates helped to keep the ecumenical question before the Council over the years, including both its implications for a renewed Catholic understanding of separated Christians, and for renewal in the Catholic Church itself. In his address at the opening assembly of the third session, September 14, 1964, Paul VI again directed some words to the observers: "We wish to assure you once more of our purpose and hope to be able one day to remove every obstacle, every misunderstanding, every hesitancy that still prevents us from feeling fully 'of one heart and one soul' in Christ, in His Church (Acts 4:32)." He pledged to strive "to understand

41. French original in *AAS*, LVI, 1964, pp. 941-43, here p. 942. English translation in "Pope's Talk to Non-Catholic Observers," September 29, 1964, *Council Daybook*, Session 3, pp. 77-78.

better and to welcome all that is genuine and admissible in the different Christian denominations that are distinct from us. And at the same time we beg them to try to understand the Catholic Faith and life better. . . ."[42]

The Pope continued in this line when meeting the observers in private audience on September 29, 1964. The Catholic Church is "disposed to study how difficulties can be removed, misunderstandings dissipated, and the authentic treasures of truth and spirituality which you possess be respected."[43] The Council, he said, "has had only words of respect and of joy for your presence, and that of the Christian communities which you represent. Nay more, words of honor, of charity and of hope in your regard."[44] These ecumenical aspirations also required renewal in the Catholic Church itself, calling for study of "how certain canonical forms can be enlarged and adapted, to facilitate a recomposition in unity of the great and, by now, centuries-old Christian communities still separated from us."[45] The Pope saw the historic meaning of these new attitudes, "if we think of the polemics of the past."[46]

Second, as just suggested, new attitudes were developing not just towards the individual observers, but also toward the separated Christian communities from which they came. Addressing the observers at a prayer service for Christian unity at the Basilica of St. Paul Outside the Walls, December 4, 1965, at the end of the Council, the Pope indicated that:

> We have come to know you a little better, and not only as the representatives of your respective confessions. Through you we have come into contact with Christian communities which live, pray and act in the name of Christ, with systems of doctrines and religious mentalities, and — let us say it without fear — with Christian treasures of great value.[47]

Third, the Pope encouraged the continuation of the new reciprocal contacts and the changing relationships with other Christian communions

---

42. *AAS*, LVI, 1964, pp. 805-16, here p. 814 and p. 815. English in "Pope Paul's Speech," September 14, 1964, *Council Daybook*, Session 3, p. 10.

43. French original in *AAS*, LVI, 1964, pp. 941-43, here p. 942. English: "Pope's Talk to Non-Catholic Observers," September 29, 1965, *Council Daybook*, Session 3, p. 78.

44. *AAS*, LVI, 1964, p. 942 and *Council Daybook*, Session 3, p. 77.

45. *AAS*, LVI, 1964, pp. 942-43 and *Council Daybook*, Session 3, p. 78.

46. *AAS*, LVI, 1964, p. 942 and *Council Daybook*, Session 3, p. 77.

47. "Discours de Sa Sainteté Paul VI" (4 décembre 1965), *Observateurs-Délégués*, pp. 59-64, here p. 61. English translation in "Pope Paul," *Council Daybook*, Session 4, p. 353.

that were beginning. He expressed joy that the SPCU had been invited to send observers to conferences and meetings "of your churches and organizations. We will gladly continue to do this," he said, "so that our Catholic organizations and our representatives may, on their side, acquire a knowledge, corresponding to truth and to charity, which are a prerequisite of a deeper union in the Lord."[48] Reflecting on his 1964 meeting with the Ecumenical Patriarch Athenagoras in Jerusalem which was followed by other moving visits from representatives of different Christian confessions, with whom there had been no contact for centuries, Paul VI considered these fraternal meetings "as an historical event of great importance and we wish to see in them the prelude to more consoling developments."[49]

Acknowledging the change that had taken place in the relations with other Christians during the four years of the Council, the Pope told the observers that "your departure produces a solitude around us unknown to us before the council and which now saddens us. We should like to see you with us always."[50] While there is still a long way to go before reaching full and authentic communion, "May we at least at the end of the council record a victory: we have begun to love each other once more."[51] Setting the stage for the continuation of ecumenical contacts in the post-conciliar period, Paul VI told the observers that their departure "does not close for us a dialogue begun silently, but obliges us, on the contrary, to examine how we can follow it up profitably."[52]

The Pope also testified to the observers' impact on the Council's formalities: "We have greatly appreciated this presence. We have felt its influence."[53] The Council fathers have had "the spiritual joy of seeing your elite group associated with the religious ceremonies of the council to the formulation of doctrinal and disciplinary expressions able to remove obstacles and to open paths as wide and smoothed as possible for a better evaluation of the Christian religious inheritance which you preserve and develop."[54]

---

48. *AAS,* LVI, 1964, p. 943. English, "Pope's Talk to Non-Catholic Observers," September 29, 1964, *Council Daybook,* Session 3, p. 78.

49. "Discours de Sa Sainteté Paul VI" (4 décembre 1965), p. 62. English translation in "Pope Paul," *Council Daybook,* Session 4, p. 353.

50. "Discours de Sa Sainteté Paul VI," p. 59; *Council Daybook,* Session 4, p. 353.

51. "Discours de Sa Sainteté Paul VI," p. 63; *Council Daybook,* Session 4, p. 353.

52. "Discours de Sa Sainteté Paul VI," p. 60; *Council Daybook,* Session 4, p. 353.

53. "Discours de Sa Sainteté Paul VI," p. 59; *Council Daybook,* Session 4, p. 353.

54. "Discours de Sa Sainteté Paul VI," p. 62; *Council Daybook,* Session 4, p. 353.

The Second Vatican Council. Observers are in the front on the left side. (Photo © Fotografia Felici, Rome)

Lutheran-Catholic joint working group at its first meeting, August 25-27, 1965, at the Institute for Ecumenical Research, Strasbourg. The group worked to prepare for the international dialogue that began in 1967. Seated (left to right) are Bishop Hermann Dietzfelbinger, Lutheran Chairman; Bishop Hermann Volk, Catholic Chairman; and Bishop Johannes Willebrands. Standing are (left to right) Bishop Hans Martensen, Dr. Victor Hayward (WCC observer), Rev. Prof. Kristen E. Skydsgaard, Rev. Prof. Warren A. Quanbeck, Rev. Dr. Kurt Schmidt-Clausen, Rev. Dr. Oswald Hoffmann (observer), Fr. Peter Blaser, MSC, Rev. Carl H. Mau, Rev. Dr. Andre Appel, Dean Jerald C. Brauer, Fr. Johannes Witte, SJ, Fr. Yves Congar, OP, Msgr. William Baum, and Dr. Vilmos Vajta. (Photo courtesy of LWF)

The joint working group in session. (Photo courtesy of LWF)

CHAPTER 2

Turning Toward Lutheran-Catholic Dialogue

The impact of the observers on the Council, and, in turn, the impact, through the observers, of the Council on the churches or Christian World Communions from which they came, created the atmosphere in which the desire for more formal dialogue could grow. In the context of such mutual impact, seeds of Lutheran-Catholic dialogue were planted. Steps toward dialogue came rather quickly.

Impact of the Observers on Conciliar Documents

What impact, then, did the observer-delegates have on the conciliar documents? According to Cardinal Bea, the discussions in the meetings of the observer-delegates "more than once proved helpful to the Council itself, since the points put forward at these meetings were later expressed in the Council hall by one or another Council father."[1]

Thomas Stransky states that, in regard to the emerging text on ecume-

---

1. In Stjepan Schmidt, SJ, *Augustin Bea. The Cardinal of Unity* (New York: New City Press, 1992), p. 457. Schmidt, on the same page in footnote 20, cites the example given by Anglican observer Bishop J. Moorman in his book *Vatican Observed: An Anglican Impression of Vatican II* (London: Darton, Longman & Todd, 1967), p. 28, that the Archbishop of Chicago, Cardinal A. Meyer, spoke in the Council expressing a thought of the Lutheran observer Kristen Skydsgaard.

nism, "the observers' input became essential in the improvements."[2] A new schema on ecumenism reached the floor in November 1963. "At no previous time had the Observers been more engaged *participantes in Concilio.*"[3] "More than any other schema, the Observers contributed detailed written suggestions to the SPCU. *De Oecumenismo* was also *their* document."[4]

Stransky recalls several major influences of the observers on the conciliar text *Unitatis redintegratio,* which was approved by the Council in November 1964. To mention three, a first concerned the decision about where the Catholic Church stood in regard to the ecumenical movement, as reflected in Chapter 1 of *UR* (entitled "Catholic Principles on Ecumenism"). "Every previous draft took for granted '*Catholic ecumenism.*' The Observers urged the change to '*Catholic principles of ecumenism.*'"[5] The change implies that the Council came to recognize that there is one ecumenical movement for all Christian churches and communions even if a church may have its own principles for its involvement in this one movement.[6] The previous expression, "Catholic ecumenism," could imply that "Catholic ecumenism" was seen in contrast to another ecumenical movement.

A second influence of the observers, according to Stransky, in order to explain the ecclesiology of the abnormal historical divisions between the churches, concerned "the shift from the dominant Pauline image of the Body of Christ and thus avoid Pius XII's *Mystici Corporis* language of *either* in *or* outside the one Church of Christ, to the Pauline image of *koinonia* and thus: *communio realis sed non plena or imperfecta.* And the emphasis is not on individuals but on *Communiones* as *ecclesial* realities. These suggested changes coincided with *De Ecclesia,* owing principally to Y. Congar." And a third influence related to "the inseparable bond between the *unity* and the *mission* of the Church," emphasized at the New Delhi Assembly, and found in no. 12.[7]

Cardinal Bea stated on various occasions, e.g., at a reception in honor

---

2. Thomas F. Stransky, "Paul VI and the Delegated Observers/Guests to Vatican Council II," in *Paolo VI e ecumenismo* (Rome: Istituto Paolo VI, Brescia/Edizione Studium, 2001), p. 139.

3. Stransky, "Paul VI and the Delegated Observers," p. 140 (emphasis original).

4. Stransky, "Paul VI and the Delegated Observers," p. 141 (emphasis original).

5. Stransky, "Paul VI and the Delegated Observers," p. 146 (emphasis original).

6. Cf. *The Decree on Ecumenism,* Chapter 1, "Catholic Principles on Ecumenism," note 9 in Walter Abbott, SJ, general editor, *The Documents of Vatican II,* 1966, p. 343.

7. Stransky, "Paul VI and the Delegated Observers," p. 146.

of the observers, in an address given before the Pope and the cardinals, and in various conversations and interviews, that the observer-delegates had "contributed in a decisive way" to the Decree on Ecumenism.[8] The Cardinal summed it up in this way in 1966, during an interview while visiting the Ecumenical Center in Geneva. Referring to the contacts between the Catholic bishops and the observers during the Council he said:

> The effect of the latter can hardly be underestimated and has not been sufficiently appreciated to date in terms of its magnitude and enormous consequences. . . . I myself am able to state publicly that the non-Catholic observer delegates made a decisive contribution to the *Decree on Ecumenism*. Of course they did not prepare this Decree and did not participate directly in Council debates and voting. But their presence at the Council and their participation in the form of prayer, study, and all types of contacts and suggestions allowed the Council Fathers to experience the ecumenical problem profoundly and from all points of view.[9]

Impact of the Second Vatican Council on the LWF

The impact of the Council, in turn, was felt within the LWF. The non-Catholic observers present at the first session in 1962 had been reassured by the honesty of genuine debate within the Council,[10] characterized by a freedom of discussion some had previously thought "incompatible with a seemingly monolithic clerical organization."[11] LWF observer George Lindbeck commented that ". . . Catholic Christians, Roman or not, have had to acknowledge that the Church of Rome possessed a greater dynamism and a greater zeal for reform than they had thought. . . ."[12] Furthermore, the main preoccupations of the Fourth LWF General Assembly, which met in Helsinki, Finland, in August 1963, were close to those of Vati-

8. Schmidt, *Augustin Bea,* pp. 481-82.

9. "The Church in New Directions: Interview with a Member of the Protestant Press Service," in Augustin Cardinal Bea and Willem A. Visser 't Hooft, *Peace Among Christians* (New York: Herder & Herder, and Association Press, 1967), pp. 129-30.

10. *History of Vatican II, Vol. II. The Formation of the Council's Identity First Period and Intersession October 1962–September 1963,* ed. Giuseppe Alberigo; English version ed. Joseph A. Komonchak (Maryknoll, NY: Orbis; Leuven: Peeters, 1997), p. 558.

11. *History of Vatican II, Vol. II,* p. 557.

12. Cited in *History of Vatican II, Vol. II,* p. 558.

can II, including the concern for Christian unity and "the question of how to present the Christian faith to contemporaries who were unbelieving, individualist, and rootless in the midst of an industrialized society."[13]

In this context, motivated by what they saw, the LWF observers at the Vatican Council were influential in shaping two decisions in the LWF that fostered deepened relations with the Catholic Church. One was the decision of the LWF to engage in theological dialogue with the Catholic Church. The other, which came earlier, was the finalizing in 1963 of the establishment of the Institute for Interconfessional Research.[14]

The Strasbourg Institute

The establishment of an institute for confessional research had already been proposed at the Third LWF Assembly in Minneapolis 1957, because of the increasing number of contacts developing between the different confessions. Instead, however, a "Special Commission for Interconfessional Research" was set up.[15] But the incipient Vatican II was already making an impact even in 1960, as a recent history of the LWF notes:

> Urged on by the events in the Roman Catholic Church [the preparation for and convening of Vatican II], concrete developments had already taken place. As early as the beginning of 1960 the Danish scholar Kristen E. Skydsgaard had been busy with theological research at the behest of the Special Commission, and had devoted himself to the question of relations with the Roman Catholic Church.[16]

Skydsgaard, assigned to the staff of the LWF, set up a Foundation for Interconfessional Research in Copenhagen. Another LWF Vatican II observer, Professor George A. Lindbeck of Yale University, replaced him two years later. In 1962 the first well-received publication of the Institute, di-

---

13. *History of Vatican II, Vol. II,* p. 540.

14. *From Federation to Communion: The History of the Lutheran World Federation,* ed. Jens Holger Schjørring, Prasanna Kumari, and Norman A. Hjelm (Minneapolis: Fortress Press, 1997), p. 255.

15. This Commission in turn was the result of the proposal by the German National Committee to establish an institute "in view of the increasingly numerous points of contact developing among the confessions." *From Federation to Communion.*

16. *From Federation to Communion.*

rected at the coming Vatican Council, appeared in English and German: *The Papal Council and the Gospel/Konzil und Evangelium,* edited by Professor Skydsgaard.[17] The Special Commission later proposed to the 1963 LWF Assembly in Helsinki the establishment of a "Lutheran Foundation for Interconfessional Research," which the Helsinki Assembly accepted. In his report at the assembly describing the purpose of the new foundation, Bishop Herman Dietzfelbinger again showed the impact of Vatican II: "the direction taken by the Roman Catholic Second Vatican Council has shown that the theological dialogue is urgently needed. It was quite logical that those entrusted with the research, Professor Skydsgaard and Professor Lindbeck, should act as observers from the Lutheran World Federation at the Council . . . joined by the director of the Department of Theology, Dr. Vilmos Vajta, who is clearly associated with our work."[18] The Institute associated with the Foundation, linked to the LWF but legally and financially independent, was founded, located first in Copenhagen in 1963, but since 1965 in Strasbourg.[19]

In the early years "the Institute's interests were directed particularly at Roman Catholic theology,"[20] though attention to Reformed, Anglican, Protestant, and others soon followed. The Institute initially provided an important resource to the LWF and even as early as the Helsinki Assembly in 1963, in connection with the Institute's work, the question was raised within the LWF as to whether a dialogue could be initiated with the Catholic Church.[21]

17. *From Federation to Communion.*

18. Bishop Herman Dietzfelbinger, First oral report, Special Commission on Inter-Confessional Research. *Proceedings of the Fourth Assembly of the Lutheran World Federation, Helsinki, July 30–August 11, 1963* (Berlin and Hamburg: Lutherisches Verlagshaus, 1965), pp. 154-55; here p. 155.

19. *From Federation to Communion,* p. 255.

20. *From Federation to Communion,* p. 256.

21. *From Federation to Communion,* pp. 256-57. The *JD* would be the best result of this dialogue. In the 1990s, the Strasbourg Institute, at the request of LWF authorities, would play a key role in assisting the LWF and its member churches in evaluating the *JD,* and in the process leading to its successful approval.

A Lutheran Evaluation of the Council: "A New Dialogue Has Begun"

The Strasbourg Institute, like the Commission it replaced, fostered knowledge about, and evaluation of, the Council. In 1965, while the Vatican Council was still in session (its fourth session had not yet met), the Lutheran observers published a volume entitled *Dialogue on the Way: Protestants Report from Rome on the Vatican Council.*[22] Its editor, George Lindbeck, in his Preface (p. v), described it as "the first extended evaluation of the Second Vatican Council by a group of Protestant observers officially delegated by their churches to attend its sessions." The original stimulus and continuing support for the book came from the Lutheran Foundation for Interconfessional Research, with its institute at Strasbourg. Just as the latter was the successor to the earlier Special Commission of the LWF which published the *Papal Council and the Gospel* in 1961, so too *Dialogue on the Way* "may in a sense be considered a continuation of the Protestant evaluation of the council," which began with *Papal Council and Gospel* (Preface, p. vii). The Institute also continued providing reflection on the Council years afterwards.[23]

The authors of *Dialogue on the Way* spoke only for themselves and not for the churches that had sent them as observers. The volume sought "to give a balanced and distinctively Protestant summary and evaluation of what so far has happened at Vatican II." Chapters described the structures and procedures of the Council and highlights of the first three sessions, and evaluated major theological themes of the Council. The authors focused on strengths of the documents published by the Council, as well as what they saw as weaknesses or ambiguities. The writers had certain differences of interpretation on some points, according to Lindbeck, but he asserted his impression "that we have here a basic consensus."[24]

Professor Edmund Schlink's chapter on "The Decree on Ecumenism"

---

22. George A. Lindbeck, ed., *Dialogue on the Way: Protestants Report from Rome on the Vatican Council* (Minneapolis: Augsburg Publishing House, 1965).

23. Cf. *Unitatis redintegratio 1964-1974: The Impact on the Decree on Ecumenism*, ed. Gerard Békés and Vilmos Vajta, Studia Anselmiana 71 (Roma: Pontificio Ateneo S. Anselmo, 1977). This publication resulted from a conference initiated by the Strasbourg Institute in cooperation with the Faculty of Theology (Specialization Dogmatic-Ecumenical Theology section) of the Pontifical University of Sant'Anselmo. Some Lutheran observers took part, e.g., Lindbeck, Skydsgaard, Vajta, Quanbeck.

24. Lindbeck, Preface to *Dialogue on the Way*, pp. v-vii.

is the longest (pp. 186-230). Schlink gives his views of strengths as well as weaknesses or ambiguities in the decree. Briefly, among important developments, are the evolution from initial references to others as non-Roman Christians, i.e., individuals outside of the Roman church who through baptism are united in spirit with the Roman church, to eventually acknowledging them corporately, as "churches and ecclesial communities," recognizing them as having greater ecclesiological importance than had traditional Roman theology (cf. pp. 214-16).

Since the observers followed with particular interest the discussion and evolution of the schema *De Oecumenismo,* it is interesting to see that Schlink, reflecting on the finished product, highlights especially the importance of the second chapter, "The Practice of Ecumenism":

> In an impressive simplicity it gives instructions for the implementation of the decree which may lead, ecumenically speaking, farther than anything else in the council's documents. . . . (p. 196)

These instructions spell out matters that are "most important in the relationship between separated Christians. . . ." This chapter shows in an especially impressive way "the seriousness of the ecumenical yearning which influenced both the Secretariat for Christian Unity and many of the council fathers" (pp. 196-97). Points that every Roman Catholic "is told to take to heart" include (1) the spiritual renewal of the heart (*UR* 6) including the acceptance of repentance, (2) prayer for unity (*UR* 7) including, if possible, common prayer with the separated brethren, prayer which, as interpreted by Cardinal Bea, leaves it to God to decide when and in which way a more complete unity can be established, (3) ecuménical instruction (*UR* 10) also about the doctrine, worship, piety, etc., related to the faith of the separated brethren, (4) dialogue with the separated brethren that must be undertaken on the basis of equality (*UR* 9, 11), in a common search for truth; especially helpful is the instruction that there exists a "hierarchy" of truths. Schlink pauses to say that these instructions on dialogue, in light of the previous reluctance of the Roman Catholic Church to enter into dialogue with other churches, "mean more than may appear to the casual observer." They are not just "pious wishes," "but an expression of the real accomplishment of this council and of something that we as observers at the council have experienced again and again" in our meetings with the fathers and the theologians of the Roman church.

22

A new dialogue has begun which is based on mutual esteem, love, and frankness and is wrestling with the problem of "what is truth." (p. 198)

And (5), further emphasis is given to the demand that Roman Catholics cooperate with the separated brethren, and a willingness to advocate giving with them a common confession before the world of faith in the Triune God, and in the incarnate Son of God (*UR* 12), a step "very important for the future of ecumenism" (pp. 197-99).

Schlink testified, furthermore, to the authenticity of this new Catholic ecumenical program. These directives in the Decree's second chapter "correspond to a large degree to the methods that have been tried and proved effective in the ecumenical movement of the non-Roman churches. This agreement in ecumenical methods is especially important because Rome did not adopt these methods from the World Council of Churches, but developed them on the basis of her own desire for a fruitful dialogue with the separated brethren" (pp. 225-26).

The Lutheran-Catholic "Joint Working Group" and the Beginnings of Official Dialogue

Secondly, besides influencing the Strasbourg Institute and its work, the LWF observers also played an important role in the Federation's decision to engage in an international dialogue with the Catholic Church. As a result of the presence of the observers, even while the Vatican Council was still in progress, two bilateral "joint working groups" between the Catholic Church and others came into existence in 1965, the first with the World Council of Churches, the second with the Lutheran World Federation.[25] Cardinal Bea, addressing the observers at the beginning of the Council's fourth session, on September 18, 1965, spoke of important ecumenical steps already begun, mentioning these two joint working groups.[26]

The joint working group between the Catholic Church and the LWF originated "from September 1964 when the LWF Executive Committee

---

25. Good relations, if not "joint working groups," were developing at this time with other communions as well.

26. Cardinal Bea's speech to observers and guests of the SPCU, September 18. French original. English translation in *Council Daybook*, Session 4, p. 28.

meeting at Reykjavik called for a dialogue with the RCC."[27] This initiative toward dialogue, as Vatican II was still in progress, "lay in the fact that the LWF had appointed three theologians — Kristen E. Skydsgaard, George A. Lindbeck and Vilmos Vajta — as observers at Vatican II, who reported regularly to the executive committee."[28] A confidential memo from Lindbeck, available to the September 1964 executive committee meeting, indicated "that there was a desire on the Roman Catholic side [Secretariat for Promoting Christian Unity] for the contacts to continue beyond the Council. Entering into conversations — bilateral church conversations of an official nature — with individual world confessional families was considered to be one form of such continuing contacts."[29] Lindbeck supported the idea, declaring that Lutherans should be willing when the occasion comes to enter "bilaterally" into the ecumenical dialogue.

Both Sides Give Formal Approval to Dialogue

The executive committee did not at once take up this idea, but asked the LWF General Secretary to be a liaison officer with the SPCU if it should seek continuation of contacts. In autumn 1964 a meeting in the SPCU proposed a joint consultation to examine the possibility of future contacts and discussions and even themes for these, and in January 1965 the LWF officers agreed to this proposal. In June 1965 the executive committee appointed Lutheran participants of a joint working group, and proposed the creation of two joint study commissions: one on "The Gospel and the Church," the other on "The Theology of Marriage and the Problems of Mixed Marriages."[30]

On the Catholic side, as this joint working group was being organized, information about it was sent to Pope Paul VI on May 22, 1965, "with a re-

---

27. "The Roman Catholic Church and the Lutheran World Federation," *IS* 1 (1967): 5. The question of bilateral conversations between Lutherans and Catholics had been raised in an address at the 1963 LWF Assembly in Helsinki, by Dr. E. Clifford Nelson, "The One Church and the Lutheran Churches," Helsinki Proceedings, 293, cited in *From Federation to Communion*, p. 257.

28. *From Federation to Communion*, p. 259.

29. *From Federation to Communion*, p. 259.

30. *From Federation to Communion*, p. 259. The joint working group agreed that both study commissions be established.

quest for authorization of the JWG."[31] On July 7th, in response, "a letter from the Cardinal Secretary of State gave the sanction of the Holy See."[32]

The joint working group's[33] first meeting, at the Strasbourg Institute, August 25-27, 1965, aimed at determining whether and in what manner "the relations which have already begun between the LWF and the RCC can be continued and intensified," and looked for "central theological issues for future dialogue" between the two, a dialogue intended as "official and special."[34] The second meeting, April 13-15, 1966, produced a joint report which Cardinal Bea presented to Pope Paul VI on May 26, 1966, for approbation, and which was similarly approved by the LWF Executive Committee, July 17-22, 1966.[35]

The LWF was the first of the world confessional bodies to officially organize a joint dialogue commission with the Catholic Church.[36] This step to bilateral international dialogue was "something new in the history of the ecumenical movement," and the international Catholic-Lutheran dialogue "became as it were, the 'parent' of all later dialogues of this kind."[37]

31. "The Roman Catholic Church and the Lutheran World Federation," *IS* 1 (1967): 5.

32. "The Roman Catholic Church and the Lutheran World Federation," p. 5.

33. Its members included, *Lutherans:* Bishop Herman Dietzfelbinger (Chairman), Revd. Prof. Jerald Brauer, Revd. Carl H. Mau, Revd. Prof. Warren Quanbeck, Revd. Dr. Kurt Schmidt-Clausen, Revd. Prof. Kristen Skydsgaard, Revd. Prof. Vilmos Vajta; *Catholics:* Bishop Herman Volk (Chairman), Msgr. William Baum, Fr. Peter Bläser, MSC, Fr. Yves Congar, OP, Bishop Hans L. Martensen, Bishop Johannes Willebrands, Fr. Johannes L. Witte, SJ; *Observers:* Revd. Victor Hayward, World Council of Churches, Revd. Dr. Oswald Hoffmann, Lutheran Church Missouri Synod; *Guest:* Revd. Dr. André Appel. "The Roman Catholic Church and the Lutheran World Federation," p. 5.

34. "The Roman Catholic Church and the Lutheran World Federation," pp. 5-6.

35. "The Roman Catholic Church and the Lutheran World Federation," p. 6.

36. Cf. Thomas F. Stransky, CSP, "The Foundation of the Secretariat for Promoting Christian Unity," in *Vatican II by Those Who Were There*, ed. Alberic Stacpoole (London: Geoffrey Chapman, 1986), p. 80.

37. *From Federation to Communion*, p. 259. The first meeting of the Lutheran-Catholic joint international commission took place November 26-30, 1967. See *IS* 3 (1967): 3. Though the Methodist-Catholic joint international commission was officially approved later than the Lutheran-Catholic commission, its first meeting took place October 15-19, 1967. See *IS* 3 (1967): 6.

The Sixteenth-Century Anathemas

Since the 1999 *Joint Declaration on the Doctrine of Justification* put the sixteenth-century mutual condemnations concerning justification in a new light, Edmund Schlink's references to the anathemas, in his commentary on the Decree on Ecumenism in 1965, are interesting. He viewed renewal in the church as limited by its dogmas. He observed that the Council fathers simply reiterated their acceptance of the Council of Trent's dogmatic decisions with all its anathemas against doctrines of the non-Roman communions. Without mentioning justification, he said that "[t]he statements of faith promulgated at Trent and the corresponding anathemas are the greatest stumbling block against reunion." Pessimistically, he felt that "we cannot hope for an abrogation of the anathemas in order to make possible the reunion with the non-Roman churches." But, optimistically, he said that today in both Protestant and Roman Catholic theology, we see "our task in a reinterpretation of these old dogmatic statements and in explaining them in their historical setting." While this Council has not attempted it, nonetheless, he said, "[t]here is a possibility for new interpretation of dogmatic expressions and for a better understanding of them, which may lead us to a consensus with the separated brethren of the Roman Church" (*Dialogue on the Way,* p. 203).

Summary of Part I

Pope John XXIII's two decisive interventions before the Council began, that is, of creating, in 1960, the Secretariat for Promoting Christian Unity, and authorizing, in 1961, that other churches and Christian World Communions be invited to send observers to the Council, made significant attention to ecumenism at the Council inevitable from the start. The care offered to the observers by Cardinal Bea and the SPCU, their access to conciliar documents and to the Council fathers, the warm contacts they had with Popes John XXIII and Paul VI, brought them into the life of the Council, opened opportunities for informal dialogue with Catholic bishops and other theologians, and practically assured that the observers, including the Lutheran observers, would have some influence especially on the ecumenical aspect of the Council's life and work. Cardinal Bea and others witnessed to the fact that the observers had an influence on the evolution of the Council's Decree on Ecumenism (1964).

Lutheran observers were among the most consistently present at the Council. Some published important studies aimed at the Council just before it began, and evaluations of the Council's published Constitutions, Decrees, and Declarations in 1965, even before the Council concluded. They evaluated the Council's achievement in a positive but constructively critical way. Having, along with the observers of other communions, some influence on the Council, the LWF observers were one of the channels through which Vatican II also had some influence on the LWF. By encouraging the LWF, while the Council was still in session, to engage in bilateral dialogue with the Catholic Church, the observers helped prepare the transition from the conciliar period to the post-conciliar period. A joint working group, approved by Paul VI and Lutheran authorities during the Council, suggested steps fostering new relationships between them, and led to the dialogue that would begin formally after the Council, and would take up important themes including justification.

While the Catholic Church became involved in international bilateral dialogues with various churches and Christian World Communions after the Council, the international Lutheran-Catholic dialogue is the only one among those churches of the Reformation for which steps and initiatives were approved officially at the highest levels during the Council. At every stage, the openness of John XXIII and Paul VI and the SPCU to the observers, and the ecumenical developments during the Council, encouraged the development of these new relationships and fostered rapprochement between the Catholic Church and the Lutheran World Federation.

The ecumenical dynamics within the Council resulting from the presence and participation of the observers, their engagement with the Council fathers, the continuing reflection of the fathers on ecumenism as seen by the evolution of the Decree on Ecumenism and the observers' influence on it, the renewal within the church in regard to ecumenism, and the steps taken during the Council to begin the Lutheran-Catholic dialogue — all of these illustrate the "conciliar foundation" on which the dialogue was built. And it was from this dialogue that, decades later, the *Joint Declaration on the Doctrine of Justification* would finally emerge.

PART II

From Centuries of Isolation to Dialogue and Mutual Respect

The Immediate Post-Conciliar Period, During the Pontificate of Pope Paul VI, 1966-1978

CHAPTER 3

Creating Partnership Between the Catholic Church and the Lutheran World Federation

Developments during the Second Vatican Council planted the seeds for a new relationship between Lutherans and Catholics. But in the previous four centuries and more before Vatican II, Lutherans and Catholics had lived to a good extent in mutual isolation, and with considerable hostility toward one another. This was still mostly the case for Lutherans and Catholics throughout the world. In the immediate post-conciliar period, starting in 1966 and extending during the rest of the pontificate of Paul VI (1966-78), a relationship between the LWF and the Catholic Church began to evolve.

In 1966, Pope Paul VI in the Apostolic letter *Finis Concilio* confirmed the SPCU as a "permanent organ of Vatican Administration." And then, as Cardinal Bea described developments in his introduction to the first issue of the SPCU's new *Information Service,* "Now the Council's directives are being put into practice throughout the world."[1]

The first meeting of the SPCU-LWF joint working group in August 1965 had already reflected on central theological issues for dialogue between Catholics and Lutherans.[2] But the second meeting, April 1966, emphasized that besides dialogue, some other important requirements for fostering the new relationship included, among others, "regular exchange of observers and consultations; regular staff consultations with broadening scope"; and a "constant projection of dialogue beyond the academic to

1. "Introduction, Augustin Cardinal Bea," *IS* 1 (1967): 3.
2. "The Roman Catholic Church and the Lutheran World Federation," *IS* 1 (1967): 6.

31

the spiritual plane with consequent openness and patience."[3] The fact that four of seven LWF members of the joint working group had been LWF observers at the Council (Skydsgaard, Vajta, Brauer, Quanbeck) embodied some continuity with the new relationships that had begun at the Vatican Council.[4] The observers would continue to contribute to other major contacts during the late 1960s, the 1970s, and even the 1980s.

The LWF and the Catholic Church began to act in partnership. They quickly established the envisioned dialogue, and took other appropriate steps to create new relationships between them, aimed at assisting their faithful to move from mutual isolation and suspicion towards mutual respect and a common concern for unity. National and local initiatives between Lutherans and Catholics towards these ends were beginning at the same time. The international Lutheran-Catholic theological dialogue began in November 1967, focusing on the theme "The Gospel and the Church."[5] Its report in 1972 would indicate that a consensus on justification could be in reach. At the same time other contacts implementing the suggestions of the 1966 joint working group's report began as well.

Exchanges of Correspondence, Observers, Visits, Invitations

A high level exchange of correspondence in 1967, and mutual exchanges of visits between LWF and SPCU leadership in 1969, 1972, and 1976, helped to foster partnership between the Catholic Church and the LWF. In 1967 Cardinal Bea initiated an exchange of correspondence with Dr. Frederick A. Schiotz, President of the Lutheran World Federation. Bea, "having spoken

3. "The Roman Catholic Church and the Lutheran World Federation," p. 6. See also "The First Official Report of the Joint Working Group Between the Roman Catholic Church and the Lutheran World Federation," *IS* 3 (1967): 26-28.

4. "The First Official Report of the Joint Working Group," p. 26. Cf. *Observateurs-Délégués et Hôtes du Secrétariat pour L'Unité des Chrétiens au Deuxième Concile Œcuménique du Vatican* (Civitas Vaticana: Typis Polyglottis Vaticanis, 1965), p. 89.

5. The second study commission concerning "The Theology of Marriage and the Problem of Mixed Marriages" took place 1970-76. It became a "trilateral" dialogue involving also the World Alliance of Reformed Churches as both began to have conversations with the Reformed in the late 1960s. See the "Historical Introduction" to the report of this dialogue found in *Growth in Agreement: Reports and Agreed Statements of Ecumenical Conversations on a World Level (hereafter GA)*, ed. Harding Meyer and Lukas Vischer (New York/Ramsey: Paulist Press; Geneva: World Council of Churches, 1984), p. 278.

about this with . . . Pope Paul VI," sent greetings to Dr. Schiotz and the LWF on the occasion of the Federation's twentieth anniversary and of the observance of the 450th anniversary of the Reformation.[6] The Cardinal, after praising the LWF observers at the Council, whose presence began a mutual fellowship that had now increased, expressed deep "regret that 450 years ago the unity of Western Christianity was broken," and said that to-day, neither wished to blame the other for the schism, but "rather, together we wish to seek ways for restoring the lost unity."[7]

While not speaking directly about justification, Bea underlined common convictions of Lutherans and Catholics about faith. "The decisive factor for you, as for us, is faith — faith in Jesus Christ. . . ."[8] "This faith is threatened in our world as never before." He expressed the hope that "we might succeed in giving a more effective witness to the world where so many feel incapable of faith in the Gospel. . . ." He noted also that Paul VI had proclaimed this year of the 1900th anniversary of the martyrdom of the Apostles Peter and Paul as the "Year of Faith." Bea then prayed that Christ "unite us in prayer so that Christian faith may be strengthened and be proclaimed with new power. Only in attending to the true message of Jesus will we find each other again."[9] Responding, Dr. Schiotz, after also referring positively to the LWF observers at the Second Vatican Council, wrote that "we recognize that the Holy Spirit has given us a precious unity in Jesus Christ. . . ." He stated that LWF member churches "will welcome participation in the 'Year of Faith' proclaimed by . . . Pope Paul VI. . . ."[10]

Exchanges of observers soon began. In 1967 Catholic observers representing the SPCU were present at an LWF Conference on World Mission,[11] and at the annual meetings of the LWF Commission on World Mission in 1968 and 1969.[12]

---

6. The Cardinal's letter and Dr. Schiotz's response are both found under "For the 450th Anniversary of the Reformation," *IS* 3 (1967): 21.

7. "For the 450th Anniversary of the Reformation," p. 21.

8. "For the 450th Anniversary of the Reformation," p. 21.

9. "For the 450th Anniversary of the Reformation," p. 21, all three quotes.

10. "For the 450th Anniversary of the Reformation," p. 21.

11. These were Dr. A. Hasler and Dr. K. Pitkatsky, SVD. See "Secretariat Observers Present at Non-Catholic Christian Gatherings," *IS* 3 (1967): 20.

12. "Joint Working Groups, with the Lutheran World Federation: Roman Catholic Observers," *IS* 7 (1969): 8. Even earlier, in 1963, two Roman Catholics (Pater Prof. Dr. Peter Bläser, MSC, and Pater Prof. Johannes Witte, SJ) were listed among the "Ecumenical Visitors" to the

The first official visit took place in 1969 when LWF General Secretary Dr. André Appel led a staff delegation to Rome.[13] Pope Paul VI's address to them included a very warm remembrance of the LWF observers at the Council. The Pope then expressed his happiness with the various ways in which cooperation and dialogue between Lutherans and Catholics were then taking place. He noted the significance of the question of Gospel and Church being studied in the international dialogue as "one of the most central which still stands between us . . . since the unhappy rupture of the time of the Reformation." He was happy that cooperation between the LWF and the Catholic Church was not limited to the theological field, but there were other ecumenical contacts. He stated that this visit was a cause of joy to him because it opened new perspectives of cooperation and dialogue.[14] He was referring to the fact that the delegation was visiting not only the SPCU, but also other Vatican offices such as the Congregations for the Doctrine of the Faith, and Evangelization of Peoples, the Secretariat of State, the Council for the Public Affairs of the Church, and the Secretariat for Non Believers. The visit therefore expanded existing contacts between LWF and Vatican offices "in line with mutual expressions for continuing relations voiced from the start of official theological dialogue."[15]

New Understanding and New Relationships Continue to Develop

Of great significance, the LWF invited Cardinal Willebrands to give one of the major addresses at its Fifth General Assembly in 1970 at Evian, France. Two of five major addresses at the Assembly focused on ecumenical issues — those of Cardinal Willebrands and of Professor Kent Knutson — and their themes were closely connected.[16] Both illustrated ways

---

LWF Assembly. *Proceedings of the Fourth Assembly of the Lutheran World Federation, Helsinki, July 30–August 11, 1963* (Berlin and Hamburg: Lutherisches Verlagshaus, 1965), p. 100.

13. "Visit of a Delegation of the Lutheran World Federation to Rome, May 28-31, 1969," *IS* 8 (1969): 10-11.

14. French original in "Allocution à la Fédération Luthérienne Mondialle (31 mai 1969)," *Documents Pontificaux de Paul VI (= Documents . . . Paul VI)* (Saint Maurice-Suisse: Editions Saint Augustine, 1969), VIII, pp. 393-95. English in *IS* 8 (1969): 11.

15. Introduction to the visit, *IS* 8 (1969): 10.

16. *From Federation to Communion: The History of the Lutheran World Federation*, ed. Jens Holger Schjørring, Prasanna Kumari, and Norman A. Hjelm (Minneapolis: Fortress Press, 1997), p. 391.

in which the Second Vatican Council helped to advance Lutheran-Catholic relations.

Significant in Willebrands's address[17] was his positive evaluation of Martin Luther, pointing to ways in which the Second Vatican Council had recognized concerns previously articulated by Luther. This caught the attention of the Lutheran listeners. Comparing the achievements of Vatican II and the growing ecumenical awareness of Luther's legacy, Willebrands rejoiced in points of agreement, without hesitating to acknowledge that areas of disagreement remained.[18] Of particular importance, Willebrands noted that just as Luther had used the Bible as the starting point of theology and Christian life, the Vatican Council had put more emphasis on the Holy Scriptures.[19] Willebrands's effort to articulate a positive understanding of Luther's achievements was an important contribution to a healing of memory, and to a new positive atmosphere between Lutherans and Catholics.

Professor Knutson in turn declared that the Second Vatican Council "constituted a challenge to the Lutheran Church unprecedented in our history," and interpreted the outcome of the Vatican Council as "being the end of the Counter-reformation and the beginning of a new era involving the Roman Catholic Church's participation in the quest for the reconciliation of all churches."[20] He gave a positive evaluation on some key statements of the Council, especially those dealing with the relation of Scripture and tradition.[21]

As an outcome, a statement prepared for Section 2, which dealt with ecumenical commitment, and in which these two addresses were discussed, recognized Cardinal Willebrands's lecture as "a unique and important step toward a deeper and more far-reaching understanding between our churches." It also pointed out that the member churches must be prepared to "acknowledge that the judgment of the Reformers upon the Roman Catholic Church and its theology was not entirely free of po-

---

17. Entitled "Sent into the World," found in *Sent into the World: The Proceedings of the Fifth Assembly of the Lutheran World Federation* (Minneapolis: Augsburg Publishing House, 1971). Reprinted in *IS* 101 (1999): 107-13.

18. *From Federation to Communion*, p. 392.

19. "Sent into the World," *IS* 101 (1999): 112.

20. Cited in *From Federation to Communion*, p. 392.

21. Even though he remarked that "the meaning of tradition is not as clear to us," *From Federation to Communion*, pp. 392-93.

lemical distortions, which in part have been perpetuated to the present day."[22]

Other gestures at the assembly illustrated ecumenical growth. Because there was no local Lutheran church to host the Evian meeting, services were held in the local Catholic church, which "in itself became a sign of ecumenical progress, an important legacy of the assembly."[23] At the invitation of local church leadership, some of the discussion groups met in Catholic schools.[24]

In 1972 the Holy See returned the 1969 LWF visit by sending a delegation, November 29–December 1, to visit the LWF.[25] Led by Cardinal Willebrands, the delegation included members from the Congregations for the Doctrine of the Faith, for Evangelization, for Catholic Education, from the Secretariat of State, and the Secretariat for Non Believers. The delegation was able to get an idea of LWF work in various fields. Discussions were held on theological questions and on ways of promoting practical cooperation between Lutherans and Catholics and of providing a better common witness to the non-Christian world. According to LWF General Secretary André Appel, "the exchange of views, instead of being a merely formal contact, became a real ecumenical dialogue, conducted with frankness and friendliness."[26]

Another LWF delegation visited Rome October 25-28, 1976, aiming "to improve continually mutual relationships."[27] They met again with principal Roman Congregations, Commissions, and Secretariats. As it had in the addresses of Cardinal Willebrands and Professor Knutson at Evian, the ecumenical importance of the Second Vatican Council's treatment of Scripture came up again, this time in Pope Paul VI's address to the delegation, and the latter's response. After expressing his profound gratitude to God for the ecumenical progress made over the last ten years, the Pope mentioned two factors that could foster further progress in the future. The first was "the special importance of Holy Scripture." Referring to *Unitatis redintegratio* 21, he said that we recognize with the Council that "in dia-

22. Cited in *From Federation to Communion*, p. 394.
23. *From Federation to Communion*, p. 389.
24. *From Federation to Communion*, p. 391.
25. "Relations with the World Lutheran Federation" (sic), *IS* 19 (1973): 10.
26. "Relations with the World Lutheran Federation," p. 10.
27. "Lutheran World Federation Visit in Rome, October 25-28, 1976," *IS* 32 (1976): 28. The reference here is to the Press statement.

logue itself, the Holy Scriptures are precious instruments in the mighty hand of God for attaining that unity which the saviour holds out to all men." Acknowledging that there are differences in interpreting Scripture "which still divide us," nonetheless, he said, the Word of God in Scripture "is able to build up and give the inheritance among all those who are sanctified (cf. Acts 20, 32, *Dei verbum* 21)."[28] Underlining a similar point, the delegation gave as a gift to the Pope a facsimile edition of Luther's Bible from 1545, saying that "it is the precious Word of God that meant so much to him, and that also guides our conversations with the Roman Catholic Church."[29]

The second factor that would foster the goal of full ecclesial communion, said the Pope, referring to *UR* 7, is the "need for authentic Christian living in accordance with the Gospel." Ecumenism cannot be limited to ecumenical dialogue and collaboration. Again referring to the Council, he recalled that the full unity of Christians has its highest exemplar and source in the mystery of the Holy Trinity. Thus Christians can more deeply and easily grow in mutual fraternal relations "to the extent that they enjoy profound communion with the Father, the Word and the Spirit (cf. *UR* 7)."[30]

This second factor was underlined when this visit was interpreted for the SPCU plenary meeting three weeks later (November 10-18, 1976). "All this goes on because the task of re-establishing union concerns 'as much the daily Christian life as it does theological and historical studies' (cf. *UR* 5)."[31]

Finally, the press release for the visit mentioned another development being prepared for the future. The Catholic Church would send observers to the Sixth LWF Assembly to be held June 13-25, 1977, in Dar-es-Salaam, Tanzania.

28. *AAS*, LXVIII, 1976, p. 667, and *IS* 32 (1976): 28.
29. Address of Mikko Juva, LWF President, *IS* 32 (1976): 29.
30. *AAS*, LXVIII, 1976, pp. 667-68, and *IS* 32 (1976): 29.
31. SPCU Plenary November 10-18, 1976, Report on "Dialogue with Lutherans at the International Level," *IS* 33 (1977): 20-22, here 22.

CHAPTER 4

Acknowledging the Growing Convergence on Justification

"Many questions . . . are now barely felt as controversial. An example of this is . . . the doctrine of justification."

Johannes Cardinal Willebrands, at Evian, 1970

Shortly after the Council, as these new initiatives for reconciliation between Lutherans and Catholics were being taken, important statements were made that also gave hope for reconciliation on the doctrine of justification, the key theological issue at the time of the Reformation. This was another sign that Lutherans and Catholics were moving away from the mutual isolation of the past.

The first official report of the Catholic Church–LWF joint working group had listed (no. 6) seven general areas for future exploration in dialogue. The fifth was "Justification and Sanctification," including four subtopics: "Law and Gospel," "The Meaning of Sin," "Baptismal Faith and Justification," and "Sacraments as Means of Grace."[1]

Writing in *L'Osservatore Romano* in July 1966 to explain this joint report about future theological dialogue, SPCU Secretary Bishop Johannes Willebrands illustrated that there was now a different context in which to assess the theological and pastoral problems that had divided the two com-

---

1. "First Official Report of the Joint Working Group Between the Roman Catholic Church and the Lutheran World Federation," *IS* 3 (1967): 26-28.

munities since the Reformation. They are still with us, he said, but "the manner in which they present themselves today is very different." The classical problems "are presented in a completely new context. The progress of the natural sciences, of history and scripture has from time to time modified their terms."[2]

Cardinal Willebrands at Evian, 1970

In 1970, Willebrands, as Cardinal and new President (succeeding Bea) of the SPCU, continued to affirm the growing convergence on justification when he addressed the LWF's Fifth General Assembly at Evian, France. Speaking on Catholic-Lutheran relations in the present and in the future, he referred also to the international dialogue, which had begun in 1967. The dialogue, he said, must always look back to the sixteenth century. There can be no doubt that "many of the controversies of that time appear in a new light today."

> Many questions, which at that time stood at the very center of controversy, have today been partly pushed towards the periphery and are now barely felt as controversial. An example of this is to be found in the doctrine of justification as such. It has been shown that extensive misunderstandings came into play on both sides and that these made a factual discussion impossible. The ecumenical dialogue has now been going on for some decades and the situation has been substantially improved.[3]

Willebrands also spoke of present-day changes in the Catholic picture of Luther. It is a good thing, he said, "to recall to mind a man for whom the doctrine of justification was the 'articulus stantis et cadentis Ecclesiae.' In this we could all learn from him that God must always remain the Lord, and that our most important human answer must always remain absolute confidence in God and our adoration of him."[4] Willebrands expressed an

---

2. Cited in "The Roman Catholic Church and the Lutheran World Federation," *IS* 1 (1967): 6.

3. "Sent into the World," Address of Cardinal Willebrands at the Assembly of the Lutheran World Federation, Evian, France, 1970. Reprinted in *IS* 101 (1999): 111.

4. "Sent into the World," p. 112. *From Federation to Communion: The History of the Lu-*

important insight concerning Luther's understanding of faith that would be helpful some years later in one of the major studies used as a resource for the development of the *Joint Declaration on the Doctrine of Justification.* "The joint research of Catholic and Evangelical theologians has nevertheless shown," he said,

> that the word "faith" in Luther's sense does by no means intend to exclude either works, or love, or hope. One may well say, and with much good reason, that Luther's concept of faith when taken in its full meaning, might not really mean anything other than what we designate by the word love in the Catholic Church.[5]

The Malta Report's Challenge on Justification, 1972

The first phase of international Lutheran-Catholic dialogue reflected on justification as a part of its agenda. In 1971, as the first phase was completing its report, the description of its fifth and final meeting published in SPCU's *Information Service* indicated that the participants had "general agreement that the long-standing controversial issue of justification need no longer divide our churches."[6] The report itself, entitled "The Gospel and the Church" (1972), the so-called "Malta Report,"[7] became "the foun-

---

theran *World Federation,* ed. Jens Holger Schjørring, Prasanna Kumari, and Norman A. Hjelm (Minneapolis: Fortress Press, 1997), p. 260, recalled this statement of Willebrands as important in the first stages of the Lutheran-Catholic dialogue.

5. "Sent into the World," p. 112. In the chapter on justification in *The Condemnations of the Reformation Era: Do They Still Divide?*, ed. Karl Lehmann and Wolfhart Pannenberg (Minneapolis: Fortress, 1990), p. 52, the authors follow this statement of Willebrands in a section arguing that Protestant doctrine understands substantially under the word "faith" what Catholic doctrine following 1 Corinthians 13:13 sums up in the triad of "faith, hope and love," and comment that, "in this case, the mutual rejections in this question can be viewed as no longer applicable today."

6. "Roman Catholic/Lutheran Relations," *IS* 14 (1971): 9-10.

7. So-called because the last session of this phase took place in Malta. Participants included: *Catholics:* W. Kasper (Co-Chairman), J. A. Fitzmyer, Bishop H. L. Martensen, E. Schillebeeckx, OP, E. Schürmann, A. Vögtle, J. L. Witte, and A. Hasler (Secretary). *Lutherans:* E. Molland, H. Conzelmann, G. Lindbeck, W. Lohff, P. E. Persson, K. Stendahl, G. Strecker, V. Vajta (Consultant), and H. Meyer (Secretary). Dr. August Hasler was the SPCU staff person responsible for relations with the LWF from 1968 to 1971.

dation for further dialogue, establishing its direction and demonstrating its feasibility."[8]

Noting that there were numerous causes for the break between Lutherans and Catholics in the sixteenth century, the Malta Report (MR) states that ultimately they "separated over the issue of the right understanding of the gospel" (no. 14). Then together they describe the foundation and center of the gospel as "constituted by the eschatological saving act of God in Jesus' cross and resurrection . . . which all proclamation seeks to explicate" (no. 24). In reference to the question of the center of the gospel it presents a concise treatment of justification, as follows:

> Today, however, a far-reaching consensus is developing in the interpretation of justification. Catholic theologians also emphasize in reference to justification that God's gift of salvation for the believer is unconditional as far as human accomplishments are concerned. Lutheran theologians emphasize that the event of justification is not limited to individual forgiveness of sins, and they do not see in it a purely external declaration of the justification of the sinner. Rather the righteousness of God actualized in the Christ event is conveyed to the sinner through the message of justification as an accompanying reality basic to the new life of the believer. (no. 26)

The report said, further, that the message of justification "must be articulated ever anew as an important interpretation of the center of the gospel" (no. 27). Also, "although a far-reaching agreement in the understanding of the doctrine of justification appears possible," other questions arise such as: What is the theological importance of this doctrine, and do both

---

8. Foreword to the report of the third phase of Lutheran-Catholic dialogue, *Church and Justification: Understanding the Church in the Light of the Doctrine of Justification* (Geneva: Lutheran World Federation, 1994), p. 7. Bishop Karl Lehmann later described the Malta Report as the "magna charta" on which all further phases of the Lutheran-Catholic dialogue had to build. Cited by Heinz-Albert Raem, "The Third Phase of Lutheran/Catholic Dialogue (1986-1993)," *IS* 86 (1994): 189.

But some aspects of the Malta Report seem not to have been adequately developed, as four participants added their special statements to the text expressing reservations on those aspects. "Report on the Joint Lutheran–Roman Catholic Study Commission on the 'Gospel and the Church' [Malta Report]," *Growth in Agreement: Reports and Agreed Statements of Ecumenical Conversations on a World Level (GA)*, ed. Harding Meyer and Lukas Vischer (New York/Ramsey: Paulist Press; Geneva: World Council of Churches, 1984), pp. 186-88.

sides similarly evaluate its implications for the life and teaching of the Church? (no. 28).

The Malta Report's claim, that a "far-reaching consensus is developing," challenged the Lutheran-Catholic dialogue to test this affirmation by more intense dialogue on justification during the next two decades. Taking up the challenge, other dialogue reports showed more clearly, with lengthy documentation, the extent of the consensus on justification, thereby creating the theological basis for the *Joint Declaration*.[9] Thus, the first of the two dialogue projects suggested in 1965-66 by the new Lutheran-Catholic joint working group produced important results.[10]

9. Two of the theological studies that were basic resources for the *Joint Declaration* indicate the challenge that the Malta Report posed. The report of the Lutheran-Catholic dialogue in the USA, *Justification by Faith: Lutherans and Catholics in Dialogue VII* (1985) (see Chapter 5 below), as its Introduction shows, responds to the Malta Report statement that a "far-reaching consensus is developing" in regard to justification, indicating that therefore "a further treatment of the subject and its implications is needed" (§2), and that "The present statement is a response to this need" (§3). The Foreword to the 1994 report of the international Lutheran-Catholic dialogue, *Church and Justification: Understanding the Church in the Light of the Doctrine of Justification,* indicates that "The Malta Report became the foundation for further dialogue" (p. 7), and "because of the developments between 1972 (Malta Report) and 1986, the Joint Commission found itself compelled to test the claim of a 'far-reaching consensus' on justification. In so doing they relied heavily on the comprehensive American dialogue statement, *Justification by Faith* (1985), and on the justification chapter of *The Condemnations of the Reformation Era — Do They Still Divide?* (1986)" (p. 9).

Also, there was a certain continuity of theological expertise from the Malta Report to the *Joint Declaration*. This is reflected in the fact that several theologians who worked on the Malta Report would also participate in the task force developing the *JD* in the 1990s (Meyer and Fitzmyer), and another officially signed it on behalf of the Catholic Church in 1999 (Kasper). Meyer also participated in the first three phases of international Lutheran-Catholic dialogue, and Fitzmyer in the USA dialogue *Justification by Faith*. Bishop Hans Martensen participated in the joint working group that prepared for the dialogue in 1965-66, and served on three phases of international Lutheran-Catholic dialogue (chairing the second phase), although he was not involved in the drafting of the *JD*.

We will point to this continuity of theological expertise in the process leading to the *JD* at several other points further on.

10. The other, on "The Theology of Marriage and the Problems of Mixed Marriages," involving also the World Alliance of Reformed Churches, met 1970-76, producing a report by that title (*GA*, pp. 277-306). While this subject was more pastoral in nature, Harding Meyer, who participated in both study commissions, referred to this report in 1999, when speaking of the significance of the *Joint Declaration*. To illustrate that the question of justification runs

Preparing the Catholic Church for Reception, 1973

With important dialogue reports beginning to emerge, not only from the Lutheran-Catholic dialogue, but also from others[11] as the Council's mandate on ecumenism was being implemented, it became clear that steps also had to be taken to begin to prepare and involve the Catholic Church as a whole for the reception of these reports, since "[t]he concern for restoring unity involves the whole Church, faithful and clergy alike" (*UR* 5). Since this kind of bilateral ecumenical dialogue was relatively new, an education process was necessary within the Catholic Church to explain the theological rationale for the dialogue itself and the nature and authority of the reports that the dialogues produced. Cardinal Willebrands addressed such issues, in the light of the teaching of Vatican II, several times in the years after the publication of the Malta Report. He did this first in the 1973 SPCU plenary meeting, and then in his addresses to the 1977 Assembly of the Synod of Bishops in Rome, thus helping to pave the way for the initial phases of reception of dialogue reports.

In his opening address to the 1973 SPCU plenary meeting, referring to *Unitatis redintegratio,* Cardinal Willebrands explained that the dialogues of today differ essentially from those in the sixteenth century, which involved controversies and were often polemical against those who were considered heretics at that time. Dialogue today is based on the teaching of the Second Vatican Council that "one cannot charge with the sin of separation those who at present are born into these communities . . . and are

---

through all controversial questions dealt with thus far in the dialogue, he recalled that the dialogue on *The Theology of Marriage and the Problem of Mixed Marriages* (1970-76) reached a critical point which at that time could not be overcome when it touched *the understanding of justification.* While for the Roman Catholic participants the indissolubility of marriage and the law of the Church *prohibited* any remarriage, the Reformed and Lutheran participants argued that, in light of the message of justification and forgiveness, *remarriage could not be excluded.* Here again *the differing understandings of justification proved to be the real issue.* At the end of the conversations both parties agreed in affirming that any promising continuation of the dialogue on marriage, especially on the issue of remarriage, ought to take as its starting point the questions of "justification and sanctification" and "law and grace" (no. 108; cf. 42, 43, 95) (emphasis his). Harding Meyer, "The Ecumenical Future: The Influence of Current Decisions," *Lutheran Forum* (Easter/Spring 1999): 38.

11. Reports were coming from the Anglican-Roman Catholic International Commission ("The Eucharist," 1971) and the Methodist-Catholic international dialogue (first report in 1971).

accepted as brothers by the children of the Catholic Church" (*UR* 3). In dialogue "everyone gains a truer knowledge and a more just appreciation of the teaching and religious life of both Communions" (*UR* 4, cf. also nos. 9, 11, 22). Putting theological dialogue in a broader perspective, he said that it must be accompanied by progress in dialogue in the form of encounter between Christians in the life of the churches. He stressed the fact that the search for perfect communion or unity in truth and charity, which will be a gift of God, involves more than an intellectual effort, because "it is from newness of attitudes of mind, from self-denial and unstinted love, that desires of unity take their rise and develop in a mature way" (*UR* 7).[12]

Concerning the authority of dialogue reports the Cardinal explained that these dialogues are not organs of the magisterium, and do not possess the authority of the church's magisterium. The conclusions found therein remain the responsibility of those who formulate them. These conclusions cannot be used, therefore, to support a line of conduct that changes the discipline of the church.[13]

Willebrands went further in his address to the 1977 Synod of Bishops, indicating the various purposes that publication could serve. With publication "the documents are offered for the critical study of specialists and of the communities concerned," and the results of this study will be "invaluable for revision or for the examination of the same theme in any subsequent dialogue." Furthermore, since dialogue is an instrument for reconciliation of the partners, "publication is an aid, at the various levels of the Church's life, in the task of assimilation of the process of convergence in practice, of understanding the method used, and the language used." Showing again that what was happening here was in line with the Council, concerning "the subject of language," he said, "it is worth recalling the norm given on this point by the Second Vatican Council in the Decree on Ecumenism: 'Catholic belief needs to be explained more profoundly and precisely, in ways and in terminology which our separated brethren too can really understand'" (no. 11).[14]

12. "Opening Address by His Eminence Cardinal Willebrands," at the SPCU plenary, November 6-14, 1973, *IS* 23 (1974): 3 and 4.

13. "Opening Address by His Eminence Cardinal Willebrands," pp. 5 and 6.

14. Contributions of the Secretariat for Promoting Christian Unity to the Work of the Synod of Bishops, 1977: Interventions of Cardinal Willebrands, "The Activity of the Secretariat for Promoting Christian Unity. Report to the Synod of Bishops, October 1977," *IS* 36 (1978/I): 6-8. Quotes just cited on 7.

Initial Evaluation of the Malta Report, 1974

Steps were taken toward reception of the Malta Report. In the same 1973 SPCU plenary meeting, the SPCU Secretary, Msgr. Charles Moeller, expressed the hope that the local churches could give a reaction to the Malta Report, and to give some indication as to what seems possible at the local level between Catholics and Lutherans in regard to practical situations of a pastoral type.[15] Also, in 1973 the initial session of the second phase of international Lutheran-Catholic dialogue (1973-84) heard reports from various countries about Lutheran-Catholic relations and determined that a main emphasis of future discussions would also include ways to implement agreements already achieved between the confessions.[16] The commission was to "evaluate the present relations of the Lutheran and Catholic churches, especially in the light of [the Malta Report]." The commission understood that its "primary purpose . . . was to initiate a process for the reception of the 'Malta Report' by the Lutheran churches, Catholic episcopal conferences and others concerned as well as to plan for an evaluation of their eventual responses." This included asking "what are the consequences of agreements already achieved for the common life of the churches; what matters need further study."[17]

In 1976, the results of this initial effort to gauge reception of the Malta Report were published. There were twenty-two Catholic responses (eight from episcopal conferences, two from ecumenical commissions, three from ecumenical institutes, nine from individual theologians) and ten Lutheran responses (three from churches, four from theological faculties, and three from individual theologians).[18] The Lutheran-Catholic joint commission studied these responses and determined that "it is still too

15. "General Report" by Msgr. Charles Moeller, *IS* 23 (1974): 12.

16. "Lutheran/Roman Catholic Joint Commission, Geneva, March 21-24, 1973," *IS* 21 (1973): 15.

17. Press release, "Lutheran/Roman Catholic Joint Commission," p. 15. The Malta Report had also been sent to study centers of both confessions as well as to LWF member churches and to Catholic episcopal conferences in countries where Lutherans are most represented. See "Dialogue with the Lutherans on the International Level," report for the 1975 SPCU plenary session, *IS* 27 (1975): 22.

18. "Dialogue with Lutherans at the International Level," a report of the SPCU plenary of November 10-18, 1976, *IS* 33 (1977): 21. It mentioned that "The restricted number of reactions from the Lutheran side may perhaps be explained, at least in part, by the fact that Lutherans in the USA and in Europe are involved in various projects for concrete union."

early to determine whether the substance of the 1972 report has gained general acceptance or been rejected by the churches."[19] However, the commission made an important observation that, "for now, the greater number of reactions positively values the fact that an official level dialogue between the Roman Catholic Church and the Evangelical Lutheran Churches has begun. The reactions further indicate that the MR has underlined the necessity of pursuing study and dialogue on a series of specific themes."[20] But by this initial effort to gauge reception of its report, the sponsors signaled that the dialogue was intended, at least, to help change attitudes of Lutherans and Catholics towards one another.

Justification and Indulgences: The Holy Year 1975

The Second Vatican Council had indicated that ecumenism involved the spiritual challenge of a conversion of mind and heart (cf. UR 7, 8), a different way of thinking about separated Christian brothers and sisters and their traditions. It would require an ecumenical spirit that would be reflected by sensitivity towards the views of the others, even when not agreeing with them. Attitudes that surfaced in the context of the Holy Year 1975 reflected that reception of these perspectives was beginning to take place in the Catholic Church, and in relationship to the question of justification.

As ecumenical convergence on the doctrine of justification was beginning to emerge in dialogue, preparations for the Holy Year 1975 raised issues that had some bearing on justification and would have to eventually be clarified. The Holy See's Central Committee for the Holy Year included an Ecumenical Commission which reported that "[g]iven the ecumenical commitment of the Catholic Church, the celebration of the Holy Year 1975 will necessarily have an effect on our relations with other Churches and Christian communities."[21] In fact, one of the questions raised by some of the latter after the announcement of the celebration of the Holy Year con-

19. "Lutheran/Catholic Joint Commission, Liebfrauenberg, France, March 15-21, 1976," *IS* 31 (1976): 11.

20. Final communiqué of the Liebfrauenberg meeting as reported to the November 1976 SPCU plenary, *IS* 33 (1977): 21.

21. "Reflections of the Ecumenical Commission for the Holy Year, Addressed to the Central Committee for the Holy Year (October 23, 1974)," *IS* 25 (1974): 13.

cerned the issue of indulgences in relation to justification. As the Ecumenical Commission said:

> We are the heirs of a centuries-old dispute over the problem of the popular interpretation of the doctrine of indulgences . . . which is linked to the understanding of justification and merit (and) is not regarded with favour by our Christian brethren of the Reform.[22]

At the same time, the Commission expressed the view that the Bull of Indiction of the Holy Year reflects a deep interest in Christian unity. For example, the Bull presents indulgences as immediately linked with Christ himself: "our indulgence, our salvation and our justice is primarily Christ himself." Moreover, particular indulgences form part of the "fullness of Christ." And care has been taken to avoid too materialistic expressions in regard to indulgences such as "the treasury of the Church."[23]

The Ecumenical Commission worked to raise ecumenical consciousness within the whole Catholic Church in regard to the Holy Year. Its first initiative was to contact the ecumenical commissions of episcopal conferences throughout the world, asking their opinions, encouraging them to study certain problems, and to collaborate with the Ecumenical Commission. One of the questions on which their opinion was asked related to the issue of justification: "how to present the doctrine of merit and the related indulgences, keeping in mind the difficulties that this matter raised among Protestants and also among Orthodox."[24]

While the issue of indulgences as an ecumenical problem was not resolved between Lutherans and Catholics at that time,[25] the fact that it was being raised, and in relationship to the doctrine of justification, testifies to the growing ecumenical awareness during that decade.

---

22. "Reflections of the Ecumenical Commission for the Holy Year," p. 13. For example, the Joint Working Group between the Catholic Church and the World Council of Churches had stated that the problem of special indulgences as an aspect of the Holy Year presents difficulties to other Christians. "Joint Working Group (RCC/WCC) Meeting 1974. Report on WCC/RC Collaboration. ©Holy Year 1975," *IS* 24 (1974): 2.

23. "Reflections of the Ecumenical Commission for the Holy Year," pp. 13-14.

24. "Reflections of the Ecumenical Commission for the Holy Year," p. 14.

25. It had still not been adequately discussed in ecumenical dialogue even by the time the *Joint Declaration on the Doctrine of Justification* was signed in 1999. A first consultation on indulgences, co-sponsored by the LWF, the WARC, and the PCPCU took place in Rome in February 2001.

Justification at Dar-es-Salaam, 1977

At the 1970 LWF Assembly in Evian, Cardinal Willebrands had suggested that the doctrine of justification need no longer be the insurmountable ecumenical problem that it had been. At the 1977 LWF Assembly in Dar-es-Salaam, Tanzania, the leading Catholic representative, Bishop Hans Martensen, Bishop of Copenhagen, a member of the SPCU and cochairman of the second phase of international Lutheran-Catholic dialogue, was able, in light of the Malta Report, to go further than Willebrands. Martensen was invited to respond to the plenary address given by Church of Norway Bishop Andreas Aarflot, entitled "The Lutheran Church and the Unity of the Church."[26] Aarflot spoke of the importance of the doctrine of justification for Lutheran identity (no. 18), stressing that in the history of the Reformation, the point with the partners was always: "Do you have the same understanding of the gospel as is expressed in the doctrine of justification by faith?" (no. 11). Martensen affirmed that, in the dialogue, "a wide field of central issues between the Lutheran and Catholic Churches has been dealt with and often an almost unexpected consensus has been reached even on those questions which seemed to be the most difficult and the most dividing issues at the time of the Reformation, such as . . . the justification by faith alone *contra* (emphasis original) a supposed Catholic concept of justification through works or merits."[27]

Thus at Evian in 1970, and even more at Dar-es-Salaam in 1977, the Holy See's representatives expressed to world gatherings of Lutherans the hopes for a consensus between Lutherans and Catholics on the doctrine of justification.

The Continuing Impact of the Observers

In this post-conciliar period, the participation of the Lutheran World Federation at the Second Vatican Council through its official observers was re-

26. Andreas Aarflot, "The Lutheran Church and the Unity of the Church," *In Christ a New Community: The Proceedings of the Sixth Assembly of the Lutheran World Federation. Dar-es-Salaam, Tanzania, June 13-25, 1977*, ed. Anne Sovik (Geneva: The Lutheran World Federation, 1977), pp. 35-47.

27. "Response by Bishop Hans L. Martensen," *Proceedings of the Sixth Assembly*, p. 48.

called more than once during contacts mentioned above, and continued to have a positive impact as a new relationship between the Lutheran World Federation and the Catholic Church took shape.

When Cardinal Bea wrote to Dr. Schiotz in 1967 on the occasion of two important anniversaries (see above), he started by praising the observers. "In Rome," he said, "we still have a vivid recollection of the inner readiness with which the LWF participated in the . . . Council through its distinguished representatives." Knowing they were present during four sessions of the Council "was always a matter of joy" for Bea and his colleagues. Numerous publications "testify to the interest and care" with which they followed the proceedings and studied conciliar decrees. This new fellowship among us, "which was made possible by the Holy Spirit, has not diminished since the end of the Council but has grown in dialogue and in cooperation."[28] Responding, Dr. Schiotz also referred to the LWF observers of the Council who "have faithfully reported on what transpired during those historic weeks. This has warmed our hearts."[29]

Addressing the LWF delegation on its first official visit to Rome (1969), Pope Paul VI said that "we hold in living memory the openness with which the Lutheran World Federation participated in the Council through representatives of quality." The Pope mentioned specifically "the second Conciliar session where Prof. Skydsgaard, representing your federation, spoke on behalf of all observers of the Council and underlined the fundamental importance for the ecumenical movement of a theology of the history of salvation." The Pope now added more detail than when meeting the observers in 1964, saying that this task "will be assumed, particularly, through the new Ecumenical Institute of Jerusalem."[30]

In 1976 when another LWF delegation visited Rome, Paul VI recalled

---

28. "For the 450th Anniversary of the Reformation," *IS* 3 (1967): 21.

29. *IS* 3 (1967): 22.

30. "Visit of a Delegation of the Lutheran World Federation to Rome, May 28-31, 1969," *IS* 8 (1969): 10-11, here 11.

In September 2005, in his address at the fortieth-anniversary celebration of Vatican II's Constitution on Divine Revelation *Dei verbum,* Cardinal Walter Kasper made the point that "The Council is concerned with the essence and significance of the word of God understood as *praeconium salutis,* a message of salvation and life," and then made the point that "During the Council it was above all two Protestant theologians Kristen E. Skydsgaard and Oscar Cullmann who emphatically highlighted this salvatory character and found a hearing above all from Pope Paul VI." *IS* 119 (2005): 121.

the observers even more warmly. He addressed the delegation as "Dear Brothers in Christ," recalling that "[i]t was with these words that Cardinal Bea greeted the observers when he met them at the beginning of the Second Vatican Council." Bea used the words "'Brothers in Christ,'" said Pope Paul, "to underline the unity that all Christians have: a unity which Christ created in Baptism itself." The Pope used the same title now to communicate his joy and gratitude for their visit, "which has for its purpose the further advancement of that mutual understanding which is so basic in the movement towards the reestablishment of full ecclesial communion."[31]

The Pope, addressing the 1976 SPCU plenary meeting a few weeks later, and underlining the importance of developing good relations with other churches and ecclesial communities, applied his words to the Lutherans, to the impact of the observers in general at the Council. "Through the presence of observers during the Council, future dialogues were outlined and our meetings with the pastors of their churches were prepared." And, "we have rediscovered one another as brothers, brothers still disunited, it is true, but really brothers who 'justified by faith in baptism are incorporated into Christ'; they therefore have a right to be called Christians."[32]

In the 1980s, the last report of the second phase of international Lutheran-Catholic dialogue, *Facing Unity* (1984), attributed the change of attitude of Lutherans towards Catholics, among other things, to "the presence of official Lutheran observers at all sessions of the Second Vatican Council," international and national dialogue, and increased cooperation at the local level, which "have led Lutherans to a new understanding of Catholic piety, church life and teaching. The Roman Catholic Church is no longer regarded as 'false church'" (no. 52).

Some of the Lutheran observers were themselves living links between the ecumenical spirit of the Council, which they experienced and to which they in some ways contributed, and the emerging new relationship between the Catholic Church and the LWF in the post-conciliar period, which they helped to shape. Thus, four of the seven Lutheran members of the new Lutheran-Catholic joint working group formed in 1964 were

31. "Address of Pope Paul VI to the Lutheran Delegation," *IS* 32 (1976): 28.
32. "Address of Pope Paul VI to the Members of the Secretariat, November 13, 1976," *IS* 33 (1977): 1.

LWF observers.[33] Some participated in the Lutheran-Catholic international dialogue that began in 1967.[34] Some were members of the second official LWF delegation that visited Rome (1976).[35]

33. Professors Skydsgaard, Vajta, Brauer, and Quanbeck. See "The First Official Report of the Joint Working Group," *IS* 3 (1967): 26; cf. *Observateurs-Délégués et Hôtes du Secrétariat pour L'Unité des Chrétiens au Deuxième Concile Œcuménique du Vatican* (Civitas Vaticana: Typis Polyglottis Vaticanis, 1965), p. 89.

34. Professor George Lindbeck took part in the first (1967-71) and second (1973-83) phases, being Co-Chair of the second, and Professor Vajta was consultant for the first phase and staff for the second.

35. Skydsgaard and Vajta; cf. "Lutheran World Federation Visit in Rome, October 25-28, 1976."

Summary of Part II

In the immediate post-conciliar period, to the end of Pope Paul VI's pontificate, the Catholic Church and the Lutheran World Federation took steps that initiated a new partnership. The Pope approved the International Catholic-Lutheran dialogue that began in 1967 and produced a significant report in 1972. Other contacts between the Pope, and SPCU presidents Cardinals Bea (up to 1968) and Willebrands (from 1969 onwards) and staff, including exchanges of correspondence, visits of high-level delegations, and invitations to important events in each other's life, helped foster new levels of friendship and mutual understanding. Paul VI fostered high-level exchanges and met LWF delegations when they came to Rome.

Concerning the doctrine of justification, it was beginning to become clear in the early 1970s, both from Cardinal Willebrands's address at Evian, and from the results of official international Lutheran-Catholic dialogue, that the centuries-old conflict over justification could be resolved. The Malta Report's statement that "a far-reaching consensus is developing in the interpretation of the doctrine of justification" was a step forward even if the report had no binding character yet for either sponsor. The efforts, in Rome during the Holy Year 1975, to present Catholic teaching on indulgences with ecumenical sensitivity in reference to the doctrine of justification, reflected a developing ecumenical spirit within the Catholic Church. Initial efforts of reception of the first dialogue results were undertaken, and attention was given in Rome to the importance of preparing the Catholic Church to receive properly the results of dialogue.

PART III

From Dialogue and Mutual Respect to Acknowledging Common Bonds of Faith and Friendship

Developments During the Pontificate of Pope John Paul II: The First Decade: 1978-1987

"In our dialogue with the Lutheran World Federation, we have begun to rediscover the deep bonds which unite us in faith. . . ."

John Paul II, February 8, 1980

CHAPTER 5

Deepening and Confirming the "Far-Reaching Consensus" on Justification

Introduction: The Pontificate of Pope John Paul II

Mutual respect continued to grow between the Catholic Church and the Lutheran World Federation, but so too did friendship and the awareness of sharing common bonds of faith. On the Catholic side, a new Pope made important contributions to this.

At the inauguration of his pontificate on October 22, 1978, Pope John Paul II assured representatives of Orthodox, Anglican, Lutheran, and many other Christian World Communions in attendance of his "firm resolution to go forward along the way to unity," and that "we must not stop before arriving at the goal . . . this unity which Christ wishes for his Church," and that "the commitment of the Catholic Church to the ecumenical movement, such as it was solemnly expressed in the Second Vatican Council, is irreversible."[1]

The pontificate of Pope John Paul II coincides with an important evolution in ecumenism: while dialogue continued and expanded, more attention was now given also to the reception of, and official response to, dialogue results. The Pope strongly encouraged both dialogue and reception. International ecumenical dialogues between the Catholic Church and var-

---

1. "Pope John Paul II to the Delegations of Other Christian Churches," *IS* 38 (1978): 56. French original: *Insegnamenti di Giovanni Paolo II,* Libreria Editrice Vaticana, Vol. I (1978): 44, 45. We will refer to the *Insegnamenti,* (volume, year, page) for the original language if other than English.

ious partners which had begun during the time of Paul VI continued under John Paul II,[2] and new dialogues began.[3]

From the beginning of his long pontificate, John Paul contributed significantly to reconciliation between Lutherans and Catholics and to calling attention to the significant bonds of faith that they shared. Continuing to support their dialogue, he eventually called for the official evaluation of the dialogue results. He continued and expanded contacts with Lutherans. Like Paul VI he met with LWF delegations, and supported growing cooperation between the SPCU/PCPCU[4] and the LWF. But John Paul II went further in fostering Lutheran-Catholic friendship. On numerous occasions, he also met the leaders and faithful of LWF member churches when they visited Rome, and/or during his pilgrimages to the Catholic Church in many countries. He met Lutherans in Germany, the Nordic countries, the USA, Brazil, and elsewhere. He was the first Pope to visit the Lutheran Church in Rome. He helped to create openness and trust by the respect he showed for the Lutheran heritage, for example, in his many positive statements about the Augsburg Confession, and in his critical evaluation of Martin Luther, acknowledging Luther's positive intentions.

During the first decade of John Paul II's pontificate, the far-reaching consensus on justification, signaled by the 1972 Malta Report, was deepened and confirmed through further dialogue. A certain reception of the Malta Report's statement on justification took place as it influenced subsequent Lutheran-Catholic dialogues. It was taken up in several of the reports of the second phase of international Lutheran-Catholic dialogue. Its challenge of a "far-reaching consensus" on justification was tested also, with significant results, in some national Lutheran-Catholic dialogues. Together, the results

2. Including bilateral dialogues with the Lutheran World Federation, the World Methodist Council, the Anglican Communion, the World Alliance of Reformed Churches, the Pentecostals, the Coptic Orthodox Church, the Church of Christ (Disciples of Christ), with some Evangelical leaders, and the multilateral dialogue of Faith and Order.

3. With the Orthodox Church (1980), the Baptist World Alliance (1984), the Malankara Orthodox Churches of India (1989), the World Evangelical Fellowship/Alliance (1993), the Assyrian Church of the East (1996), the Mennonite World Conference (1998), the family of Oriental Orthodox Churches (2004), the Union of Utrecht of Old Catholic Churches (2004), and informal consultations with Seventh Day Adventists (2000).

4. John Paul II's Apostolic Constitution *Pastor Bonus* in 1988 authorized a reorganization of the Roman Curia, in which the SPCU was renamed the Pontifical Council for Promoting Christian Unity (PCPCU), though its responsibilities remained the same. In referring to an event before 1988 we will use SPCU, and from 1988 and after, PCPCU.

of dialogue were gradually illustrating common bonds of faith on a doctrine once considered so divisive between Lutherans and Catholics.

The Malta Report's Statement on Justification in the Second Phase of International Dialogue

The second phase of international Lutheran-Catholic dialogue (1973-84) was co-chaired respectively by Dr. George Lindbeck and Bishop Hans Martensen.[5] The publication of its six reports, between 1978 and 1985, coincided with the first years of John Paul II's pontificate.[6]

This second phase of international dialogue did not treat justification at length, but four of its six reports explicitly recall the Malta Report's statement of the emerging "far-reaching consensus" on justification. Each refers to it in a different context, suggesting how the growing consensus on justification could foster fellowship and reconciliation between Lutherans and Catholics. The other two reports seem to allude to it.[7]

5. Msgr. Alois Klein was the SPCU staff person responsible for relations with the LWF 1979-84.

6. Six reports were published: *The Eucharist* (1978), *Ways to Community* (1980), *All Under One Christ* (1980), *The Ministry in the Church* (1981); they are found in the order just mentioned in *GA,* respectively pp. 190-214, pp. 215-40, pp. 241-47, and pp. 248-75. *Martin Luther — Witness to Jesus Christ* (1983), and *Facing Unity: Models, Forms and Phases of Catholic-Lutheran Church Fellowship* (1985) are found together in *Facing Unity: Models, Forms and Phases of Catholic-Lutheran Church Fellowship* (Geneva: Lutheran World Federation, 1985), and in *IS* 52 (1983): 84-88, and *IS* 59 (1985): 44-73.

Catholic members besides Martensen: Bishop P. W. Scheele, J. Hoffmann, J. Hotchkin, S. Napiorkowski, V. Pfnür, C. Mhagama (except '78); Staff: H. Schütte (Secretary '78, then consultant), A. Klein (except '78), P. Duprey (except '78, '80), C. Moeller (*Ways to Community* only); Consultants: H. Legrand (except '78). W. Kasper ('81 only), P. Bläser, MSC ('81 only). *Lutheran members* besides Lindbeck: Bishop D. H. Dietzfelbinger, K. Hafenscher, P. Nasution, L. Thunberg, B. Weber, I. K. Nsibu (except '78); Staff: V. Vajta (Secretary '78, then staff '80-81, consultant '83), C. Mau (except '78), D. Martensen ('80-81), G. Gassmann ('83), E. Brand ('84); Consultants: H. Meyer, G. Forell (*Ways to Community* only), U. Kühn ('80-81), W. Lohff ('81), J. Vikstrom ('81).

7. One of these, *The Eucharist* (1978), refers to the "important convergences and a certain consensus" expressed in MR without mentioning justification specifically (*Introduction,* no. 1, *Growth in Agreement: Reports and Agreed Statements of Ecumenical Conversations on a World Level* (*GA*), ed. Harding Meyer and Lukas Vischer (New York/Ramsey: Paulist Press; Geneva: World Council of Churches, 1984), p. 192. The other, *Ways to Community* (1980), states that the dialogue between our churches "has led in the last few years to the production

With *All Under One Christ* [AUOC] (1980), the international dialogue commemorated the 450th anniversary of the Augsburg Confession (CA) (1530). It put the "far-reaching consensus" on justification in the broader historical perspective of the Lutheran Reformation itself, also stressing that this ecumenical development on justification is part of a larger emerging consensus on basic aspects of Christian doctrine.

It explains that in 1530, when the CA was presented, the unity of the Western Church had not yet been shattered, and despite conflicts, the religious parties of that time "still felt themselves to be 'under one Christ' and committed to that church unity" (no. 2). Afterwards, differences between them that sharpened in doctrine, practices, church structures, along with non-church factors, led to an estrangement that lasted for centuries (cf. nos. 3-6). But since the Second Vatican Council, with the emergence of a new ecumenical situation, "there is a new sense among us that we are 'all under one Christ'" (no. 6). In this new context it is possible to look again at the ecumenical purpose of the CA, which is "the basis and point of reference for other Lutheran confessional documents (and) reflects as no other confession does the ecumenical purpose and catholic intention of the Reformation" (no. 7). The express purpose of the CA is to bear witness to the faith of the one, holy, catholic, and apostolic church. Its concern "is not with peculiar doctrines nor indeed with the establishment of a new church (CA VII, 1) but with the preservation and renewal of the Christian church in its purity — in harmony with the ancient church and 'the church of Rome,' and in agreement with the witness of Holy Scripture" (no. 10). While saying that theological research and ecumenical dialogue have shown that "the Augsburg Confession in large measure fulfills this intention and to this extent can be regarded as an expression of the common faith" (no. 11, cf. 12), AUOC also admits that there are still open and unresolved problems, since CA "does not adopt a position on the number of sacraments, the papacy, or on certain aspects of the episcopal order and the church's teaching office" and on other questions (no. 23).

Nonetheless, it is possible to appeal to CA in speaking of "a common mind on basic doctrinal truths which points to Jesus Christ, the living centre of our faith" (no. 17). Among other things, "together we confess the faith in the Triune God, and the saving work of God through Jesus Christ

---

of documents in which it has been possible to make joint statements on questions of faith where church-dividing contradictions previously prevented unity" (no. 75), citing in note 49 "Cf. especially Malta and *The Eucharist*," *GA*, pp. 231, 240.

in the Holy Spirit, which binds all Christendom together (CA I and III)" (no. 13). And referring to the Malta Report 26 (in note 5), it includes among these basic doctrinal truths that

> A broad consensus emerges in the doctrine of justification, which was decisively important for the Reformation (CA IV): it is solely by grace and by faith in Christ's saving work and not because of any merit in us that we are accepted by God and receive the Holy Spirit who renews our hearts and equips us for and calls us to good works. (no. 14)

AUOC states that, with all the limitations mentioned, this amounts to a "newly discovered agreement in central Christian truths . . ." (no. 25).[8]

In *The Ministry in the Church* (1981), MR 26 is recalled in the context of mission. Before three sections of the text which discuss the nature of ministry, an introductory section reflects on the message to be proclaimed by ministers: "The Saving Act of God Accomplished Through Jesus Christ in the Holy Spirit." Discussing the central truth of "salvation once for all" in Jesus Christ (nos. 6-8), the text indicates (no. 9) the possibilities today of common witness to this central truth because of the breakthrough reflected in MR 26. "The doctrine of the justification of sinners," it says, "was the central point of controversy in the sixteenth century." But, citing MR 26, "Today, however, a far-reaching consensus is developing in the interpretation of justification." This consensus "also helps us to see the earlier attempts to achieve unity in the doctrine of justification in a new light." And, "consequently, we now have a *joint starting point* (italics original) for the question of the communication of salvation in history."[9]

The joint commission published *Martin Luther — Witness to Jesus Christ* (= *Witness*) in 1983 on the occasion of Luther's 500th birthday, intending "to emphasize some central concerns of Luther and to bring out his ecumenical significance, to draw attention to the new understanding resulting from Lutheran and Catholic studies" (Preface). It cites Cardinal Willebrands's statement at the 1970 LWF Evian Assembly as reflecting this new attitude toward Luther (no. 23). The liberating message of the gospel, *Witness* states, as expressed in the doctrine of the justification of the sinner

---

8. The "Resources" for the 1999 *Joint Declaration on the Doctrine of Justification* (see note 1 in *JD*) indicate that, in parts 3 and 4 of the *JD*, formulations from different Lutheran-Catholic dialogues are referred to. *All Under One Christ* is one of these.

9. *GA*, p. 250.

through faith alone "was the central point" of Luther's theological thinking and of his exegesis of Scripture (cf. no. 9). But his "interpretation and preaching of justification by faith alone came into conflict with prevailing forms of piety which obscured God's gift of righteousness" (no. 13). But today, marked by an intensive Catholic re-evaluation of Luther and his Reformation concerns, "it is widely recognized that he was justified in attempting to reform the theology and the abuses in the church of his time and that his fundamental belief — justification given to us by Christ without any merit of our own — does not in any way contradict genuine Catholic tradition . . . found, for example, in St. Augustine and Thomas Aquinas" (no. 22). Thus, there is deeper mutual understanding today between Catholics and Lutherans of the central concerns of the Lutheran Reformation. And here *Witness* refers to MR 26 as reflected in *All Under One Christ:* summarizing what had already been jointly affirmed by Catholic and Lutheran theologians in 1972 *(The Gospel and the Church),* the joint statement on the Augsburg Confession says that: "A broad consensus emerges in the doctrine of justification, which was decisively important for the Reformation (CA IV)" (no. 11).

Facing Unity: Models, Forms and Phases of Catholic-Lutheran Church Fellowship (1984) was the last report of the second phase. While the Malta Report and previous documents of the second phase had either indirectly (most of them) or directly (*Ways to Community,* 1980) contributed to reflection on the goal of church fellowship, *Facing Unity* "strives for clarity regarding the nature of church unity and a concept of that goal which implies neither absorption nor return but rather a structured fellowship of churches."[10] In this context, *Facing Unity* indicates the importance of MR 26 for the goal of unity, which is the aim of the dialogue.

To set the stage, the preface gives a brief overview of what the dialogue had achieved since 1967. The achievement of the first round, the Malta Report, was that it "established an extensive consensus in the interpretation of justification and also a convergence of views in the controversial question of the relationship between Scripture and Tradition" (p. 5). Indicating later some of the steps needed for growth in fellowship and unity, *Facing Unity* states that "common witness to the apostolic faith is of fundamental importance" (no. 56). Thus, the dialogue has focused on issues relating to the

---

10. *Facing Unity: Models, Forms and Phases of Catholic-Lutheran Church Fellowship* (1984), Preface, p. 6.

Christological and Trinitarian center of the foundation of the Christian faith, and mutual rethinking has led to convergence or consensus on some basic aspects of faith. Among them, "it extends to our understanding of the gospel expressed during the Reformation particularly in the doctrine of justification," citing at length MR 26: "Today a far-reaching consensus is developing in the interpretation of justification . . . the Holy Spirit who renews our hearts and equips us for and calls us to good works" (no. 57).

Thus, reports of the second phase of international Lutheran-Catholic dialogue related the Malta Report's claim of a "far-reaching consensus" on justification to the growing "common mind on basic doctrinal truths which points to Jesus Christ" *(All Under One Christ)*, to a common view of the message, to be proclaimed by ministers, of the "saving act of God accomplished through Jesus Christ" *(Ministry in the Church)*, to the growing common appreciation of Luther's basic concerns *(Martin Luther — Witness to Jesus Christ)*, and to the basic agreement in faith required to achieve the goal of church fellowship *(Facing Unity)*.

The Malta Report and National Lutheran-Catholic Dialogues

Reception of Malta Report no. 26 took place also within some national dialogues, in particular in the USA and Germany. The Lutheran Catholic dialogue in the United States dedicated its seventh round (1978-83) to justification. Challenged by the Malta Report's statement that "today . . . a far-reaching consensus is developing in the interpretation of justification," the Introduction to its report, *Justification by Faith* (1985), states that "further treatment of the subject and its implications is needed. The present relationship between the Catholic and Lutheran traditions calls for a greater clarity about the way to understand and speak of justification than has yet been achieved in official discussions. . . . The present statement is a response to this need."[11] This dialogue, especially in light of its report's achievement and extensive treatment of justification, has been described, in historic perspective, as the first time in which this question has been taken up in an official dialogue by the Catholic Church and the Evangelical

---

11. *Justification by Faith: Lutherans and Catholics in Dialogue VII*, ed. H. George Anderson, T. Austin Murphy, and Joseph A. Burgess (Minneapolis: Augsburg Publishing House, 1985). Introduction to the Common Statement, nos. 2 and 3, p. 15.

Lutheran Church since the dispute at Worms and at Regensburg (1540-41).[12] In responding to the need to test the growing consensus by further work, *Justification by Faith* encompassed the present level of convergence up to that time in regard to (1) the history of the question, (2) reflection and interpretation of the issues, and (3) perspectives for reconstruction. "What has emerged from its work," said this report, "is a convergence (though not uniformity) on justification by faith in and of itself, and a significant though lesser convergence on the application of the doctrine as a criterion of authenticity for the church's proclamation and practice (no. 121)."[13] This became one of several basic studies that would contribute to formulations in the *Joint Declaration* a decade later,[14] and a resource for other key studies that came shortly afterward.

In Germany, inspired by a meeting between Pope John Paul II and Lutheran leaders in Germany during the Pope's visit there in 1980 (see Chapter 7), an ecumenical study group of Protestant and Catholic theologians was organized, focusing on questions of justification, sacraments, and ministry from the perspective of whether the sixteenth-century mutual condemnations expressed in the confessions of the Lutheran and Reformed churches, and in the doctrinal decisions of the Council of Trent on these issues, still apply today. As this study began in 1981, there was already a sense of the results it could achieve when Joseph Cardinal Ratzinger, then Archbishop of Munich, and Bishop Eduard Lohse, the two chairmen of the joint ecumenical commission, wrote together that "[a]ccording to the general conviction, these so-called condemnations no longer apply to our partner today. It must be established by the churches in binding form."[15]

12. Pawel Holc, *Un ampio consenso sulla dottrina della giustificazione: Studio sul dialogo teologico cattolico-luterano* (Roma: Editrice Pontificia Università Gregoriana, 1999), p. 74. Holc reviews the report and the reactions to it especially in the USA, pp. 67-131.

13. *Justification by Faith,* Common Statement, no. 152.

14. *Justification by Faith* is listed in the "Resources" of the *JD* as a report whose formulations are referred to in parts 3 and 4.

Another aspect of its continuity with the Malta Report was the participation, in this national dialogue, of Malta Report participants Dr. G. Lindbeck and Fr. J. Fitzmyer. Furthermore, several participants in this dialogue participated in the 1990s in the drafting group that produced the *JD. Catholics:* J. Fitzmyer and G. Tavard; *Lutherans:* E. Brand and John Reumann. Another, H. G. Anderson, was a signatory of the *JD.*

15. Their letter to the theological directors of the ecumenical study group of Protestant and Catholic theologians doing this study is found in *The Condemnations of the Reformation Era: Do They Still Divide?* (Minneapolis: Fortress Press, 1990), p. 169 (see note 16).

The study group worked for five years and published its report *Lehrver-urteilungen — kirchentrennend?*[16] in 1986. It became another primary source used in formulating the *Joint Declaration*.[17] It shared and cited the position presented in the American document *Justification by Faith*, that the way to get beyond the "barricades" held with intransigence on justification is to remain unswervingly on the Christological foundation:

> Christ and his gospel are the source, center and norm of Christian life, individual and corporate, in church and world. Christians have no other basis for eternal life and hope of final salvation than God's free gift in Jesus Christ, extended to them in the Holy Spirit.[18]

This study[19] gave more attention to why the ancient condemnations no longer apply to the partner today. It stated that "a number of differences were caused by insufficient mutual understanding — in part also by misinterpretation and excessive mistrust. Others were due to different modes of thought and expression. But undoubtedly difficulties remain and they still have to be worked through."[20]

The Third Phase of International Lutheran-Catholic Dialogue

The third phase of international Lutheran-Catholic dialogue, which began in 1986, relied significantly on the reports of the USA and German dialogues.

A joint LWF/SPCU meeting in Rome, March 19-20, 1985, which

16. *Lehrverurteilungen — kirchentrennend?* ed. Karl Lehmann and Wolfhart Pannenberg (Freiburg im Breisgau: Herder; Göttingen: Vandenhoeck & Ruprecht, 1986). English, *The Condemnations of the Reformation Era: Do They Still Divide?* References in this text are to the English version.

17. It is listed in the "Resources" of the *JD* as a report whose formulations were referred to in parts 3 and 4 of the *JD*. A certain continuity of theological expertise from the Malta Report to the *JD* is again seen because two MR participants, Walter Kasper and Harding Meyer, took part in this study group. Several participants took part in the drafting team in the 1990s that produced the *JD*: Bishop Paul-Werner Scheele and Harding Meyer.

18. *The Condemnations of the Reformation Era* refers on p. 36 to *Justification by Faith*, Common Statement, no. 156, 1 (p. 71).

19. For a discussion of this study see Holc, *Un ampio consenso*, pp. 133-223.

20. *The Condemnations of the Reformation Era*, p. 42.

planned this third phase,[21] understood that the dialogue, which in the second phase had led to the question about models, forms, and phases of Catholic-Lutheran church fellowship, "has brought us to a point from which it is no longer possible to go back" and "thus the question about the actualization of Catholic-Lutheran church fellowship should be the framework for the further dialogue and the themes which it will take up."[22]

The dialogue[23] took up the interrelated issues of justification, ecclesiology, and sacramentality, returning "to a specific theme of its 'Malta Report' (1972), namely justification," but with the "present point at issue . . . the relationship between this doctrine of justification and the doctrine of the Church."[24] At its first meeting in 1986, in light of the Malta Report's claim (no. 26) concerning justification, the Commission established a subcommittee to assess the statements made on justification in Lutheran-Catholic dialogue on the international and national levels in order to try to set forth this "far-reaching consensus" developing on justification.[25] The subcommittee worked in September 1986, and by the second meeting (1987) the commission had before it the subcommittee's draft of a statement, "Ascertaining the Wide Ranging Agreement on Justification."[26] The 1988 meeting reported that this latter was to be a platform from which the joint commission could deal with its assignment, i.e., to work on the

---

21. LWF representatives were General Secretary Carl Mau, Eugene Brand, Andreas Aarflot, George Lindbeck, and Harding Meyer; SPCU representatives were the Secretary, Pierre Duprey, Alois Klein (nineteenth only), and John A. Radano.

John A. Radano was the SPCU/PCPCU staff person responsible for relations with the LWF and other Lutherans 1984-90, 1997-98.

22. "Joint Memorandum: The Future Work of the Roman Catholic–Lutheran Joint Commission" (nos. 1 & 2), Rome, March 20, 1985, attached to "Report, Roman Catholic–Lutheran Planning Meeting, Rome 19-20, 1985," written by Eugene L. Brand. Manuscript dated March 25, 1985 (PCPCU Archive).

23. Catholic Co-Chair was Bishop K. Lehmann (1986-87), then Bishop P.-W. Scheele (1988-93); Lutheran Co-Chair was Bishop J. Crumley. Others: *Catholics:* Bishop H. L. Martensen, Bishop A. Nossol, C. Mhagama, V. Pfnür, L. Ullrich, J. Wicks; Consultants: A. Klein, H. Legrand; Staff: B. Meeking ('86-87), J. Radano, H.-A. Raem (from 1990). *Lutherans:* J. Boendermaker, G. Brakemeier, Bishop M. Buthelezi, I. Lönning, D. Wendebourg, Bishop U. Wilckens; Consultants: R. Jensen, H. Meyer; Staff: E. Brand.

24. "Lutheran/Catholic International Commission, February 15-21, 1987," IS 63 (1987): 13.

25. "Lutheran–Roman Catholic Relations," staff report to SPCU plenary meeting, February 1-6, 1988, IS 67 (1988): 78.

26. IS 63 (1987): 13.

nature of the church and its role in salvation, addressing the ecclesiological theme from the perspectives of sacramentality and justification. To build this platform, the paper attempted "to test the assertions of the 1972 Malta Report about the doctrine of justification," drawing heavily on the American report, *Justification by Faith,* and the German report, *The Condemnations of the Reformation Era. Do They Still Divide?,* which had worked on the issue while dealing with mutual condemnations of sixteenth-century Protestant and Roman Catholic confessional documents.[27] Thus the broad convergence on justification signaled by the Malta Report was developing further and deepening as a result of reports from other dialogues, national and international.

After its completion in 1993, the international joint commission published its report: *Church and Justification: Understanding the Church in the Light of the Doctrine of Justification.*[28] This report, too, is cited in the *Joint Declaration* as a resource. These international and national reports together provided the theological rationale for affirming that a consensus on basic truths of the doctrine of justification could be claimed.

27. "Lutheran–Roman Catholic Joint Commission, March 7-11, 1988," *IS* 67 (1988): 92. This 1988 "platform statement" on justification can be found in Holc, *Un ampio consenso,* pp. 377-89.

28. Geneva: The Lutheran World Federation, 1994, and *IS* 86 (1994): 128-81. For an analysis of *Church and Justification* see Holc, *Un ampio consenso,* pp. 233-313.

CHAPTER 6

John Paul II and the Lutheran Heritage

The 450th anniversary of the Augsburg Confession, and the 500th anniversary of the birth of Martin Luther, occurred during the early years of John Paul II's pontificate. The Pope seized the opportunity to address these anniversaries in positive ways, seeking to promote friendship and deeper fellowship between Lutherans and Catholics. He addressed these anniversaries both in Catholic contexts and in ecumenical settings involving Lutherans. Considering the importance of justification for Luther, and the prominent place of justification as an article of faith and doctrine in the Augsburg Confession (Art. 4), the positive attention given to these anniversaries by Catholic authorities would also be another form of support for efforts to achieve agreement on the doctrine of justification.

450th Anniversary of the Augsburg Confession, 1980

The significance, especially for Lutherans, of the Pope's references to the Augsburg Confession during this anniversary celebration, and also of the dialogue statement *All Under One Christ*, mentioned above, is suggested by events in the years leading up to the anniversary. In the 1970s a number of Catholic and Lutheran theologians in Germany, joined later by others in the USA, began to explore the question of whether the Catholic Church could also recognize the Augsburg Confession as a particular expression of the common Christian faith.[1] At the 1977 LWF Assembly in Dar-es-Salaam, the SPCU representative, Bishop Hans Martensen, made reference to this study process in his address to the Assembly,[2] but also cautioned "that he did not want to give the impression that Roman Catholic recognition of the Augsburg Confession was just around the corner."[3] Nonetheless, the Assembly passed an optimistic statement, noting "that distinguished Roman Catholic theologians consider it possible for their Church to recognize the Confessio Augustana as a particular expression of the common Christian faith."

> The Assembly — conscious of the importance of this initiative — welcomes endeavours which aim at a Catholic recognition of the Confessio Augustana, expresses the willingness of the Lutheran World Federation to engage in dialogue with the Roman Catholic Church on this subject, and requests that the Executive Committee promote and carefully follow the progress of all studies of this matter, its possibilities, its problems and its wider ecumenical implications.[4]

Cardinal Willebrands also welcomed the dialogue on this question, expressing the hope that "unprejudiced historical and theological investigations will clarify the meaning of the CA so that it becomes possible to restore unity in diversity. . . ."[5] But he cautioned that "official reaction by

1. A translation of the German essays, *Katholische Anerkennung des Augsburgischen Bekenntnisses?* (1977), with several additional contributions from American theologians, is found in Joseph A. Burgess, ed., *The Role of the Augsburg Confession: Catholic and Lutheran Views* (Philadelphia: Fortress Press; New York/Ramsey/Toronto: Paulist Press, 1980). Theologians contributing these essays were among those intimately involved in the official international or national Lutheran-Catholic dialogues that produced reports leading eventually to the *Joint Declaration* (Pfnür, Pannenberg, Schütte, Lindbeck, Vajta, Jorissen, Dulles, Kasper, Meyer, Jensen). Harding Meyer was also one of the *JD*'s drafters, and Walter Kasper signed the *JD*.

2. "Response by Bishop Hans L. Martensen," in *In Christ a New Community: The Proceedings of the Sixth Assembly of the Lutheran World Federation. Dar-es-Salaam, Tanzania, June 13-25, 1977*, ed. Anne Sovik (Geneva: The Lutheran World Federation, 1977), nos. 81 and 82, p. 49.

3. "Abridged and Consolidated Minutes of the Plenary Sessions" (Chapter 5), *Proceedings of the Sixth Assembly*, no. 78, p. 191.

4. "Statements of the Assembly" (Chapter 4), "Recognition of the Confessio Augustana by the Roman Catholic Church," *Proceedings of the Sixth Assembly*, nos. 18, 19, p. 175.

5. Cardinal Willebrands's Foreword in Burgess, *The Role of the Augsburg Confession*, p. vii.

the Catholic Church can only take place after a thorough consideration of all aspects of the problem." In fact, within a short time it was becoming clear that a simple recognition of the CA by the Catholic Church was not so feasible.[6]

Nonetheless, John Paul II referred to the CA a number of times in 1980. Just as the dialogues were reporting, more and more, a far-reaching consensus on the doctrine of justification, the Pope's statements during the 450th anniversary year of the Augsburg Confession also underscored the fact that Lutherans and Catholics have now reached a point of acknowledging that they share deep bonds of faith. Thus, on February 8, 1980, in Rome,[7] John Paul reminded the plenary meeting of the SPCU that "[t]his year is the 450th anniversary of the Augsburg Confession," and stated that in the dialogue with the LWF "we have begun to rediscover the deep bonds which unite us in faith and which were masked by the polemics of the past." He also urged that "if, after 450 years, Catholics and Lutherans could arrive at a more exact historical evaluation of this document and establish better its role in the development of ecclesiastical history, it would be a considerable step forward in the march towards unity."[8] He spoke of the anniversary at a general audience on June 25, 1980, recalling that the efforts to avoid tensions that had arisen between the Roman Catholic Church and the evangelical reform 450 years ago had not been successful at that time. Nonetheless, he was grateful that even if there had not been any success then in reconstructing a bridge, "the storms of that age spared important piers of that bridge." And the Lutheran-Catholic dia-

---

6. Msgr. Charles Moeller, SPCU Secretary, giving an update of the Lutheran-Catholic dialogue to an SPCU plenary meeting, November 13-18, 1978, reported that at the most recent international dialogue meeting, in October 1978 at Sigtuna, Sweden, in principle "reaction was favorable to the idea of the international commission taking part, in 1980, in the celebration of the anniversary of Augsburg Confession. But at Sigtuna there was no longer any question of 'recognition,' *Anerkennung*, of that document." Instead, the commission would propose, within the setting of the anniversary celebrations, "some kind of joint reading of the text, which would allow it to take into account the concrete scope of declarations of faith." Report of the Secretary to the Plenary, *IS* 39 (1979): 10.

7. This was just before *All Under One Christ*, dated February 23, 1980, was released. *Growth in Agreement: Reports and Agreed Statements of Ecumenical Conversations on a World Level*, ed. Harding Meyer and Lukas Vischer (New York/Ramsey: Paulist Press; Geneva: World Council of Churches, 1984), p. 246.

8. "The Pope's Address to the Plenary, February 8, 1980," *IS* 43 (1980): 67. French original: *Insegnamenti*, III, 1 (1980): 341-42.

logue since Vatican II "has enabled us to discover how great and solid are the common foundations of our Christian faith."[9]

He referred to the anniversary on trips abroad, in Brazil[10] and in Germany. During his visit to Germany, November 15-19, 1980, he mentioned the anniversary in five different addresses[11] and twice more when he returned home, in describing his trip.[12] Addressing the Council of the Evangelical Church in Germany in Mainz, on November 17, 1980, he reiterated, in light of CA, basic aspects of Christian faith held in common, namely, that "Jesus Christ is the salvation of us all. He is the only mediator, 'whom God put forward as an expiation by his blood, to be received by faith' (Rom 3:25). 'We have peace with God through our Lord Jesus Christ' (Rom 5:1) and among ourselves. By virtue of the Holy Spirit we are his brothers, really and essentially sons of God. 'If children, then heirs, heirs of God and fellow heirs with Christ' (Rom 8:17). . . . Reflecting on *Confessio Augustana*, and through numerous contacts, we have realized anew that we believe and profess all that together."[13]

The Pope stated at least twice that it was his particular wish to make his pastoral visit to Germany precisely during the anniversary year of the Augsburg Confession.[14] The LWF Executive Committee in 1981 expressed

9. "General Audience, June 25 (450th anniversary of the Confession of Augsburg)," *IS* 44 (1980): 91. German original: *Insegnamenti*, III, 1 (1980): 1840-41.

10. "Brazil: At Porto Alegre, July 4 (1980)," *IS* 44 (1980): 87. Portuguese original: *Insegnamenti*, III, 2 (1980): 118-19.

11. On his arrival, November 15, at Cologne-Bonn Airport; at his meeting on the 17th in Mainz with the Council of the Evangelical Church in Germany; at his meeting on the 17th in Mainz with other Christian denominations; in his address to the German Episcopal Conference in Fulda on the 17th; and in his final address at Munich airport on the 19th. "Visit to Germany, November 15-19," *IS* 45 (1981): 4-11. German original: *Insegnamenti*, III, 2 (1980): 1186, 1255-57, 1260, 1291, 1376.

12. At his Angelus address on November 23rd, and at the general audience on November 26th, saying at the latter that the anniversary "became for me a particular reason to be present, precisely in this year, in the country of the Reformation. . . ." *IS* 45 (1981): 11. Italian original: *Insegnamenti*, III, 2 (1980): 1392, 1423.

13. "Meeting with Council of the Evangelical Church, Mainz, November 17," *IS* 45 (1981): 6. German original: *Insegnamenti*, III, 2 (1980): 1255. His words reflected *All Under One Christ* (nos. 13 and 17). His affirmations reflect aspects of what would be the Christological basis of the *JD* (cf. no. 15).

14. At the general audience on November 26, 1980, *IS* 45 (1981): 11, Italian original: *Insegnamenti*, III, 2, (1980): 1423, and in an address at the German-Hungarian college in Rome, October 18, 1981, *IS* 47 (1981): 101. German original: *Insegnamenti*, IV, 2 (1981): 462.

its gratitude for the Pope's statements on CA during the anniversary year, as it did for the international Lutheran-Catholic dialogue statement *All Under One Christ,* and its claim that there is agreement on central doctrinal truths.[15] The Pope recalled this anniversary again in 1984,[16] and in 1987, during his second pastoral visit to the Federal Republic of Germany. He said in a homily during the 1987 visit: "The anniversary of the Augsburg Confession, celebrated a few years ago, provided us with a reminder of how broad and firm the common foundations of our Christian faith still are." He continued with a challenge that, one can say now, has been partially answered with the signing of the *JD* in 1999: "The genuine ecumenical spirit calls upon us to discover anew and promote the common elements of our faith, particularly the elements of the apostolic tradition that represent a profound link among all Christians."[17]

500th Anniversary of Martin Luther's Birth, 1983

In 1983, Lutherans celebrated the 500th anniversary of Martin Luther's birth. They also hoped to do this in an ecumenical way, with the participation of the Catholic Church in the celebrations. In some cases they extended formal invitations.[18] Pope John Paul II used the anniversary to foster deeper relations with the Lutherans. Of particular importance were the Pope's letter, dated October 31, 1983, to Cardinal Willebrands concerning the fifth centenary of the birth of Luther, and his visit to the Lutheran church in Rome the following December. But John Paul also referred to this anniversary in several addresses: to the Bishops of Bavaria, Germany, during their Ad Limina visit to Rome in January 1983; to Church leaders of Austria in Vienna, September 11, 1983; to participants in a study convention on Luther in March 1984. Cardinal Willebrands gave an address at the quincentenary celebration in Leipzig, Germany, on November 11, 1983. And, as seen

15. The Executive Committee statement, at its Turku, Finland, meeting, August 4-13, 1981, was cited in a report on Lutheran-Catholic dialogue at the SPCU plenary meeting, November 1981, *IS* 47 (1981): 125.

16. In an address to the international Lutheran-Catholic dialogue commission meeting in Rome, March 1984, *IS* 54 (1984): 10.

17. "Homily at Mass in Augsburg, May 3, 1987," *IS* 64 (1987): 56. German original: *Insegnamenti,* X, 2 (1987): 1571.

18. "Plenary Meeting of the Secretariat January 31–February 5, 1983," Report on "Lutheran/Roman Catholic Dialogue," *IS* 51 (1983): 27.

before, the international Lutheran-Catholic dialogue commission, co-sponsored by the SPCU, published the statement: *Martin Luther — Witness to Jesus Christ* in May 1983. All of these together acknowledged the more nuanced picture of Luther and his intentions resulting from contemporary study by Lutheran and Catholic scholars, thus continuing to foster a new atmosphere for Lutheran-Catholic relations. The Pope's statements reiterated again the common understanding on basic aspects of faith. The joint commission's statement underscored the emerging consensus on justification.

John Paul's letter to Cardinal Willebrands took up what the Pope saw as an ecumenical challenge and opportunity. He responded "with satisfaction" to the desire of "notable personalities and institutions of Lutheran Christianity" that this anniversary be marked by a genuine ecumenical spirit, and by discussion on Luther that might contribute to Christian unity.[19]

The Pope gave tribute to results of recent scientific research by both Evangelical and Catholic scholars, who "have already reached notable points of convergence," and have put things in a new perspective. There is "a more complete and more differentiated picture of Luther's personality and of the complex texture of the social, political and ecclesial historical realities of the first half of the sixteenth century." Consequently, "there is clearly outlined the deep religious feeling of Luther, who was driven with burning passion by the question of eternal salvation." But the Pope judges "that the breach of Church unity cannot be traced back either to a lack of understanding on the part of the authorities of the Catholic Church, or solely to Luther's lack of understanding of true Catholicism, even if both factors played their role." Rather the decisions taken had deeper roots. "In the dispute about the relationship between Faith and Tradition, there were at stake fundamental questions on the correct interpretation and the reception of the Christian faith which had within them a potential for ecclesial division which cannot be explained by purely historical reasons."

For these reasons the Pope proposed that a twofold effort was necessary, both in regard to Martin Luther and also for the re-establishment of unity. First, he called for an accurate historical work in order "to arrive at a true image of the reformer, of the whole period of the Reformation, and of

---

19. He perceived therein "a fraternal invitation to arrive together at a deepened and more complete vision of the historical events and at a critical assessment of Luther's manifold legacy." In "Pope John Paul II's Letter on Fifth Centenary of Birth of Martin Luther," *IS* 52 (1983): 83.

the persons involved in it." "Only by placing ourselves unreservedly in an attitude of purification by means of the truth can we find a shared interpretation of the past and at the same time reach a new point of departure for the dialogue of today." Second, he underscored the importance of the dialogue of faith in which we are jointly engaged, the dialogue which, "according to Evangelical-Lutheran confessional writings, has its solid basis on that which unites us even after the separation, namely, in the Word of Scripture, in the Confessions of faith, and in the Councils of the ancient Church." He asked that the dialogue be conducted "in fidelity to the Faith freely given, which implies penitence and a readiness to learn from listening."[20]

Cardinal Willebrands's address in Leipzig, November 11, 1983, referred to the Holy Father's letter, noting that it "paid tribute to the merits of the Luther research carried out by both Catholic and Protestant scholars,"[21] and stated that he wanted to pass on this word of recognition to all those, past or present, who had dedicated themselves to this research. Urging that this research continue, and recalling that at Evian in 1970 he had already drawn attention to some of its results, the Cardinal made some additional points, also citing Luther's theology. Concerning Baptism, since it is in Baptism we are brought into the Body of Christ, so too Luther, in Baptism "was 'added' to the body of the Lord Jesus Christ in the concrete form of his Church. And thus he became our brother in Christ. And even though later he did not remain in full ecclesial communion, this brotherhood in Christ was not destroyed." The Cardinal cites Luther on the significance of baptism: "The most important thing for us is Baptism through which we are received into Christianity. . . . God himself makes it a point of honour, and puts into it his own strength and power (Large Catechism)." "In it God pours out on us superabundant and inexhaustible riches of his grace, riches which he himself calls a new birth, so that we may be freed from the tyranny of the devil, saved from sin, death and hell, become sons of life, heirs of all God's gifts, sons of God himself and *brothers of Christ* (Small Catechism)" (emphasis original). Willebrands recalls another of Luther's main concerns, saying that the basic power of evil, the impotence of man, and the all-pervading might of God "were the central questions of life that

20. "Pope John Paul II's Letter on Fifth Centenary of Birth of Martin Luther," pp. 83-84.
21. "Address of Cardinal Willebrands on the Occasion of the 500th Anniversary of the Birth of Martin Luther, Church of St Thomas, Leipzig, Nov. 11th, 1983," *IS* 52 (1983): 92-94, here 92.

Martin Luther, professor of theology, man of prayer, preacher and pastor, posed himself. He pursued them with such passion and coherence that, in this respect, one is in a certain sense justified in describing him as the standard bearer of the majesty, the honour and the judgeship of God and, at the same time, as the spokesman of man, who — mortal and turned inwards onto himself — can rely on nothing other than God's mercy. A merciful saving God and man weighed down by guilt." Many of our contemporaries, the Cardinal said, have lost sight of the reality conveyed by those words. In light of this Willebrands offered a challenge relating to common mission: "I ask whether the time is not more than ripe for us to join hands in trying to see to what extent, face to face with this world of ours, we can today bear a joint witness to the good news of our redemption, the message that the Church is intended to serve. Ought we not, driven on by the memory of history and guilt, jointly to mould and shape our present?"

Willebrands pointed also to "another fundamental programmatic feature in Luther's theology and spirituality," namely the theology of the cross. Showing convergence between Luther's view and Catholic thought, the Cardinal asked whether the mystery of the cross has not been placed in a new light "by what the Second Vatican Council had to say about the Church as the people of God on a pilgrimage between the 'already' of the coming of the last age of salvation and the 'not yet' of its being brought to perfection? The Cross implies suffering, but also penance and conversion." Was it not true, Willebrands asked, that the intentions of the Reformation and the Counter-Reformation "met in the one basic concern they had in common, namely in the call for repentance and conversion conveyed to us by Holy Scripture"? Here he cited *Unitatis redintegratio* 4, that every Catholic must aim at Christian perfection, so that the church, which bears in her own body the humility and dying of Jesus, "may daily be more purified and renewed, against the day when Christ will present her to Himself in all her glory, without spot or wrinkle." We have a common commitment, said Willebrands, "for it behooves both of us to bear witness to and proclaim weakness, misery, challenge, persecution and suffering as manifestations of the hidden dynamics and the victorious force of our crucified and resurrected Lord."[22]

22. "Address of Cardinal Willebrands on the Occasion of the 500th Anniversary of the Birth of Martin Luther," pp. 92-94. By coincidence, some of the aspects of Luther's thought on which the Cardinal showed convergence with Catholic thought closely reflect positions

While showing these important convergences between Lutheran and Catholic thought, Willebrands also did not hesitate in the same address to recall that the church of his time put Luther under the ban of excommunication "to show in an unmistakable manner that there were errors and mistakes in the teachings and the personal attitude" of Luther. The historical data is there for all to see, but even these, said the Cardinal, "may today appear in a new light as far as this or that aspect is concerned, and prove open to a deeper and more comprehensive appreciation of the truth."

The year ended with a powerful symbolic act as John Paul, on December 11, 1983, made the first papal visit to the Lutheran church in Rome. The visit itself may have been a more powerful symbol of reconciliation than any words he spoke. But, sympathetically he referred to "the difficult history of the Evangelical-Lutheran community in Rome, its painful beginnings and all the light and shade of its development in the surroundings of this city." Once more he spoke of shared faith: "With gratitude we recall our common origin, the gift of our redemption, and the common goal of our pilgrim way." Echoing the international dialogue's report on the Augsburg Confession *All Under One Christ,* he stated that "we are all under the grace of Our Lord Jesus Christ. He is the center, the hinge, in which the whole existence, meaning and salvation of this world are contained." Once again he spoke of his ardent desire for unity and the need to make every effort to attain this unity. He spoke of penance, and used the Advent season to offer a vision of unity:

---

expressed in the *JD* as aspects of faith that Lutherans and Catholics now confess together. Concerning Baptism, compare *JD* 28: "We confess together that in baptism the Holy Spirit unites one with Christ, justifies, and renews the person" with Willebrands's citation from the Small Catechism: ". . . in it God pours out on us superabundant and inexhaustible riches of his grace, riches which he himself calls a new birth, so that we may be freed from the tyranny of the devil, saved from sin, death and hell, become sons of life, heirs of all God's gifts, sons of God himself. . . ." Concerning the question "How can I find a merciful God?" and Luther's central questions, as described by Willebrands, namely, "The basic power of evil, the impotence of man and the all pervading might of God," the *JD* states: "We confess together that the faithful can rely on the mercy and promises of God. In spite of their own weakness and the manifold threats to their faith, on the strength of Christ's death and resurrection they can build on the effective promise of God's grace in Word and Sacrament and so be sure of this grace" (no. 34); "We confess together that all persons depend completely on the saving grace of God for their salvation" (no. 19); "We confess together that sinners are justified by faith in the saving action of God in Christ" (no. 25).

From afar there seems to arise like a dawn, on this 500th anniversary of the birth of Martin Luther, the Advent of a restoration of our unity and community. This unity is the fruit of the daily renewal, conversion and penance of all Christians, in the light of the eternal word of God. It is also the best preparation for the coming of God in our world.

Thus, reminding them of John the Baptist calling his hearers to "Make straight the way of the Lord," the Pope urged his listeners: "Let us follow the call to reconciliation with God and with each other."[23]

Though his letter to Cardinal Willebrands and his visit to the Lutheran church attracted the most attention during the Luther year, the Pope's reflections on other occasions relating to this anniversary also illustrate his efforts at reconciliation with Lutherans. Speaking to Bavarian Bishops on January 28, 1983, the Pope referred to the theme, "Penance and Reconciliation," of the 1983 Synod of Bishops Assembly, urging them to take the opportunity to preach in greater depth on sin, penance, and salvation. But he also suggested the ecumenical significance of this during the Luther year in regard to the controversial issue of indulgences. Namely, "it could be shown clearly that indulgences, which are at the origin of division between Christians and which this year once again come face to face with the thought of Luther, make no claim to be anything more than a concrete response to the fundamental truth of faith which the Council of Trent formulated in these terms: 'The whole Christian life ought to be a continual penance' (DS 1694)."[24] Addressing Church leaders of Austria during his visit to Vienna in September, he referred to the fifth centenary of Luther's birth to speak of common faith that we share: "*After centuries of polemics and hostility* or . . . indifference we have *'rediscovered' each other in the true sense of the word* in our common foundation of faith in the one Lord and Redeemer, Jesus Christ. . . ."[25]

The Pope offered further reflections in March 1984 when receiving participants in a study convention on Luther that was meeting in Rome.

---

23. "Address of Pope John Paul II at the Lutheran Church in Rome, Sunday, December 11th, 1983," *IS* 52 (1983): 95. German original: *Insegnamenti*, VI, 2 (1983): 1326-27.

24. "To Bavarian Bishops 'ad limina' (January 28)," *IS* 51 (1983): 5, 6. German original: *Insegnamenti*, VI, 1 (1983): 261-62 (citing *Enchiridion Symbolorum*, Denzinger/Schönmetzer [DS] [Freiburg im Breisgau: Herder, 1965], n. 1694).

25. "To Church Leaders of Austria, Vienna (Sept. 11)," *IS* 52 (1983): 70 (emphasis original). German original: *Insegnamenti*, VI, 2 (1983): 455.

First, he affirmed that the 1983 holy year theme, commemorating the Redemption, provided another clue for seeking reconciliation. In speaking of the many initiatives and historical inquiries that had been taken during the Luther anniversary to re-evaluate "in a spirit of Christian love serenely open to the truth the . . . events . . . of the Reformation era," in order "to settle a still-open account from the past," while looking toward "that full unity for which our Saviour prayed," John Paul pointed to a further way forward. He spoke of the Redemption, relating his comments to the "two-fold commitment" mentioned in his letter to Cardinal Willebrands concerning the Luther anniversary:

> The spiritual movement of the Holy Year of the Redemption, open to all reality, makes a particular contribution to this interior attitude. "Celebrating the Redemption we go beyond historical misunderstandings and contingent controversies, in order to meet each other on the common ground of our being Christians, that is, redeemed" (Discourse to Roman Curia, 23 Dec., 1982). Reconciliation is a dimension that characterizes the Year of the Redemption, reconciliation with God and with our brothers and sisters.[26]

Second, taking note of developments in Europe, aimed at the "construction of a united Europe," and the fact that the Christian tradition had united the peoples of Europe, the Pope suggested that "there is growing among divided Christians an awareness of the urgency of regaining their historical unity in order to build together the dwelling of the family of European peoples. The unity of Christians is profoundly connected to the reunification of the continent; this is our vocation and our historical task at the present moment." He offered a challenge expressing the hope that the Luther convention might result in new impulses for fostering the unity of Christians, reconciliation among men, and for "developing the process of European integration in all its richness."[27]

Thus both John Paul II and Cardinal Willebrands indicated new efforts within the Catholic Church to look at the reformer in a new light. It is also appropriate here to indicate briefly what the international dialogue said about Luther. *Martin Luther — Witness to Jesus Christ* linked this com-

---

26. "To Participants in Study Convention on Luther (March 24)" *IS* 54 (1984): 13. Italian original: *Insegnamenti*, VII, 1 (1984): 752.

27. "To Participants in Study Convention on Luther," p. 14 and pp. 753-54.

memoration of Luther to that of the Augsburg Confession three years earlier. That document stated that research had led toward a more positive Catholic attitude toward Luther, who "is beginning to be honored in common as a witness to the Gospel, a teacher in the faith and a herald of spiritual renewal" (no. 4). The celebrations of the CA in 1980 "made an essential contribution to this perspective" because the CA is "inconceivable without the person and theology of Luther." The insight "that the Augsburg Confession reflects 'a full accord on fundamental and central truths' (Pope John Paul II, 17 November, 1980) between Catholics and Lutherans facilitates the common affirmation of fundamental perceptions of Luther" (no. 5).

Concerning justification, *Witness* recalls that Luther's study led him to a "renewed discovery of God's mercy." This "Reformation discovery" "consisted in recognizing that God's righteousness is, in the light of Romans 1:17, a bestowal of righteousness, not a demand that condemns the sinner." It is "a joyful message, that is, 'gospel.'" This discovery was confirmed for Luther by the Church father Augustine (no. 8). Its "liberating message," as the "doctrine of the justification of the sinner through faith alone," was the "central point of his theological thinking and of his exegesis of Scripture" (no. 9). The beginnings of an agreement on this fundamental concern of Luther "were already apparent in the theological discussions at the time of the Reformation" though not effectively accepted by either side (no. 10). But research in our time has opened the way "for a mutual understanding of the central concerns of the Lutheran Reformation." There is a "widespread recognition among Catholics that Luther's ideas, particularly on justification, are a legitimate form of Christian theology." For this reason, recalls *Witness*, summarizing what Catholic and Lutheran theologians had affirmed in 1972 (*The Gospel and the Church*), the Catholic-Lutheran statement of the Augsburg Confession in 1980 — *All Under One Christ* — says that "[a] broad consensus emerges on the doctrine of justification . . ." (no. 11).

Seeking to present a balanced picture, *Witness* also indicates Luther's weaknesses. Lutheran churches today are also aware of his limitations in person and work, and of certain negative effects of his actions. They cannot approve of his polemical excesses, and are aghast at the anti-Jewish writings of his old age. They see that his apocalyptic outlook led him to judgments that they cannot approve, e.g., on the papacy, the Anabaptist movement, and the Peasants' War. In addition, certain structural weaknesses in Lutheran churches have become obvious, especially in the way in which their administration was taken over by princes or the state — which Luther himself wanted to think of as simply an emergency arrangement (no. 20). Thus, with a balanced approach, *Witness* seeks to bring Lutheran-Catholic relations a step forward.

Both Catholics and Lutherans commented on the importance of the Pope's references to Luther during the Luther year. At the SPCU plenary meeting, November 12-17, 1984, Cardinal Willebrands stated that "[f]or the first time" the celebration of Luther's birth "took on an ecumenical character." Mentioning the Pope's letter to him, his visit to the Lutheran church in Rome, and his own address in Leipzig, he said that these "showed progress in fraternal relations between the Catholic Church and the Lutheran churches."[28] The staff report to the plenary on Lutheran–Roman Catholic dialogue, while mentioning the same events as receiving particularly strong public echoes, also said that in many countries, "Catholics showed a surprisingly great interest in Luther's person and work, and this was reflected in a lively participation in educational events, symposia, exhibitions, publications and church celebrations."[29] And Cardinal Willebrands, addressing a Lutheran Church in America Convention in Toronto in July 1984, described the significance of the Pope's words and gestures during those celebrations in 1980 and 1983 in terms of reception: "They are signs and examples of the efforts the Catholic Church is making to promote the reception of insights that are of great importance for the rapprochement and mutual recognition of our churches and their communions. Today we must continue to build on them and collect new elements that will pave the way to full church communion."[30]

A Lutheran appreciation was offered by Dr. George Lindbeck, Lutheran co-chairman of the international Catholic-Lutheran dialogue commission when the Pope received the commission on March 2, 1984. Addressing them, the Pope recalled the Vatican Council during which the Catholic Church renewed her commitment to Christian unity. At that time

28. "Prolusio of His Eminence Cardinal Johannes Willebrands," at the SPCU plenary meeting, November 12-17, 1984, *IS* 56 (1984): 96-97.

29. Staff report to the same plenary on "Lutheran/Roman Catholic Dialogue," *IS* 56 (1984): 108. The report also mentioned a pastoral letter of the Berlin Episcopal Conference in February 1983 as having received strong public echoes.

30. "Address of Johannes Cardinal Willebrands to the Convention of the Lutheran Church in America. Toronto, Canada, July 3, 1984," p. 7 in *Ecumenical Documents of the Lutheran Church in America 1982-1987* (New York: Lutheran Church in America, 1987).

"our first tie was with the esteemed Delegated Observers at the Council." This led to the official dialogue with the LWF and the "special, official relations we see as a necessity and as a gift of God." The Pope commented on the two anniversaries. Concerning that of the Augsburg Confession, he said that the dialogue has noted "an agreement on certain central truths of faith. What unites us and what we hold in common encourages us in the hope that we shall find still further unity in those areas of faith and Christian life in which we are as yet divided." Referring to the 1983 Luther commemoration, he said that we have been able to discern that research offers us "a more complete picture of the person and teaching of Luther" and a more adequate view "of the complicated historical events of the sixteenth century." He prayed that the commission's work would "be richly blessed and . . . bear much fruit."[31]

In response, Dr. George Lindbeck, speaking "as one who was a delegated observer from the Lutheran World Federation to the Second Vatican Council," expressed the gratitude of the joint commission for the Pope's "encouragement of the closer relations between our Churches." "Your statement on the Augsburg Confession in 1980," he added, "your letter to Cardinal Willebrands on the occasion of the 500th anniversary of Martin Luther, and your visit as Bishop of Rome to the Lutheran congregation in this city have evoked warm responses from both Lutherans and Catholics throughout the world and have greatly strengthened the bond between our Churches." The commission, he added, was increasingly impressed "by how deeply Lutherans and Roman Catholics are united by their shared commitment to the Christ-centered Trinitarian faith testified to by the Scripture and expressed in the creeds of the early Church. . . ."[32]

31. "To Catholic-Lutheran International Commission (March 2)," *IS* 54 (1984): 10.
32. "Address to the Holy Father of Prof. Dr. George Lindbeck, Lutheran Co-Chairman," *IS* 54 (1984): 11.

The Catholic-Lutheran international dialogue (second phase, 1973-1984) meets Pope John Paul II in Rome, March 2, 1984. Dr. George Lindbeck, Lutheran Co-Chair, exchanges gifts with the Pope. On the right, Bishop Martensen, Catholic co-chair, looks on. Behind Dr. Lindbeck are Rev. John Hotchkin (Catholic, USA) and Rev. Dr. Eugene Brand (LWF). (Photo © Servizio Fotographic de "L'O.R.," Vatican City)

Cardinal Johannes Willebrands, President of the Secretariat for Promoting Christian Unity (center), at the Lutheran Church in America Assembly in Toronto, Canada, 1984, with Msgr. Dr. Alois Klein of the Secretariat (left) and Dr. William G. Rusch, LCA Director for Ecumenical Relations (right). (Photo courtesy of LCA Office for Communications)

Pope John Paul II and LCA Bishop James Crumley in the Pope's library, November, 1984. Crumley was co-chair of the third phase of the international Lutheran-Catholic dialogue, 1986-1993. (Photo courtesy of *L'Osservatore Romano* and *The Lutheran*)

Delegation of the Lutheran World Federation visits Rome, March 3-5, 1988. From left, Dr. Eugene Brand; Rev. Dr. Jonas Jonson; Dr. Gunnar Stålsett, General Secretary; Bishop Johannes Hanselmann, President; Pope John Paul II; Bishop Andreas Aarflot; Dr. Paul Wee; and Dr. Walter Allgaier; accompanied by Msgr. John Radano (right) of the Pontifical Council for Promoting Christian Unity. Decisions taken by the LWF and PCPCU leadership during this visit opened the way for a later commitment to develop a joint declaration on justification. The delegation met with the Pope on March 4, 1988. (Photo © Servizio Fotografico de "L'O.R.," Vatican City)

Bishop Hanselmann (center) and Dr. Gunnar Stålsett exchange a gift with the Pope, March 4, 1988. (Photo © Servizio Fotografico de "L'O.R.," Vatican City)

An ecumenical Vespers service in St. Peter's Basilica, October 5, 1991, on the occasion of the sixth centenary of the canonization of St. Bridget of Sweden. Seated from left are Bishop H. Brandenburg, Catholic Bishop of Stockholm, Sweden; Archbishop Bertil Werkström, Lutheran Archbishop of Uppsala, Sweden; Pope John Paul II; Archbishop John Vikström, Lutheran Archbishop of Turku, Finland; and Bishop P. Vershuren, Catholic Bishop of Helsinki, Finland.
(Photo © Servizio Fotografico de "L'O.R.," Vatican City)

At the ecumenical Vespers service, October 5, 1991, Archbishop Werkström, Archbishop Vikström, and Pope John Paul II all preached. (Photo © Servizio Fotografico de "L'O.R.," Vatican City)

Some of the worshippers gathered at the same Vespers service, October 5, 1991. At the right, front is Rev. Dr. Heinz-Albert Raem, the staff person of the Pontifical Council for Promoting Christian Unity responsible for Lutheran-Catholic relations during 1990-97. (Photo © Servizio Fotografico de "L'O.R.," Vatican City)

CHAPTER 7

John Paul II and the Lutheran Family:
Fostering Bonds of Friendship and Reconciliation

Pope John Paul II, assisted primarily by the SPCU, also promoted friendship, deeper fellowship, and reconciliation between Lutherans and Catholics by supporting a broad range of contacts with the LWF, and by his own direct contacts with LWF member churches in different parts of the world.

Building on Paul VI's contacts with the leadership of the LWF, John Paul II met LWF leaders but also leaders of national and local Lutheran churches from different countries, either when they visited Rome, or during his own pastoral visits to different countries, including visits to some nations with a high percentage of Lutherans. This most traveled Pope in history insisted that pastoral visits to the Catholic Church in many countries include ecumenical contacts, and at times, prayer services, as a normal part of his program. He therefore had important contacts with Lutherans living, at that time, in very different cultural and ecclesiological contexts. Lutherans in Germany were rooted in the motherland of the Reformation. In the Nordic countries Lutheran folk churches were interrelated with the state which in some ways tended to dominate the church. Lutheran churches in the USA lived in a context of separation of church and state; and during the 1980s three Lutheran churches there were in a process of merging into one. During these various meetings the Pope usually made strong appeals for Christian unity. These and other contacts supported the often-significant Lutheran and Catholic contacts already taking place in local and national settings, or added some new dimensions to those relationships. This in turn helped to strengthen mutual understanding between the Holy See and the Lutheran World Federation, its international partner in Lutheran-Catholic dialogue and cooperation. While this chapter describes these many contacts during the first decade of John Paul II's pontificate, such meetings continued and were significant in the next decade as well.

An indication of the liveliness of these contacts can be seen in the fourteen-month period from July 1984 to September 1985. During that span the Pope sent a greeting to the LWF Assembly meeting in Budapest (July 23, 1984),[1] and received a number of Lutheran leaders in Rome. These included Bishop James R. Crumley, Jr., President of the Lutheran Church in America (November 1984), Archbishop John Vikström, Primate of the Lutheran Church of Finland (January 1985, with Finnish Orthodox and Catholic bishops), Archbishop Bertil Werkström, Primate of the Lutheran Church of Sweden (March 1985),[2] a delegation related to the American Lutheran Church (April 29, 1985),[3] Bishop Dr. Zoltan Kaldy, President of the Lutheran World Federation, Dr. Carl Mau, General Secretary of the Lutheran World Federation (June 27, 1985), and Bishop Dr. Lohse, President of the Council of the Evangelical Lutheran Church in Germany (June 1985).[4] In an address on ecumenism to the Roman Curia (June 28, 1985) he mentioned meeting other Christians during his apostolic journeys, including "the visit in Germany," and then "the contacts which I have had with the Lutheran bishops of the United States of America," and "the visit to the Lutheran community of Rome at the Christus-Kirche in December 1983."[5] An exchange of letters between himself and Bishop James R. Crumley, Jr., President of the Lutheran Church in America (LCA), was published on September 27, 1985, and on that same day the Pope received a delegation of bishops from the LCA on their ecumenical journey to Geneva, Istanbul, Canterbury, and Rome.[6] While this might be an unusual concentration of

---

1. *IS* 55 (1984): 51. Also *"In Christ — Hope for the World,"* Official Proceedings of the Seventh Assembly of the Lutheran World Federation, Budapest, Hungary, July 22–August 5, 1984 (Geneva: Lutheran World Federation, 1985), p. 152.

2. "Lutheran/Catholic Relations," staff report given to the SPCU plenary of February 3-8, 1986, *IS* 61 (1986): 126.

3. "To Group from American Lutheran Church (April 29)," *IS* 57 (1985): 12-13.

4. "Lutheran/Catholic Relations," p. 126.

5. "The Twenty-Fifth Anniversary of the Secretariat for Promoting Christian Unity: Pope John Paul II's Address to the Roman Curia, June 28, 1985," *IS* 59 (1985): 4.

6. "Exchange of Letters with Bishop James Crumley, Lutheran Church in America," *IS*

contacts between the Pope and leaders of one Christian tradition, it illustrates the increasing facility of these contacts.

As will be seen below, during some of these contacts, even early ones, something significant occurred relating to the eventual development of the *Joint Declaration on the Doctrine of Justification*, or somehow signaling its importance.

Deepening Relationships with the Lutheran World Federation

During this first decade of John Paul's pontificate, the SPCU and the LWF initiated, in 1986, the third phase of international dialogue, under the co-chairmanship of Bishop James R. Crumley, Jr., and Bishop Karl Lehmann, Bishop of Mainz, Germany (succeeded in 1988 by Bishop Paul Werner Scheele, Bishop of Würzburg, Germany). This phase was initiated "with the conscious intention of fostering fellowship between the two communions."[7] Its 1994 report[8] was a major theological contribution to the *JD*.

But other significant encounters during these years also fostered fellowship. These included exchanges of invitations to major events in the life of the other. The LWF invited Cardinal Willebrands to address its Seventh General Assembly at Budapest, July 1984. Illustrating growing friendship, the Pope, at the Sunday Angelus, July 22, 1984, at Castel Gandolfo, greeted the Assembly and offered a public prayer for its success, inviting those present and those listening to his voice "to pray to the Holy Spirit for the Assembly in Budapest, that its works may bear fruit and contribute to the restoration of full unity among all Christians."[9] In 1985, the Catholic Church invited the Lutheran World Federation and the other churches and Christian World Communions with which it was in dialogue, to send fraternal delegates to the extraordinary assembly of the Synod of Bishops in Rome, called to commemorate the twentieth anniversary of the closing of

---

59 (1985): 17-20. The exchange of greetings on meeting the LCA bishops immediately follows the letters, pp. 20-21.

7. Johannes Cardinal Willebrands, "The Catholic Church and the Ecumenical Movement," *A Day of Dialogue* (New York: Department for Ecumenical Relations of the Lutheran Church in America, 1987), p. 17.

8. *Church and Justification: Understanding the Church in the Light of the Doctrine of Justification* (Geneva: Lutheran World Federation, 1994).

9. "After Sunday Angelus, July 22," *IS* 55 (1984): 51. Italian original: *Insegnamenti*, VII, 2 (1984): 113-14.

the Second Vatican Council. Bishop Andreas Aarflot of the Lutheran Church of Norway represented the LWF. The fraternal delegates together were invited to draft and present a statement to the assembly, and to participate in an ecumenical prayer service at the assembly.[10]

Two important events took place during 1986. At the first, in October 1986, Pope John Paul invited leaders of churches and Christian World communions; as well as leaders of all the great world religions, to a day of prayer for peace, in Assisi. The LWF General Secretary, Dr. Gunnar (Stålsett), and LWF Vice President, Mrs. Susannah Telewoda, represented the Federation. The events were organized in such a way as to avoid any syncretism. Thus, during the second part of that day, the different religions went to different locations in Assisi to pray according to their own traditions. At the Christian prayer service, the leaders of all the Christian communions present participated, each leading a prayer, or an intercession, or doing a reading, as did Dr. Stålsett and Mrs. Telewoda. For the third part of the day, all the religions assembled together outside the lower basilica of St. Francis, and each took turns offering prayer in the presence of the others. A few representatives of each tradition represented the others. For the Christian prayer only four participants took part: Pope John Paul II, Metropolitan Methodios of Thyateira and Great Britain representing the Ecumenical Patriarchate, the Archbishop of Canterbury Dr. Robert Runcie, and Mrs. Telewoda of the LWF.[11]

The second important event that year took place in December 1986, when the LWF invited the Catholic Church and the Anglican Communion to join with it in an important effort of common witness and service in support of the Lutheran, Catholic, and Anglican churches in Namibia at a period when that country was seeking independence from South Africa. The LWF invited a delegation of about thirty persons, ten from each of the three churches, to come to Europe and meet with church and political leaders from various countries to explain the situation in Namibia and ask for support. The SPCU agreed to assist. After a conference organized by the LWF in Hanover, Germany, and a discussion with German church leaders, the whole delegation went also to Rome (and the Vatican) and London. At one point the delegation split up into smaller groups and went to a variety of European capitals to speak of their situation. Their program in Rome in-

10. "The Extraordinary Synod of Bishops November 25–December 8, 1985: Ecumenical Aspects," *IS* 60 (1986): 19-22.
11. "Assisi: World Day of Prayer for Peace," *IS* 62 (1986): 155-81; cf. 169, 171, 172-75.

cluded an audience with Pope John Paul II, who gave support to their cause;[12] they visited the section of the Secretariat of State with responsibilities for relations with States, the SPCU, the Commission for Justice and Peace, among other contacts. They met with Italian political figures as well. This cooperation was of great benefit for the Namibian churches.

In 1987, the Pope's letter to Dr. Gunnar Stålsett congratulating the LWF on the occasion of its fortieth anniversary celebration at Lund, Sweden, July 4-5, affirmed the growing communion developing with the Federation. The Catholic Church, he wrote, "cherishes its many contacts with the Federation, which help to deepen the real, though imperfect, communion already existing between us." Of particular importance, he said, "is the theological dialogue, co-sponsored by the Secretariat for Promoting Christian Unity and the Federation . . . for it aims at seeking unity in faith, so basic for achieving full communion." His prayer on this occasion was "that together we will find ways to strengthen our commitment to the search for Christian unity."[13] The following September Stålsett replied to the Pope, also saying that "we value highly" the theological dialogue with the Roman Catholic Church, and, with a special mention of Cardinal Willebrands, said that "[t]he efforts of many dedicated persons have opened doors that we had for too long shut against one another."[14]

In 1988, the LWF sent a delegation to Rome led by President Bishop Hanselmann and General Secretary Stålsett. As will be seen further on(chapter 9), a mutual decision made on that occasion might be considered a turning point in that it gave a new impetus to steps that would lead eventually to the drafting of the *JD*.

Contacts with German Lutherans

Pope John Paul II visited Germany three times (1980, 1987, 1996). All three were primarily pastoral visits to the Catholic Church in Germany. But looking back at these journeys, one can see that events in each case helped prepare the way for the eventual development of the *Joint Declaration*.

12. "To Representatives of Catholic, Anglican and Lutheran Churches of Namibia (December 3, 1986)," *IS* 62 (1986): 192.

13. "Celebration of the Fortieth Anniversary of the Lutheran World Federation," *IS* 64 (1987): 62.

14. Dated September 14, 1987, found in "Celebration of the Fortieth Anniversary," p. 62.

An encounter during his first visit in 1980 sparked a study process that led to the 1986 publication of a report that was one of the primary resources used in the development of the *Joint Declaration*. When the Pope met Protestant leaders in Mainz, November 17, 1980, Regional Bishop Eduard Lohse, chairman of the Evangelical Church in Germany, brought to the Pope's attention the urgent need for improved cooperation with regard to Sunday services, Eucharistic fellowship, and mixed marriages. Since such cooperation was hindered because of the mutual doctrinal condemnations of the sixteenth century, especially in regard to questions of justification, sacraments, and ministry, the need to solve these problems spurred the creation of a joint ecumenical commission to face these issues. While there was already a growing conviction that these condemnations no longer applied to the partner today, this had to be established by the churches in a binding way. The significance of the resulting report published in 1986: *Lehrverurteilungen — kirchentrennend?* (English, 1990: *The Condemnations of the Reformation Era: Do They Still Divide?*) has already been noted (cf. Chapter 5, and *JD* 41). This origin of the study process is mentioned in the "Editor's Preface" to the report, p. 2.

During his second visit to Germany in April 1987, the Pope acknowledged the work done on this study, and began to call for reception of its results. In Augsburg, with Lutherans present at an ecumenical service, he expressed gratitude "for all the steps that have brought us closer to greater unity in recent years." He expressed thanks, in particular, for the intensive ecumenical study on the reciprocal condemnations recently completed in Germany, and asked for response to its findings: "Let us reward the careful and responsible work of the dialogue commission established for this purpose after my first pastoral journey by studying, evaluating its results at the levels of our respective jurisdictions and arriving at a possible agreement." Furthermore, he speculated on how different things might have been if discussions there in 1530 had bridged the differences and clarified the points of contention. Saying, however, that it is not for us to speculate, but rather to hear Jesus' words that "[t]he exact time is not yours to know," he urged that "we have been commanded to do today what is due today so that which is needed tomorrow can happen tomorrow."[15]

Also, in Cologne and Munich, on the occasion of beatifying Fr. Rupert

---

15. "Homily During the Ecumenical Service, Augsburg, May 4," *IS* 64 (1987): 57. German original: *Insegnamenti*, X, 2 (1987): 1591-92.

Meyer and Edith Stein, the Pope's addresses included references to some fundamental agreements in faith, such as the sole mediation of Christ. Addressing Catholic bishops in Cologne, and citing the Augsburg Confession, the Pope spoke of the sole mediation of Christ when referring to the ecumenical question of devotion to Mary and veneration of the saints. It is often the practice and not the doctrine, he said, which offends our separated brothers and sisters. For, in fact, true veneration of Mary and the saints cannot, and does not, seek to detract from the sole mediation of Jesus Christ. Rather, Mary and the saints provide Christian life "with a comprehensive and convincing tradition of the imitation of Christ," and so it is fitting that "we should take their lives as models and draw encouragement from them." This belief is inherent also in the Confessio Augustana, which says: "Concerning the veneration of saints, we teach that the saints should be commemorated so that our faith may thereby be strengthened, so that we see how grace was given them and how they were helped through faith. Furthermore their good works should serve as an example to each for his own sphere of life (*CA*, 21)."[16]

When the Pope visited Germany a third time, in 1996, the development of the *Joint Declaration* was well underway, and as will be seen later (chapter 10), he used that occasion to support the process leading to the declaration.

Contacts with American Lutherans

John Paul II and also Cardinal Willebrands had important contacts with American Lutheran churches and their leaders in the first decade of the pontificate. They took these opportunities to emphasize again the degree of faith shared by Lutherans and Catholics, and on some occasions to speak of the emerging consensus on the doctrine of justification.

On September 8, 1982, three Lutheran churches in the USA, the Lutheran Church in America, the American Lutheran Church, and the Association of Evangelical Lutheran Churches, voted to become a single church in 1988, and established a process to work out the details.[17] This was the

16. "To the Bishops at Cologne, April 30 (1987)," *IS* 64 (1987): 55. German original: *Insegnamenti*, X, 1 (1987): 1479-80.

17. "Lutheran/Roman Catholic Dialogue," staff report to the SPCU plenary meeting of January 31–February 5, 1983, *IS* 51 (1983): 26.

situation of the majority of American Lutherans when significant contacts between American Lutherans and Rome took place during the 1980s.

While the Pope met leaders or representatives of several American Lutheran churches during the 1980s, his most frequent and fruitful contacts were with the Lutheran Church in America.[18] From 1980 to 1987, a series of significant encounters took place. LCA Bishop James R. Crumley, Jr., who had met Pope John Paul II in 1979 at an ecumenical service during the Holy Father's pastoral journey to the USA,[19] visited the Pope and the SPCU on several occasions in the early 1980s, usually as part of a longer journey in which the Bishop was also promoting relations with church leaders in Constantinople, Canterbury, and Geneva. The first visit was in 1981. Then in 1983, Bishop Crumley had conversations with Cardinal Willebrands in Utrecht before visiting Rome where he met Pope John Paul II and also Joseph Cardinal Ratzinger, Prefect of the Congregation for the Doctrine of the Faith. In 1984 the LCA invited Cardinal Willebrands to address its Convention meeting in July, in Toronto, on the question of Lutheran and Catholic relations.[20] Crumley's meeting with the Pope and the SPCU in November 1984 was particularly important because it led to an exchange of correspondence between the Pope and the Bishop which was published in 1985. Willebrands's address in Toronto, and the exchange of letters between Bishop Crumley and Pope John Paul in 1985, explicitly affirmed the direction towards reconciliation underway between Lutherans and Catholics.

In his address to the LCA Convention, Willebrands praised the LCA for its ecumenical commitment. He praised the Lutheran-Catholic dialogue in North America in which the LCA was one of the participating Lutheran churches, stating that the extent of this dialogue "has no counterpart in any other regional or national dialogues." He cited several of its reports published over the years, "not least, 'Justification by Faith,'" reports which, he said, "are all highly qualified and add further impetus to bilateral dialogue at the world level." He praised the fact that the North American dialogue is not merely academic, but is embedded in and carried

18. An example of contact with another Lutheran church can be seen in: "To American Lutheran Church, April 29 (1985)," *IS* 57 (1985): 13.

19. Crumley mentions this in his letter to the Pope dated May 22, 1985 (see below).

20. Cf. William G. Rusch, Director of Ecumenical Relations, LCA, in his preface to Cardinal Willebrands's Toronto Address, *Ecumenical Documents of the Lutheran Church in America 1982-1987* (New York: Lutheran Church in America, 1987).

forward "by the will of many local communities to achieve greater communion in everyday church life."

The Cardinal gave an overview of recent developments in Lutheran-Catholic relations on an international level. He recalled the celebrations of the Augsburg Confession in 1980 and cited the Pope's statement in Mainz, in November 1980, relating to the CA, that we can rejoice "to discover not only partial consent on some truths, but also agreement on the fundamental and central truths." He recalled the celebrations during the Luther year 1983, including the Pope's letter to him affirming the results of common Luther study and the new, more differentiated picture of Luther that emerges. These were signs, he said, of the Catholic Church's efforts to promote reception of insights that are of great importance for rapprochement of Lutherans and Catholics. He reported that the joint ecumenical commission set up in Germany after the Pope's visit there, re-examining the mutual condemnations of the sixteenth century, was posing now, to itself, the question "to what extent, if any, these statements still have validity in the present-day reality of our churches." He stated that in contrast to centuries of separation, dialogue has become "an ecclesial fact of great importance," having a far-reaching impact on our mentalities, but also affecting the practical life of the churches. But the Cardinal devoted most of the address to a discussion of the concept of reception, a concept which he said "has assumed new meaning and a new urgency in the ecumenical movement." This was an important address on the meaning of reception at a time when reception of dialogue reports by the Catholic Church was beginning to take place. The churches need to receive the ecumenical movement and ecumenical documents. He explained that the whole church is in some way involved in reception. He pointed to ways in which some degree of reception had taken place, thus far, in the ambit of Lutheran-Catholic relations.[21]

During Bishop Crumley's visit to Pope John Paul in November 1984, the suggestion was raised as to whether there might be some kind of common witness on their part in order to encourage the developing relations between Catholics and Lutherans (particularly the LCA), especially in the USA. This resulted in an exchange of correspondence between them, de-

---

21. "Address of Johannes Cardinal Willebrands to the Convention of the Lutheran Church in America. Toronto, Canada, July 3, 1984," in *Ecumenical Documents of the Lutheran Church in America 1982-1987*, especially pp. 7-8. More of what the Cardinal said about reception in Toronto will be seen in Chapter 8.

scribed as perhaps "unprecedented" because "in the form of personal letters, a bishop of a bi-national Lutheran church and the Pope have shared with each other, and now their churches, their assessment of the present state of ecumenical progress between their churches and their hopes for the future."[22] Bishop Crumley's letter dated May 22, 1985, and the Pope's letter dated July 22, were published simultaneously in September 1985, on the occasion of an LCA delegation's visit to Rome.

Among other things, both letters witness to the convergences on faith that had been realized in recent years. In his letter,[23] Bishop Crumley, acknowledging that he is not speaking on behalf of all Lutheran churches, but only of the LCA, recalls with appreciation the Pope's words to him on two occasions: "We must remember that there is far more that unites us than divides us." He expresses his view that the results of dialogue show that even if there are still outstanding issues between us, "a legitimate and complementary diversity exists between Lutherans and Roman Catholics," an insight that was not obvious in 1965. Because of our dialogues, Crumley wrote, "Lutherans and Roman Catholics can acknowledge substantial convergences in the areas of justification, baptism, eucharist and ministry. These convergences make us increasingly aware of how close we are to each other in the 'heart of the Gospel,' in proclaiming Jesus Christ as Saviour to the world." Crumley recalled the Pope's statement, relating to the 450th anniversary of the Augsburg Confession, "on June 25, 1980, in a general audience that the important piers of that bridge between Lutherans and Roman Catholics were not destroyed in the sixteenth century — words acknowledged by the Executive Committee of the Lutheran World Federation in August 1981, in Turku."

In his letter Pope John Paul spoke about the importance, in conversations, of reflecting on the scriptures, since Christians must be nourished by the good news of salvation contained therein. At several points he recalled words of the Malta Report (1972): that "the unity of the church can be a unity only in the truth of the Gospel" (no. 14), that "ultimately Lutherans and Catholics separated over the issue of the right understanding of the Gospel" (no. 14), and therefore that the quest for unity today is also a

22. William G. Rusch, in his Preface to "A Correspondence Between Pope John Paul II and Bishop James R. Crumley, Jr.," in *Ecumenical Documents of the Lutheran Church in America 1982-1987*.

23. Both letters found in "A Correspondence Between Pope John Paul II and Bishop James R. Crumley, Jr.," and in *IS* 59 (1985): 17-20.

search to be more truly evangelical, and to allow ourselves "to be formed by the Word of God." He acknowledged with gratitude that Bishop Crumley had recalled his statement on June 25, 1980, on the occasion of the 450th anniversary of the Augsburg Confession. Referring to Bishop Crumley's own reminder "that dialogue has made us increasingly aware of how close we are to each other in the 'heart of the Gospel,'" the Pope recalled "the Malta Report's affirmation of what the center of the gospel is: 'The eschatological saving act of God in Jesus' Cross and Resurrection' (no. 24)," adding that "for the progress that has been made in this common affirmation we must be grateful."

The Pope encouraged continuing dialogue, also recalling his words to the Council of the German Evangelical Church on November 17, 1980, that gratitude for what unites us requires that we examine together what still divides us, "not to widen the gaps but to bridge them" because "we are called . . . to full unity in faith. Only full unity gives us the possibility of gathering with the same sentiments and the same faith at the Lord's one table." For these reasons he expressed his happiness that the dialogue continues in the United States, and referred to its achievements, singling out the report on justification: "It has produced a number of impressive statements such as the recent *Justification by Faith*." The national-level dialogues such as the Lutheran–Roman Catholic dialogue in the United States, he wrote, are "important not only for the region in which they are undertaken but also for the contribution they can make to the relationship of our respective Christian families at the international level." Also, "along with the contributions of dialogues in other countries, and in continuing liaison with the Secretariat for Promoting Christian Unity and the Lutheran World Federation, your dialogue in the United States can contribute to the task of achieving that unity in faith which is our goal."

The Pope also praised the other types of collaboration taking place between Lutherans and Catholics in the USA. And, as the LCA with other Lutheran churches in the USA were proceeding toward a new ecumenical relationship in the next few years (toward the formation of the Evangelical Lutheran Church in America in 1988), the Pope expressed his prayers for that effort.

The correspondence was published on September 27, 1985, on the occasion of the visit to Rome of an LCA delegation that included nine LCA bishops. As part of this ecumenical journey, which had been planned in 1984, the delegation had traveled to Strasbourg, Geneva, Istanbul, Rome, and Canterbury. But at the audience in Rome, Bishop Crumley's greetings[24] and the address of the Pope both mentioned the correspondence. The Pope also, once again, spoke to them of shared faith, expressing his joy "because the Lutheran-Catholic dialogue over the last twenty years has made us increasingly aware of how close we are to each other in many things that are basic." He expressed sorrow too, "because there are important issues which still divide us. . . ."[25]

LWF General Secretary Gunnar Stålsett suggested the importance of this correspondence for the larger Lutheran family. The Pope's encouragement expressed in his letter, said Stålsett, must be seen "as an encouragement also to what we are doing internationally. . . . This exchange of letters is another mark of our continuing path to unity."[26]

A further mark, illustrating changing attitudes that foster unity, was a seemingly small gesture of the LCA at the main Eucharistic celebration during its thirteenth Biennial Convention in August 1986. The Archbishop of Canterbury, Dr. Robert Runcie, had addressed the Convention. He was present and took a prominent role as a concelebrant in the Eucharist, joining Bishop Crumley the presiding minister, and other participants including the Presiding Bishop of the Episcopal Church. The inside cover of the booklet used for the Eucharist singled out the presence of the Archbishop: "The Lutheran Church in America welcomes the Archbishop of Canterbury to this service. His presence and participation are a visible sign of the ongoing progress of the ecumenical movement. . . ." Of particular interest were "The Prayers," seven intercessions following the recitation of the Nicene Creed. One intercession was for Church leaders, including the Pope and Dr. Runcie. But it listed the Pope first in a kind of primacy of honor:

> We give thanks for John Paul, Bishop of Rome; Robert, Archbishop of Canterbury; Dimitrios, Ecumenical Patriarch, and other patriarchs of

---

24. Read in his absence by Dr. William Rusch, who coordinated the delegation.

25. The two addresses are found in *IS* 59 (1985): 20-21. Besides meeting the Pope, the delegation had encounters elsewhere with the Ecumenical Patriarch Dimitrios I, the Archbishop of Canterbury Dr. Robert Runcie, and with WCC Deputy General Secretary, Todor Sabev. The pilgrimage reflected the determination of the LCA to make its leadership aware of the larger ecumenical picture. Another would take place the following year with other participants. For a description of the LCA pilgrimage see "The Pilgrimage: Reflections on an Ecumenical Journey," in *Ecumenical Documents of the Lutheran Church in America 1982-1987*.

26. *Lutheran World Information*, 39/85, p. 5.

the Orthodox churches; and all leaders of the Church throughout the world. Renew us all in the unity of Holy Baptism, that together the whole Church may proclaim to the world the death and resurrection of Christ. Lord, in your mercy, hear our prayer.[27]

The Pope expressed his thanks to the LCA "for including a prayer for me during the Lutheran Church in America Convention" when another LCA-sponsored ecumenical pilgrimage to European church centers came to Rome in October 1986. He asked them to "convey my gratitude for that, and for his message just read, to Bishop James Crumley, to whom I extend my best wishes."[28]

During the Pope's second pastoral visit to the USA, September 10-19, 1987, ecumenical events took place on September 11 in Columbia, South Carolina. One was a prayer service in the local stadium attended by about 60,000 persons.[29] The other event was a private meeting of the Pope with some twenty-seven leaders of a variety of American churches and denominations — Orthodox, Protestant, and others. Among these were five Lutherans, representing three churches and one church about to be born: Bishop James R. Crumley, Lutheran Church in America, Presiding Bishop David W. Preus, of the American Lutheran Church, Dr. Ralph Bohlman, President of the Lutheran Church, Missouri Synod, Bishop Herbert W. Chilstrom, first elected Presiding Bishop of the newly formed Evangelical Lutheran Church in America, to be inaugurated in 1988, and Revd. Dr. William G. Rusch, Director for Ecumenical Relations, Lutheran Church in America. One speaker addressed the Pope on behalf of all twenty-seven, and the Pope in turn gave his address in response. The contacts were important even if the occasion did not allow them to be more than brief.

While the Pope left immediately after that meeting for another part of the USA, some of the local planners had taken advantage of the presence of Cardinal Willebrands, who had accompanied the Pope, to organize a "Day of Dialogue," on September 12 — co-sponsored by the Bishops Committee on Ecumenical and Interreligious Affairs of the U.S. Conference of Catholic

27. Booklet: *Holy Eucharist,* Thirteenth Biennial Convention of the Lutheran Church in America August 25-30, 1986, Milwaukee, Wisconsin.

28. "To Ecumenical Pilgrimage Sponsored by the Lutheran Church in America," *IS* 62 (1986): 182.

29. The Holy Father presided and preached, and leaders of a broad range of American churches and denominations participated.

Bishops, the Lutheran Church in America, and an LCA seminary, Lutheran Theological Southern Seminary. The program featured an address by Cardinal Willebrands concerning the Catholic Church and the ecumenical movement, and a response by Bishop James R. Crumley, Jr., of the LCA.[30] While each covered various topics, both also gave an assessment of how the doctrine of justification was being treated in current dialogue. After first reviewing some highlights of the first and second phases of international Lutheran-Catholic dialogue, the Cardinal turned to the third phase, which began in 1986. One of its tasks, he said, "is to assess whether consensus can now be claimed between Lutherans and Catholics on the notion of justification." This assessment was taking place in light of the work done in various dialogue reports, including the Malta Report, the USA document *Justification by Faith,* and in work done on justification by the mixed commission in Germany. Another task is "to study the implications of the doctrine of justification for the doctrine of the Church," and this work was underway.

Since the third phase of international dialogue "has been initiated with the conscious intention of fostering fellowship between the two communions," Willebrands commented on the importance of personal contacts such as those mentioned above. Thus, "while dialogue is important in fostering fellowship, so too are many other things." He mentioned the Pope's contacts with leaders of various churches and ecclesial communities such as those during his present journey to the USA, and the visits of church leaders to Rome to meet him, which were all invaluable contacts. He also mentioned the ecumenical pilgrimages of LCA bishops to Canterbury, Constantinople, Geneva, and Rome in 1985 and 1986. "The visitors and those who received them learned much. This is another important way of building fellowship. These contacts must continue."[31]

The remarks of Bishop Crumley, present also in his capacity as co-chairman of the International Lutheran-Catholic dialogue, complemented the Cardinal's own by focusing only on the American study *Justification by Faith.* Illustrating its impact, he said that when it was published, many Lutherans suffering from decades of stereotypes of Roman Catholics thought they must have misread one of the summary conclusions (citing from paragraphs 157 and 164 of that text):

---

30. *A Day of Dialogue.* Some 380 persons from many denominations attended.
31. Johannes Cardinal Willebrands, "The Catholic Church and the Ecumenical Movement," *A Day of Dialogue,* pp. 16-17.

Our entire hope of justification and salvation rests on Christ Jesus and on the Gospel whereby the good news of God's merciful action in Christ is made known: we do not place our ultimate trust in anything other than God's promise and saving work in Jesus Christ.

Or,

We are grateful at this time to be able to confess together what our Catholic and Lutheran ancestors tried to affirm as they responded in different ways to the biblical message of justification. A fundamental consensus on the gospel is necessary to give credibility to our previous agreed statements on baptism, on the eucharist, and on forms of church authority. *We believe that we have reached such a consensus.* (emphasis his)

None of us, Crumley concluded, "would say that the dialogical task is finished. But it has given substantial results."[32]

Contacts with Nordic Lutherans

The most significant contacts between Pope John Paul II and Nordic Lutherans took place during his visit to the five Nordic countries in June 1989, and in subsequent contacts, which will be discussed afterwards (chapter 9). But contacts during the first decade of his pontificate already reflected a thaw in the isolation of previous centuries. The Pope could say to the Catholic bishops of Scandinavia, when meeting them in February 1987, and reflecting earlier contacts with Nordic countries, including Lutheran leaders, that "[t]he centuries-long hostilities between confessions have finally been overcome. . . . They have been replaced by a growing spirit of ecumenical open-mindedness and cooperation, which just recently received an official confirmation through the establishment of diplomatic relations between three Scandinavian countries and the Holy See."[33] In the same address the Pope acknowledged that the Christian witness to the truth and the mission of the church for the salvation of mankind will become more convincing and effective when the disciples of

---

32. "A Response by Bishop James R. Crumley, Jr.," *A Day of Dialogue,* pp. 28-29.

33. "To Bishops of Scandinavia, February 26, 1987," *IS* 63 (1987): 7. German original: *Insegnamenti,* X, 1 (1987): 429.

Christ are one, and therefore he prayed ". . . that this unity . . . will become ever more a reality in your countries. . . ."

Since Nordic Lutheran churches have had, since the Reformation, a very close relationship with the state, sometimes a delegation to Rome from those countries would include leaders of both church and state. Or, the Pope would include theological concerns in his addresses to ambassadors from those countries. Thus, receiving on October 30, 1980, a delegation from Sweden that included Prince Bertil and Princess Lilian, the Archbishop of Uppsala, other church representatives, and the ambassador of Sweden to Italy, the Pope also expressed his greetings to members of the Swedish Lutheran Church residing in Rome, and asked his visitors to join him "in my prayer that God will . . . hasten the day when full unity of faith and Christian life will be established between us."[34] Receiving successive Swedish ambassadors to the Holy See in 1983 and 1987, he could encourage ecumenical cooperation in promoting spiritual and moral values of the gospel.[35] In March 1985 the Pope received the recently appointed Archbishop of Uppsala, Right Revd. Bertil Werkström.[36] Similar opportunities for encouraging ecumenism came in receiving successive ambassadors from Denmark to the Holy See in 1982, 1986, and 1988. To the first Danish ambassador in 1982, he said that "the Lutheran Christian faith, to which the great majority of your fellow countrymen for the last four centuries officially belong, shares a common source with our own faith."[37]

To the first Norwegian ambassador to the Holy See, in February 1983, the Pope stated that "[i]n your fellow countrymen who today adhere in great majority to the Lutheran confession, the Catholic Church loves to see brothers, seeking along with us the unity willed by our common Lord. . . ."[38] To the succeeding Norwegian ambassador in 1986 the Pope in-

---

34. "To Royal Visitors from Sweden, October 30," *IS* 45 (1981): 1.

35. "To the Swedish Ambassador (March 24)," *IS* 51 (1983): 10. Cf. "To the Ambassador of Sweden, January 9, 1987," *IS* 63 (1987): 6.

36. Staff Report on Lutheran-Catholic relations for SPCU plenary, Feb. 3-8, 1986, *IS* 61 (1986): 126.

37. "Receiving the First Danish Ambassador to the Holy See on December 18, 1982," *IS* 51 (1983): 6. French original: *Insegnamenti*, V, 3 (1982): 1630. Cf. also "To the New Danish Ambassador to the Holy See, June 23 (1986)," *IS* 61 (1986): 104, and "Pope Receives Credentials of Ambassador of Denmark, October 20, 1988," *IS* 69 (1989): 3-4.

38. "To Norwegian Ambassador (February 17)," *IS* 51 (1983): 6. French original: *Insegnamenti*, VI, 1 (1983): 452.

troduced other themes referring to the common heritage of Lutherans and Catholics, profoundly marked by the Christian faith: "in particular, the beautiful figure of Saint Olaf II, King, symbolizes for ever the belonging of the Norwegian People to Christ, after the baptism of their nation almost a thousand years ago." He suggested that this heritage can be the basis of common witness: "all the human projects regarding the well-being of the peoples . . . must rely for support on spiritual and moral values in the consciences of the citizens and . . . their leaders at the various levels," and thus man in Europe "should never forget that his Christian roots are an integral part of his identity and summon him to a new creative synthesis between the Gospel and the present conditions of his life. . . . I invite all Catholics to engage themselves in this way . . . [since] moral and spiritual values are certainly the object of the same preoccupation in the other Christian churches."[39]

A continuing contact between the Lutheran Church of Finland and Rome began in January 1985, when a Finnish delegation comprising the Primate of the Lutheran Church in Finland, Archbishop Dr. John Vikström, the head of the Orthodox Church, Metropolitan John, and the Catholic Bishop of Helsinki, Bishop Verschuren, came to Rome to establish a chapel in which the Finnish people in Rome could celebrate annually on January 19, the feast of St. Henrik, the patron saint of Finland. This event has continued over the years, for the most part, as a Lutheran and Catholic celebration, since they comprise most of the Finns in Rome. Each year a Catholic and a Lutheran churchman (occasionally also an Orthodox) from Finland come together to Rome for this service, joining those in Rome. Besides the service, which takes place in a chapel in the Basilica of Santa Maria sopra Minerva (dedicated — with the permission of the Dominican Community which is responsible for the Basilica — for this celebration of St. Henrik), the delegation has invariably visited the Pontifical Council for Promoting Christian Unity and has had a private audience with the Pope. The Finnish ambassadors to Italy and to the Holy See have supported and have helped to organize this annual celebration.

39. "To Norwegian Ambassador to the Holy See (January 20)" (1986), *IS* 60 (1986): 2. French original: *Insegnamenti*, IX, 1 (1986): 157-59.

Contacts with Lutherans in Other Countries

The Pope also had contacts with Lutherans from other countries, among them Latvia, Namibia,[40] Poland,[41] and Hungary. The Pope explained the meaning of these contacts in his address to the Roman Curia, June 28, 1985. On the one hand, they serve a very general though important purpose: "It is all a continuous network of relationships which establish mutual respect on the level of reciprocal knowledge." At the same time, they are important in supporting dialogue: they "favor approaches on the strictly theological level in opportune places and at agreed times."[42]

40. "Address to Latvian Pilgrims Celebrating the Eighth Century of the Evangelization of Latvia, June 26," (1986), *IS* 61 (1986): 104-5. "To Representatives of Catholic, Anglican and Lutheran Churches of Namibia, December 3 (1986)," *IS* 62 (1986): 192.

41. During his 1991 visit to Poland, for the first time an ecumenical service during a visit to Poland took place in a Protestant church, specifically the Lutheran Church of the Holy Trinity in Warsaw. In his address the Pope recalled the memory of some of the former Lutheran bishops who had served there. *IS* 78 (1991): 126. Polish original: *Insegnamenti*, XIV, 1 (1991): 1620ff.

42. "Pope John Paul II's Address to the Roman Curia," *IS* 59 (1985): 4.

CHAPTER 8

Reflections on the Question of Official Reception During This Decade

As initial efforts of reception were made in the 1970s after the publication of the Malta Report, so too the question of reception of dialogue reports was addressed in the 1980s. In the period 1978-88 the reports of the second phase of Lutheran-Catholic international dialogue invited reception, and Cardinal Willebrands, in several important contacts with Lutherans, gave significant addresses about the meaning of reception.

In the early and mid-1980s the question of official response to dialogue reports became a serious consideration in the Catholic Church, and the processes of official response to other dialogue documents were undertaken. Pope John Paul II supported efforts of ecumenical reception from the beginning of, and throughout, his pontificate. The SPCU studied the question of reception carefully during this same period. Its plenary meeting of November 13-18, 1978, the first during John Paul's pontificate, focused on the dialogues, their value, the problems they raised, and how their results were to be communicated.[1] The Pope supported this plenary's purpose, saying to it that "after these years of many-sided efforts . . . it is good to survey the ground so as to assess the results obtained and make out the best routes for further progress." Recalling that "the Council demanded a particular effort in teaching theology and forming the outlook of future priests (cf. *Unitatis redintegratio,* 10)," the Pope asserted that "this

---

1. Introduction to "Plenary Session of the Secretariat, November 13-18, 1978," *IS* 39 (1979): 1.

is especially important now, when this teaching must take account of the work of the dialogues which are in progress." He gave a pastoral reason: Once they are in ministry, how will priests be able under their bishops' direction "to find judicious and pastorally responsible ways of informing the faithful about the dialogues and their progress, if they have not been initiated into them during their training?"[2] Cardinal Willebrands, reflecting in his plenary address on twelve years of ecumenical dialogue, recalled that in these meetings between Christians and their churches, "we have built on the theological and ecclesiological foundation laid by the Second Vatican Council," and that the Popes of the Council, John XXIII and Paul VI, "by their words and their acts," had set dialogue in motion.[3]

The publication of the *Final Report* of the Anglican–Roman Catholic International Commission (ARCIC) in 1981, and the World Council of Churches' Faith and Order convergence text *Baptism, Eucharist and Ministry* (BEM) in 1982, raised, for the Catholic Church, the challenge of making an official response. Cardinal Willebrands reported initial steps in this direction to a 1983 SPCU plenary.[4]

While these efforts did not yet include formal reception of reports of the Lutheran-Catholic international dialogue, the reports issued by the second phase of Lutheran-Catholic dialogue make a strong appeal for reception. *The Eucharist* (1978) concludes with a section called "Reception" which requests the faithful and fellow Christians to examine the report, improve its reflections where needed, "and make them their own in so far as possible" (no. 77, *GA*, 212). *Ways to Community* (1980) states that the "reception of these results of the dialogue by our churches is an urgent task" and gives some suggestions on how it may occur (no. 75, *GA*, 231). *Facing Unity* (1985) asks the churches to examine, correct, supplement, and finally give authority to these documents (Preface of co-chairmen).[5]

On three occasions involving contacts with Lutheran church bodies, twice in 1984 and once in 1987, Cardinal Willebrands underscored the importance of reception and reflected on its meaning. In his address to the

2. "Address of Pope John Paul II," *IS* 39 (1979): 1-2. French original: *Insegnamenti,* I (1978): 177.

3. "Prolusio of His Eminence John Cardinal Willebrands," *IS* 39 (1979): 5.

4. "Plenary Meeting of the Secretariat, January 31–February 5, 1983, Cardinal President's Prolusio," *IS* 51 (1983): 12-16.

5. Cf. William G. Rusch, *Reception: An Ecumenical Opportunity* (Philadelphia: Fortress Press, 1988).

LWF Seventh Assembly in Budapest, 1984, the Cardinal referred to reception briefly, in light of the 1972 Malta Report, which stated that what we are engaged in is a "process of gradual rapprochement . . . in which various stages are possible" (paragraph 73). Commenting, he said, "If this process is really to be anchored in the life of the churches, the question of 'reception' acquires great significance and urgency, increasingly so today."[6]

Several weeks earlier, in his July 3, 1984, address to the LCA Toronto Convention cited above, Cardinal Willebrands gave a major presentation of a Catholic view of the notion of ecumenical reception, and also commented on recent Catholic reception efforts relating to Lutheran-Catholic relations.[7] Willebrands rooted the notion of ecumenical reception in the teachings of Vatican II. The ecumenical movement, described in *Unitatis redintegratio* 4, and its results "should be accepted, confirmed and received" by all Christians. In the ecumenical movement, reception, "especially as regards the results of a dialogue between two or more churches," has a new meaning. "One church receives from another. In the narrower sense it refers to the formal decision of the competent church authorities, though in the wider sense it embraces all the phases and aspects of the process by means of which a church adopts the results of such a dialogue" (p. 8).

Referring to *Lumen gentium (LG)* 12, the Cardinal stated that "just as the faith of the individual Christian is a supernatural gift of God . . . so too is this true of the 'sense of faith' of the Church as a whole." The Council used a quotation from Saint Augustine to circumscribe the People of God when it said 'from the bishops down to the last member of the laity' (*LG* 12). The People of God is thus understood not in a quantitative manner, but rather qualitatively in the hierarchical sacramental structure given to it by the Lord. The Spirit of God enriches the entire People with his different gifts, the charisms (p. 9). Reception is not the exclusive prerogative of the official magisterium, but "remains a process of the entire people of God

---

6. "Ecumenical Commitment: A Roman Catholic Perspective," "*In Christ — Hope for the World*," Official Proceedings of the Seventh Assembly of the Lutheran World Federation, Budapest, Hungary, July 22–August 5, 1984, Carl H. Mau, Jr., General Editor (Geneva: Lutheran World Federation, 1984), pp. 128-36, here p. 135.

7. "Address of Johannes Cardinal Willebrands to the Convention of the Lutheran Church in America. Toronto, Canada, July 3, 1984," in *Ecumenical Documents of the Lutheran Church in America 1982-1987*, pp. 8-12. The pages on which the Cardinal's statements are found will be cited in the text.

and in this sense it also has certain aspects of a sociological process" (p. 10).

Willebrands summarized a concept of reception in this comprehensive way:

> In *Catholic understanding* reception can be circumscribed as a process by means of which the People of God, in its differentiated structure and under the guidance of the Holy Spirit, recognize and accept new insights, new witnesses of truth and their forms of expression because they are deemed to be in the line of the apostolic tradition and in harmony with the *sensus fidelium* — the sense of faith living in the whole People of God — of the Church as a whole. Because such witnesses of new insights and experiences are recognized as authentic elements of apostolicity and catholicity, they basically aim at acceptance and inclusion in the living faith of the Church. The Decree on Ecumenism of Vatican II says that divisions among Christians make it more difficult for the Church to express in actual life her full catholicity in all its aspects (*UR* 4). In its full form reception embraces the official doctrine, its proclamation, the liturgy, the spiritual and ethical life of the faithful, as well as theology as systematic reflection about this complex reality. (p. 10; emphasis original)

Willebrands gave several examples in which reception processes "have already taken place between our churches" since Vatican II. He included recent Catholic attention to the Lutheran heritage, concluding with a somewhat prophetic statement:

> The recent rapprochement in the assessment of the Augsburg Confession and the historical judgment of Martin Luther is likewise not without its importance. By the grace of God, this first brief history of reception in the ambit of Lutheran-Catholic relations is going to have its sequel both in the present and in the future. (p. 10)

Bishop James Crumley, LCA President, in closing remarks as host, linked the Cardinal's description of reception to reception of dialogue results on justification. He appreciated the Cardinal's view that reception is not simply the dialogic convergence among scholars, but "has to involve the whole people of God." Referring to an annual meeting of Lutheran and Roman Catholic bishops in the USA to evaluate the dialogues and what should be done with them, Crumley said that "there was particular satisfaction as we met last year with the document on 'Justification by Faith' produced by our dialogues in the United States." It was decided that "this is a document of such great importance in our history that we must provide for it to be used among our congregations and also arrange to provide materials so that that study could take place."[8]

The Cardinal also addressed reception at the LCA co-sponsored "Day of Dialogue" on September 12, 1987, in Columbia, South Carolina, after the Pope's visit. Whereas in Toronto he had described a theology of reception, here he described an application of that theology as reflected in the Catholic response, completed in 1987, to the Faith and Order text *Baptism, Eucharist and Ministry*. He showed the various steps required within the Catholic Church to achieve that response, including the participation of the SPCU and the Congregation for the Doctrine of the Faith (CDF).[9] Again, his interlocutor was Bishop Crumley, who responded first by repeating the comments of the Director of the WCC's Faith and Order Commission, Dr. Günther Gassmann, on receiving the Catholic response to BEM, that "[f]or the first time in the history of the ecumenical movement the Roman Catholic Church has responded officially to an ecumenical document. . . . The critical comments . . . are presented as suggestions for further work of Faith and Order in which Roman Catholic theologians are fully involved. These comments are made on the basis of definitions that may lead to a fruitful debate also within the Roman Catholic Church concerning its own doctrinal and ecumenical position. The response clearly affirms large sections of the BEM document and sees in them, if accepted also by other churches, both a means of deepening the already existing, though imperfect communion between the churches and the opening of further advance toward the goal of full visible unity."

Gassmann's remarks, said Crumley, suggest what is involved in a response process that may hopefully grow into reception in the churches: the theological work is studied carefully; the progress toward agreement, convergence, or actual consensus is noted; problems are noted; the process

---

8. "Bishop Crumley's Closing Remarks," in *Ecumenical Documents of the Lutheran Church in America 1982-1987*, p. 15.

9. "The Catholic Church and the Ecumenical Movement: An Address by Johannes Cardinal Willebrands," in *A Day of Dialogue* (New York: Department for Ecumenical Relations of the Lutheran Church in America, 1987), pp. 22-24.

does not glide over real differences if they exist; and the churches them-selves assist in pointing to the work yet to be done.[10]

Thus, when, in the 1990s, an official reception and response process was undertaken for the *Joint Declaration,* significant officials and offices of the Holy See had previously given serious thought to reception, and had some important experience with it. And, Lutherans and Catholics had had some discussion together on these concerns.

10. "A Response by Bishop James R. Crumley," *A Day of Dialogue,* pp. 29-30.

Summary of Part III

During the period 1978-87, reports of international and national Lutheran-Catholic dialogues, which had taken up the Malta Report's challenge of a "far-reaching consensus" on justification, strongly confirmed the Malta Report's assessment. Some of the reports that would be used a decade later in formulating the language of the *Joint Declaration* were already published during this period: *All Under One Christ* (1980), *Justification by Faith* (USA, 1985), and *The Condemnations of the Reformation Era: Do they Still Divide?* (1990; original German: 1986). Some of the LWF observers at Vatican II participated in and made important contributions to dialogues producing these reports.

Lutherans and Catholics continued to move away from the mutual isolation of the past by developing closer relations, fellowship, and deeper mutual understanding. Together they reflected on the Augsburg Confession and on Luther. Though official mutual acceptance of the Augsburg Confession as a common confession of faith did not result from this reflection, such reflection helped them uncover and express the significant amount of the common apostolic faith which they mutually shared. Significant authorities in the Catholic Church spoke of the positive intentions of Luther, though not uncritically, and called for further common study and understanding about his teaching and role. In both instances Pope John Paul II made significant statements. Lutherans and Catholics both expressed appreciation of the Pope's statements about Luther and the Augsburg Confession, and this contributed to a healing of memory.

Partnership between the LWF and the Catholic Church deepened. They continued to have contact at high official levels, and began to cooperate, even if in a limited way, in common service on specific issues. They continued to invite each other into specific events in each other's life. Pope John Paul II's contacts with LWF member churches in different parts of the world extended and deepened the development of mutual understanding and the creation of new relationships. His contacts with Lutherans during his first trip to Germany inspired a dialogue process leading to the 1986 report on the sixteenth-century condemnations that proved important later in the development of the *Joint Declaration.*

Concerning the difficult question of reception of dialogue results, Cardinal Willebrands, at events organized by Lutherans, called attention to its importance, lectured on a Catholic understanding of reception, described the way the Catholic Church had undertaken it in a particular case, and indicated a certain level of reception regarding Lutheran-Catholic relations in the recent reassessment by Catholics of the Augsburg Confession and on the historical judgment of Luther.

And now, official reception of the Lutheran-Catholic dialogue reports would be requested.

PART IV

From Acknowledging Common Bonds of Faith and Friendship to Mutual Commitment

Developments During the Pontificate of John Paul II, 1988-1999, Leading to the Joint Declaration

"... I share the hope that the fruit of our ecumenical work through national and international dialogues will be such that we can enter the 21st century free of the mutual condemnations on justification. ..."

Edward Idris Cassidy, 1990

CHAPTER 9

Towards Official Reception of Dialogue Results, 1988-1993

The Decade of the *Joint Declaration*

As bonds of friendship continued to develop between Lutherans and Catholics, and dialogue illustrated, more and more, the degree of Christian faith they shared in common, questions were being raised about which next steps could be taken together toward a deeper level of unity. Were they ready to make binding commitments through an official reception of dialogue results?

During the period 1988-99, the proximate steps were taken leading directly to the *Joint Declaration on the Doctrine of Justification* and its official acceptance by Lutheran churches and the Catholic Church. The period 1988-99 can be seen in three distinct, though somewhat overlapping parts. During the first, 1988-93, the highest Catholic and Lutheran authorities made statements clearly expressing the *desire for* official reception of and response to Lutheran-Catholic dialogue results, and took some concrete steps toward that goal. At the same time, leaders also made statements indicating that *the time was ready* for response and reception of dialogue results concerning specifically the doctrine of justification. And thus, in 1993 the LWF and the PCPCU agreed to a project of a Joint Declaration on Justification.

During the second part, 1994-98, the PCPCU and the LWF created a small joint Lutheran-Catholic task force charged with making a first draft of a declaration, and then, later, a more expanded joint commission developed a final version by 1997. During the third part, 1998-99, the Catholic Church, and Lutheran churches through the LWF, made their official responses to the *Joint Declaration* (1998), then negotiated to be sure that they were agreeing to the same thing before a definitive, official common signing of the *Joint Declaration* took place on October 31, 1999, in Augsburg, Germany.

A Turning Point: The LWF Delegation in Rome, March 3-5, 1988

During 1988-93 closer contacts and cooperation developed between the Lutheran World Federation and the Pontifical Council for Promoting Christian Unity. The Pope's contacts with some LWF member churches deepened, and especially, during 1989 and 1991, his contacts with Nordic Lutherans.

An LWF delegation's official visit to Rome, March 3-5, 1988, led by President Landesbischof Johannes Hanselmann, and General Secretary Dr. Gunnar Stålsett, marked a turning point toward the *Joint Declaration*.[1] Discussions with PCPCU President Johannes Cardinal Willebrands, Secretary Reverend (later Bishop) Pierre Duprey M.Afr., and staff resulted in two important mutual decisions, opening the way toward the possibility of mutual commitment. First, realizing that neither communion had yet undertaken a formal reception process of international Lutheran-Catholic dialogue results, they decided to begin preparing for reception, agreeing, as an initial step, to constitute an ad-hoc staff working group to develop strategies for dealing more officially and more locally with Catholic-Lutheran dialogue documents. Second, they decided to convene regular informal staff meetings between the PCPCU and the LWF. Those attending would include the LWF General Secretary, the PCPCU Secretary (and after two years also the Cardinal President), and respective staff including the co-secretaries of the international dialogue. In these annual meetings, each could update the other on respec-

---

1. "Visit of a Delegation of the Lutheran World Federation to Rome, March 3-5, 1988," *IS* 67 (1988): 90-91. Others in the delegation included Bishop Andreas Aarflot, Chair of the LWF Standing Committee on Ecumenical Affairs, Dr. Jonas Jonson and Dr. Paul Wee, Assistant General Secretaries, respectively, for Ecumenical and for International Affairs, Dr. Eugene Brand, Secretary for Interconfessional Dialogue and Co-Secretary of the international Lutheran-Catholic dialogue, and Dr. Walter Allgaier, assistant to Bishop Hanselmann.

tive activities, speak of tensions in the relationship, and together develop ideas for future mutual projects. Later, in the 1990s, the LWF and the PCPCU would make important decisions together in these joint staff meetings, helping to guide the development of the *Joint Declaration on Justification,* and keeping in close contact concerning response and reception of it in the two communions.

Receiving the delegation, Pope John Paul II gave his encouragement in stating that since Vatican II, Lutherans and Catholics had made much progress in overcoming the barriers of separation between them and in building visible bonds of communion. The Pope pointed to advances made, including some important for Catholic and Lutheran rapprochement on the doctrine of justification: "In theological dialogue significant work has been done in regard to matters on which we must achieve unity and faith, such as the Eucharist, ministry, and justification by faith: as also in facing other matters, including the mutual anathemas pronounced in the sixteenth century. . . . Such dialogue and collaboration must continue."[2]

Decisions taken at this 1988 meeting turned the partners decisively toward reception of Lutheran-Catholic dialogue results, and set in motion steps leading, in a few years, to the development, and a decade later, to the signing, of the *Joint Declaration.* They began to implement these decisions quickly, scheduling the first informal joint staff meeting for October of that same year.[3] One agenda item was a substantial discussion of strategy for reception. At this meeting they formed the ad-hoc group to work on strategies for reception, named the participants, and gave it direction and a time frame for an initial phase of its work.[4]

2. "To Lutheran Delegation, March 4, 1988," *IS* 67 (1988): 61.

3. October 28-29, 1988, in Geneva, hosted by the LWF. Present for the LWF were General Secretary Revd. G. Stålsett, Dr. E. Brand, Dr. J. Jonson, Dr. P. Wee, and Dr. H. Meyer of the LWF-related Strasbourg Ecumenical Institute. PCPCU representatives were the Secretary, Very Revd. P. Duprey, and Msgr. J. Radano.

Other PCPCU members who would also take part in these meetings in the years ahead included Cardinal Cassidy (1990-2001), Msgr. H.-A. Raem (1990-97), Bishop W. Kasper (1999ff., both as PCPCU Secretary and from 2001 Cardinal President), and Revd. Dr. M. Türk (1999ff.). Other LWF participants would later consistently take part, including the new General Secretary, Revd. Dr. I. Noko (1994ff.), Revd. S. Oppegaard (1997ff.), and the Strasbourg Institute's Dr. M. Root and Prof. T. Dieter.

4. The ad-hoc group consisted of E. Brand, H. Meyer, J. Radano, and A. Klein. Brand and Radano were asked to prepare a draft for the first meeting of the group the following

Authorities Request Official Evaluation
of Lutheran-Catholic Reports, 1989-1990

In 1989, during his pastoral visit to the Catholic Church in the Nordic countries (June 1-9), which included important contacts and ecumenical events with Lutheran folk churches in each country, the Pope again called for evaluation of the Lutheran-Catholic dialogue results.[5] In 1990, the Eighth Assembly of the Lutheran World Federation called for reception of bilateral dialogue agreements as well.

The Pope's visit to five predominantly Lutheran countries, Norway, Iceland, Finland, Denmark, and Sweden, though first of all a pastoral visit to the Catholic Church in those countries, had an important ecumenical aspect because of the predominant Lutheran presence there. This enabled him to continue to foster fellowship with Lutherans. Throughout the visit he invoked the theme that he came "as a brother in Christ," stressing "*my own commitment, and the commitment of the entire Catholic Church,* to work for *the restoration of unity among Christians,* in accordance with the Lord's will" (emphasis original).[6] On different occasions he stressed the common heritage that Lutherans and Catholics in those countries continue to share, either through baptism, by which they are incorporated into Christ,[7] or "*those elements of the apostolic heritage* which, despite our divisions, we still hold in common,"[8] or in their mutual high regard and reverence for the patron saints of those countries such as St. Olav in Norway,[9] St.

---

spring. Its product would be discussed at the next joint staff meeting in October 1989. The first meeting of this task force on strategies took place April 6-7, 1989, in Rome.

5. As already noted, in a homily at an ecumenical service in Augsburg, Germany, in 1987, the Pope, looking toward agreement, had called for evaluation of the German ecumenical group's study on the sixteenth-century condemnations (cf. *IS* 64 [1987]: 57).

6. "Ecumenical Meeting in Copenhagen, June 7, 1989." "The Pope's Address," *IS* 71 (1989): 103. See also his addresses on arrival in Norway, June 1, 1989, *IS* 71 (1989): 83, in the "Ecumenical Prayer Service in Oslo, June 1, 1989," *IS* 71 (1989): 86, "Ecumenical Prayer Service in the Lutheran Cathedral of Uppsala, June 9, 1989," *IS* 71 (1989): 108. The Pope gave most of his addresses in the Nordic countries in English.

7. "Ecumenical Service at National Shrine of Thingvellir (Iceland), June 3, 1989," *IS* 71 (1989): 93.

8. "Ecumenical Service in the Lutheran Cathedral of Turku (Finland), June 5, 1989," *IS* 71 (1989): 97 (emphasis original).

9. "Ecumenical Prayer Service in Oslo, June 1, 1989," *IS* 71, p. 85; "Ecumenical Meeting in Lutheran Cathedral of Nidaros at Trondheim, June 2, 1989," *IS* 71 (1989): 88.

Henrik in Finland,[10] or St. Bridget and St. Eric in Sweden.[11] He also recalled the observer-delegates at the Second Vatican Council, including those from the Lutheran World Federation, whose presence "gave great impetus to the ecumenical relations which have developed since then."[12] Meeting with the Lutheran bishops of Denmark, he addressed the excommunication of Luther, pointing out that in the understanding of the Catholic Church, every excommunication ceases with the death of an individual since it is an action taken with respect to an individual during his or her lifetime. He recalled his 1983 letter to Cardinal Willebrands, the year of the 500th anniversary of Luther's birth, in which he was able to affirm, in regard to questions raised by Luther, that scientific research has already reached notable points of convergence concerning Luther's personality and the complex historical situation of his time. Also, concerns of Luther in regard to reform and renewal have found echo with Catholics in various ways, as, for example, when the Second Vatican Council speaks of the necessity "for continuous renewal and reform . . . ," citing *Unitatis redintegratio* 6 to illustrate.[13]

Fostering Lutheran-Catholic fellowship, the Pope referred to the international Lutheran-Catholic dialogue in four of these countries. Reminding the Danish bishops that it was the first international bilateral discussion involving the Catholic Church after the Council, and that the Danish professor and observer at the Council, Kristen Skydsgaard, was one of its main initiators, he commented that "these discussions have furthered in many ways the collaboration between our Churches."[14] In Iceland he expressed encouragement for the international dialogue and asked support and prayers for its success.[15] Twice during the journey he called for official evaluation of dialogue results. This international dialogue, he recalled in Oslo, is concerned with justification, ecclesiology, and sacramentality. "The results of this dialogue must eventually be *eval-*

10. "Meeting with the President of Finland," June 4, 1989, *IS* 71 (1989): 95.
11. "Ecumenical Prayer Service in the Lutheran Cathedral of Uppsala, June 9, 1989," *IS* 71 (1989): 108.
12. "Ecumenical Service in the Lutheran Cathedral of Turku, June 5, 1989," *IS* 71 (1989): 97. Cf. "Ecumenical Prayer Service in Oslo, June 1, 1989," *IS* 71 (1989): 86.
13. "Meeting with the Bishops of the Danish Lutheran Church, June 6, 1989," *IS* 71 (1989): 101. German original: *Insegnamenti*, XII, 1, (1989): 1548ff.
14. "Meeting with the Bishops of the Danish Lutheran Church," p. 101.
15. "Ecumenical Service at National Shrine of Thingvellir, June 3, 1989," *IS* 71 (1989): 93-94.

uated officially by the authorities which commissioned it."[16] Likewise in Finland he asked that "at the proper time" both the international Lutheran-Catholic and Orthodox-Catholic dialogues "be studied by the Churches themselves, in order to see how far the dialogues have taken us toward unity in faith."[17]

Regarding Lutheran concerns about reception, in 1990 the Eighth LWF Assembly's Message stated that "[w]e commit ourselves anew, in urgent efforts, to the quest for Christian Unity in witness and service for the sake of the gospel, searching always for the removal of barriers that block the realization of full communion. . . . We urge our churches to encourage and nurture greater local awareness, practice and reception of the agreements and results emerging from bilateral . . . dialogues" (LWF Report, No. 28/29, pp. 81f.).[18] The Eighth Assembly also took another step vital both for LWF internal life and for processes of ecumenical reception: it changed the LWF Constitution to describe the LWF no longer as "a free association of Lutheran churches" (Constitution 1984), but now as a "communion of churches which are in pulpit and altar fellowship," with a constitutive obligation "to serve Christian unity throughout the world" (Constitution 1990, III). Although the LWF member churches continue to be autonomous, the new Constitution challenges them to work out the implications of communion, towards a deeper sense of interdependence among them.[19]

The good relations developing quickly between Lutherans and Catholics, evidenced by the warm welcome the Pope received from Lutherans in the Nordic countries,[20] also helped foster good conditions for official eval-

16. "Ecumenical Prayer Service in Oslo, June 1, 1989," *IS* 71 (1989): 86 (emphasis original).

17. "Ecumenical Service in the Lutheran Cathedral of Turku, June 5, 1989," *IS* 71 (1989): 98.

18. Curitiba, Brazil (January 30–February 8). Cited in *Strategies for Reception,* no. 4. *IS* 80 (1992): 42 (see below).

19. A staff report to the PCPCU plenary of January 28–February 2, 1991, commented on the ecclesiological implications of this change in the LWF constitution, that member churches are called to an "inescapable interdependency" (LWF Executive Committee Report for Curitiba), and that "[t]his development is to be seen with great interest from our side, because it might also have consequences for the binding character of the LWF teaching some day." "Lutheran–Roman Catholic relations 1988-1990," *IS* 78 (1991): 156.

20. The Pope told the Roman Curia that this pastoral journey "up to a short time ago would have been unimaginable." "Address to the Roman Curia, December 22, 1989," *IS* 75 (1990): 131. Italian original: *Insegnamenti,* XII, 2 (1989): 1595. The PCPCU perceived this pastoral visit as having had "great importance" for Lutheran-Catholic relations and "that public

uation of dialogue reports. In his message to the LWF Curitiba Assembly, the Pope noted that "even in the short period between your last Assembly in Budapest in 1984 and this Assembly in Curitiba deeper relationships have developed between the Lutheran World Federation and the Holy See's Council for Promoting Christian Unity, both in pursuing the vital theological dialogue and in finding means of closer collaboration." He described his warm reception by Lutherans in the Nordic countries as "a sign of the increasing awareness among us of the real, though imperfect communion that already exists between Lutherans and Catholics."[21]

Strategies for Reception, 1991

While the LWF and the PCPCU were each developing their own understanding of ecumenical reception,[22] they also took steps together toward understanding reception. The reception of their dialogue results was one major agenda item in the first three meetings (1988-90) of the newly established LWF-PCPCU joint staff group,[23] and in subsequent meetings.

The staff group appointed to work on common strategies for reception of Lutheran-Catholic dialogue reports finished its working paper in October 1991.[24] Though only a working paper, and not an officially agreed text, *Strategies for Reception* provided useful information on the meaning of reception, and alerted the two partners to some of the difficulties they could encounter as they embarked on reception of Lutheran-Catholic reports.

---

opinion in those countries had changed for the better as a consequence of the Papal visit." Opening address of PCPCU President Archbishop Edward Cassidy to the PCPCU plenary meeting, January 28–February 2, 1991, *IS* 78 (1991): 135.

21. "To Bishop Johannes Hanselmann, President of the Lutheran World Federation, January 13, 1990," *IS* 75 (1990): 133.

22. The *Directory for the Application of Principles and Norms on Ecumenism* published by the PCPCU in 1993 includes a description of what is entailed in reception (nos. 179-82).

23. October 28-29, 1988, Geneva, October 5-6, 1989, Rome, and October 12-13, 1990, Geneva, "Lutheran–Roman Catholic Relations 1988-1990," staff report to the 1991 PCPCU plenary meeting, *IS* 78 (1991): 158.

24. *Strategies for Reception: Perspectives on the Reception of Documents Emerging from the Lutheran-Catholic International Dialogue.* Working Paper Presented to the Joint Staff Group Pontifical Council for Promoting Christian Unity, Lutheran World Federation, October 1991, *IS* 80 (1992): 42-45, and Geneva: Lutheran World Federation, Office of Ecumenical Affairs. Hereafter *Strategies.*

To underscore the importance of reception of the international Lutheran-Catholic dialogue reports, *Strategies* refers to statements, mentioned above, of the Pope in the Nordic countries (no. 3), and to the LWF Eighth Assembly Message (no. 4). Discussing the meaning of reception it distinguishes between the churches' responses to dialogue results and the integration of their insights into a church's life (no. 5). Among the various types of response, carrying different weight,[25] "the official responses from the churches are of ultimate importance" since "our ecumenical goal is church fellowship" (no. 6).

Strategies suggested complexities that Lutherans and Catholics would encounter in undertaking official response to a common text. The procedures of reception, especially for official church response and integration, "will be different in our two communions according to their structure" (no. 8). The description of Lutheran processes reflected the current evolution of LWF self-understanding, and its need to work out the implications of being a communion. Thus, "[t]hough the Lutheran churches are autonomous bodies, in the Lutheran World Federation they have an expression of their communion, and an instrument for common action . . . [which] is positioned to play a crucial role in the official reception of international dialogue results . . ." (no. 9). Its description of the Roman Catholic position reflects stronger bonds of communion in the whole church: "reception must reflect the bonds of communion based on shared faith and sacramental life that exist within the whole church. Local churches are presided over by bishops who are in communion with one another and with the bishop of Rome, who within the collegiality of bishops, presides over the whole church" (no. 11).

The Lutheran description candidly points to a gap in its reception process. Fundamental "will be interaction between the communion as a whole and its constituent churches." While the LWF has regularly sent dialogue results to member churches for study and response, as a "first step toward arriving at a common mind," a simple tallying of responses would not suffice for official reception because that "would diminish the character of the communion as a whole." Thus, "[a]n intermediate step is needed between the initial responses and discerning the common mind of the Lutheran communion — a step not yet in place. Only on the basis of both

25. For example, those of individual theologians, of institutes or theological faculties, or official responses from the churches.

these steps could the Lutheran communion take the action desired." It "is imperative that the Lutheran communion agree upon the nature of the intermediate step . . ." (no. 10).

In the Roman Catholic perspective, the whole church should participate in reception. The PCPCU, the Holy See's office charged with promoting Christian unity, "would coordinate the development of the official Catholic response to ecumenical documents, taking into account views expressed by the local churches and, when doctrine is involved, collaborating with the Congregation for the Doctrine of the Faith in order to bring the response to its final form" (no. 11).[26]

Strategies shows that the two differ also on the question of taking steps toward visible unity on a regional basis.[27] Furthermore there are several examples of local or regional official receptions of dialogue results between Lutherans and other Reformation churches, e.g., the Leuenberg Agreement (1973), but few examples of similar actions between Roman Catholics and Lutherans. But "[o]f particular significance are the pronouncements of Pope John Paul II taking up the statements of a pastoral letter of the Roman Catholic German Bishops' Conference (1980) and of the LWF Executive Committee (1981) on the occasion of the 450th anniversary of the Augsburg Confession. Significant too were the same Pope's pronouncements on Martin Luther in 1983" (no. 13).

According to *Strategies*, Lutheran-Catholic collaboration, which has developed on many levels as they have given common witness to the gospel, also fosters reception of dialogue results. The dialogue has fostered collaboration, and the collaboration makes it urgent that the two communions respond to the dialogue results (no. 14).[28]

---

26. This description summarizes briefly the process used in developing the Catholic response to the Faith and Order text *Baptism, Eucharist and Ministry*. See John A. Radano, "The Catholic Church and BEM, 1980-1989," *Mid-Stream* (April 1991): 139-56.

27. For Lutherans regional steps toward global unity "would require the approbation, even the encouragement of the entire communion. Otherwise the conciliarity essential to being a communion of churches would be violated" (no. 12). For the Catholic Church much more than approbation or encouragement is needed. Given its framework, "which links each local church to all other local churches . . . a regional union between Lutheran and Catholic churches would also entail union between those Lutherans and the universal Catholic Church" (no. 12).

28. Significant examples of collaboration on the international level are mentioned (previously cited in Chapter 7), including collaboration in 1986 in support of the efforts of Namibian churches — Lutheran, Catholic, Anglican — to give pastoral assistance to their

Strategies proposed that the formal process of reception should begin upon completion of the current international joint commission's document on ecclesiology (the third phase of international dialogue, completed in 1993), and that the documents to submit for reception are that ecclesiology text, the platform paper on justification (perhaps expanded), *The Eucharist* (1978), and *Ministry in the Church* (1981) (no. 30), which together form "a conceptual whole" (no. 31). They should be introduced by a paper "which would put them in perspective historically," describe how they are interrelated, and "set forth the understanding of consensus with which the documents operate." A description of the latter anticipates the notion of a "differentiated consensus" underlying the *Joint Declaration:*

a) consensus does not always mean uniformity of expression;

b) the consensus required for church fellowship may include an agreement that the remaining differences are not church dividing. Furthermore, the paper should indicate that the agreements reached necessarily imply that doctrinal condemnations of the past *(Lehrverurteilungen)* against the other church and its teachings no longer apply, and that the recognition of this fact is indispensable to remove canonical hindrances to church fellowship (the *Lehrverurteilungen* document prepared by the Protestant-Catholic commission in the Federal Republic of Germany should be used in an appropriate way) (no. 31).

Perceptions of Each Other's Capability for Reception, 1992

While reflecting together on common strategies for reception, each raised questions in 1992, though for different reasons, about the other's capability for official reception.[29] The LWF's ability to make authoritative, binding decisions regarding dialogue results on the world level was questioned

---

people during that nation's struggle for independence; and LWF acceptance of Pope John Paul II's invitation in 1986 for the Assisi Day of Prayer for Peace. Also, in 1989 they cooperated concerning a delegation organized by the LWF, with Catholic participation, that visited six Central American countries in support of the peace plan initiated by President Arias of Costa Rica (no 15). More examples are given in no. 16.

29. As will be seen, these questions would linger even when the official responses to the JD were published in 1998.

during an LWF delegation's April 22-24, 1992, visit to Rome.[30] When the delegation visited the CDF, and discussed reception of ecumenical reports with Joseph Cardinal Ratzinger, the Cardinal questioned the capacity for authoritative and binding decision making on the Lutheran side. He pointed to the asymmetry between the LWF and the Catholic Church. The latter, at the universal level, had authoritative decision-making authority on doctrinal questions, whereas for the Lutherans, dialogue results are received on the local and regional level.[31]

Addressing this Catholic (and Lutheran) concern at a twenty-fifth anniversary celebration of the Lutheran–Roman Catholic international dialogue in Eisenach, Germany, in November 1992, Gunnar Stålsett echoed the gap suggested in *Strategies for Reception:*

> The Lutheran World Federation needs to develop a consensus within its membership that it can act as one to one in its relation to the Roman Catholic Church in the process of reception. It seems imperative that when the final word is to be spoken there has to be compatibility on the authoritative level of each communion, both having the authority and mandate needed, at the same time congenial to the nature and structure of each ecclesial reality.[32]

Stålsett also raised some Lutheran concerns, during that same visit to Rome, about the way the Catholic Church engages in reception. As he told the LWF Council meeting a few months after the visit, he expressed to Cardinals Cassidy and Ratzinger the delegation's disappointment with the

---

30. The delegation included LWF President Revd. Dr. G. Brakemeier, General Secretary G. Stålsett, Landesbischof C. Stier (Chair, Standing Committee for Ecumenical Affairs), Revd. Dr. J. R. Crumley, Jr. (Co-Chair, Lutheran–Roman Catholic International Commission), LWF staff members Revd. Dr. E. Brand, Dr. M. Kanyoro, Mr. B. W. Nelder, and Revd. Dr. P. Wee.

31. Stålsett afterwards related this conversation to the PCPCU leaders, as did Heinz-Albert Raem, PCPCU staff member, who accompanied the LWF delegation at the meeting.

32. "Address by Dr. Gunnar Stålsett, General Secretary of the Lutheran World Federation on the occasion of the 25th Anniversary Roman Catholic–Lutheran Dialogue, Eisenach, November 9, 1992" (manuscript). Cf. "General Secretary Reflects on Future of Lutheran-Catholic Dialogue," *LWI* (Nov. 19, 1992): 5. Stålsett raised this question again in his report to the LWF Council meeting in Kristiansand, Norway, June 20-30, 1993, saying that "as yet we have no instrumentality to deal adequately with doctrinal issues on the level of the Lutheran communion." *LWI* 13/93 (June 24, 1993): 4-5, here 5. Cardinal Cassidy and Bishop Karl Lehmann also addressed this 25th anniversary celebration.

Vatican's response to the *Final Report* of ARCIC, seeing in it "an inflexibility due to the lack of evaluating such a document on its own terms."[33] The Lutherans tended to interpret the Vatican response as driven by the question of whether or not the content of the dialogue report was identical with the Catholic Church's position. Cardinal Cassidy had assured them in that discussion that the Vatican response pointed to progress made, and did not close the door.[34] Stålsett also had harsh criticism for the 1992 CDF text, "Some Aspects of the Church Understood as Communion."[35] In regard to reception and the need to create a "receptive climate in our churches and congregations for closer relations with other Christian World Communions," he said to the Council that he felt that with these two documents a "serious problem" had emerged on the side of the Roman Catholic Church (no. 76). Cardinal Cassidy, in his address on November 9, 1992, at the celebration of the twenty-fifth anniversary of the Lutheran-Catholic dialogue, expressed his concern and sympathy for the way Stålsett and others felt about the CDF text, but cautioned them to not misunderstand that document and to keep in mind its limits.[36]

Focus on Justification, 1990-1993

Strategies for Reception was correct in saying that reception of documents on ecclesiology, justification, Eucharist, and ministry "is a necessary step toward unity" (no. 32). Nonetheless, because of the substantial progress already made on justification in international and national dialogue, both Lutherans and Catholics could see that agreement on justification was close at hand. An even wider ecumenical convergence on justifica-

33. "Report of Dr. Gunnar Stålsett" at the LWF Council meeting, Madras, India, September 1992, no. 77 (manuscript). Cf. "Vatican Letter Problematic for Lutheran-Catholic Relations, LWF General Secretary Says," *LWI* (September 17, 1992): 6.

34. The Cardinal's efforts to reassure the Lutherans were affirmed by the *Clarifications* relating to the Vatican response to ARCIC published in 1994: *IS* 87 (1994): 237-42.

35. He called this CDF text a "skandalon (stumbling block) in the true sense of the word." It is "unaware and totally insensitive to the progress toward unity made." "Report of Dr. Gunnar Stålsett" at Madras. Cf. "Vatican Letter Problematic for Lutheran-Catholic Relations, LWF General Secretary Says," p. 7.

36. "Top Vatican Official Seeks to Lessen Frustration over Lutheran-Catholic Relations," *LWI* (Nov. 19, 1992): 4.

tion was developing with reports published, for example, in 1986 by the Anglican-Roman Catholic International Commission[37] and in 1990 by the Reformed-Catholic international dialogue.[38] Between 1990 and 1993 Catholic leaders such as Pope John Paul II, PCPCU President Archbishop Edward Idris Cassidy, and Secretary Bishop Pierre Duprey made public statements about the emerging Lutheran-Catholic agreement on justification. Furthermore, the 1992 report of an international commission of Catholic scholars, organized by the PCPCU to evaluate the German condemnations study, agreed with that study's conclusion that the sixteenth-century condemnations on justification did not condemn exactly what the other held.

Archbishop Edward Idris Cassidy,[39] successor to Cardinal Willebrands in December 1989 as President of the PCPCU, accepted the invitation of John Cardinal O'Connor, Archbishop of New York, and Bishop William H. Lazareth, Bishop of the Metropolitan New York Synod of the Evangelical Lutheran Church in America, to address the topic of Lutheran-Catholic relations in November 1990 in New York. His address included a brief progress report on the dialogue on justification. He mentioned the international Lutheran-Catholic dialogue's "platform" paper: "Ascertaining the Far-Reaching Consensus on Justification by Faith" completed in 1988 (but not published), expressing gratitude for the valuable contribution made to it by the American dialogue's *Justification by Faith*. He referred also to the statements on justification in the 1990 report of the Reformed-Catholic international dialogue. Thus, he said, "If we consider the work already done on justification in different quarters, we see that it has brought us to a hopeful point. The 'far-reaching consensus' suggested by the 'Malta Report' seems to have been documented even further."[40] The response to and reception of these results, he said, ". . . is the task before us now," adding that "in terms of the Lutheran/Catholic international dialogue, it would

37. *Salvation and the Church, IS* 63 (1987): 33-41.

38. *Towards a Common Understanding of the Church, IS* 74 (1990): 91-118. Chapter 2 treats "Justification by Grace Through Faith" and "The Calling of the Church: Its Role in Justification by Grace Through Faith" (nos. 77-88).

39. Archbishop Cassidy, named a Cardinal in 1991, previously served in the diplomatic service of the Holy See. As the Holy See's Substitute Secretary of State in 1989, he had accompanied the Pope to the Nordic countries.

40. Edward I. Cassidy, "Lutheran–Roman Catholic Relations," *Mid-Stream* (October 1991): 307-8, citations on 308.

seem that a key to the reception process is the outcome of this third phase of dialogue which deals with the issues of justification and ecclesiology."[41]

He went further, referring to a proposal made in April 1990 by Bishop William H. Lazareth. Noting that 1997 would be the 450th anniversary of the Council of Trent's decree on justification, Lazareth said that "it would be glorious if we could enter the year 2000 . . . with officially binding declarations on all three sides that neither the decrees of the Council of Trent nor the condemnations of the classical sixteenth-century Protestant confessions are any longer *currently applicable* to the normative faith of our present churches in the twenty-first century."[42] Archbishop Cassidy commented that "I share the dream embodied in the proposal of Dr. Lazareth." While it was not clear at the moment, he indicated, whether a bilateral, trilateral, or multilateral approach was best for achieving officially binding declarations, nonetheless he continued:

> . . . I share the hope that the fruit of our ecumenical work through national and international dialogues will be such that we can enter the 21st century free of the mutual condemnations on justification and other issues that have burdened our relationships for centuries. I pray that the Holy Spirit will enlighten us to move in this direction.[43]

In his opening address to the 1991 PCPCU plenary meeting, reviewing various developments in Lutheran-Catholic relations, Archbishop Cassidy said that "[t]he study of the doctrine of justification has also revealed how much there is in common even on this central element of division."[44] He

---

41. "Lutheran–Roman Catholic Relations," pp. 307-8.

42. Cited in "Lutheran–Roman Catholic Relations," 308-9. Lazareth, addressing Episcopal, Lutheran, and Roman Catholic ecumenists, and taking into account the American and German studies on justification, the ARCIC report *Salvation and the Church,* and the work of the American Episcopal-Lutheran dialogue, had proposed a trilateral Catholic, Lutheran, and Episcopal reception of the convergences of these communions on the doctrine of justification. "Trilateral Reception of Justification by Faith," *Ecumenical Trends* (October 1990): 137-44.

43. "Lutheran–Roman Catholic Relations," pp. 308-9; citation 309.

44. "Plenary Meeting Pontifical Council for Promoting Christian Unity January 28– February 2, 1991, Prolusio of the Council's President," *IS* 78 (1991): 135. He mentioned the international dialogue's manuscript: "Ascertaining the Far-Reaching Consensus on the Doctrine of Justification," and the PCPCU's current "in-depth evaluation" of the German study document, *The Condemnations of the Reformation Era — Do They Still Divide?*

also reminded the plenary that the understanding of justification through faith is similarly finding an important place in many discussions: with the Anglicans, the Lutherans, the Methodists, and the Reformed Alliance.[45]

During that same year, Pope John Paul II helped focus attention on justification when meeting Nordic Lutherans. At the celebration in Rome, October 3-7, 1991, of the 600th anniversary of the canonization of St. Bridget of Sweden, the Pope said that Lutherans and Catholics were "very close" to a common understanding of justification.

To celebrate this anniversary, the Bridgettine Sisters[46] organized a number of events during 1991 in Rome, with Lutheran participation. St. Bridget of Sweden founded the order and opened its original monastery in Vadstena, Sweden, about 1346. In 1595, after Sweden accepted the Reformation, the order was officially banished from Sweden. Only in the twentieth century were the Bridgettines able to re-establish houses in Sweden.[47] Remarkable, then, was the fact that this celebration became also something of a national event for Sweden, with participation of Sweden's royal family,[48] as well as a Lutheran and Catholic ecumenical event,[49] even if the Lutherans did not share all aspects of the Catholic understanding of canonization.

---

45. "Plenary Meeting Pontifical Council for Promoting Christian Unity," p. 136.

46. The order of the Most Holy Saviour, whose motherhouse on Piazza Farnese in Rome is located at the site where St. Bridget lived when she came to Rome in the fourteenth century.

47. "Bridgettines," *New Catholic Encyclopedia* (New York: McGraw-Hill, 1967), vol. 2, p. 800.

48. The ambassador of Sweden to the Holy See, Ambassador Lars Bergquist (the first Swedish ambassador to actually reside in Rome after the recent establishment of diplomatic relations between Sweden and the Holy See), took a major role in organizing some events, and the Swedish Royal family visited Rome on two occasions to participate. On May 3rd, 1991, King Carl XVI Gustaf and Queen Sylvia of Sweden had an audience with the Pope. On May 4 the King opened an exhibition in the Vatican Museum on the life and era of St. Bridget. An International Congress took place October 3-5, and a papal Mass at Piazza Farnese on October 6th. For materials in the exhibition, and coverage of the October ecumenical event in St. Peter's, and other aspects of the celebration, see *Santa Brigida profeta dei nostri tempi: Sesto centenario della canonizzazione di S. Brigida* (Roma: Casa Generalizia Suore di S. Brigida, Piazza Farnese 96, 1994), and *Saint Bridget: Prophetess of New Ages*, Proceedings of the International Study Meeting, Rome, October 3-7, 1991 (Rome: Casa Generalizia Suore Santa Brigida, Piazza Farnese 96, no date). Title and volume in both English and Italian.

49. "Ecumenical Celebration on the Occasion of the 600th Anniversary of the Canonization of St. Bridget of Sweden," *IS* 80 (1992): 17-28.

The celebration included an ecumenical vespers service in St. Peter's on October 5. The Pope, the Lutheran Archbishop of Uppsala, Bertil Werkström, and the Lutheran Archbishop of Turku, Finland, John Vikström, all gave homilies. The Lutheran Bishop of Oslo, Andreas Aarflot, was also present. This was the first time that the Pope and Lutheran leaders participated together in a vespers service in St. Peter's Basilica. The Swedish Royal family participated, and Queen Sylvia read one of the Scripture lessons.

Both the Pope and Archbishop Werkström made references to a common understanding of justification. The Pope spoke about the "vast heritage of faith which unites us," shown by theological dialogue, and that "together we confess the same God, One and Three; the Son of God, who became incarnate and died on the Cross for our salvation; we proclaim together the same *Apostles Creed.*" A common understanding of justification is close:

> Everyone knows that the Protestant Reformation began from the doctrine of justification and that it destroyed the unity of Christians of the West. A common understanding of justification — and we think we are very close to this goal — will, we are sure, help us to resolve the other controversies directly or indirectly linked to it.[50]

Archbishop Werkström went further:

> The moment has come to declare that the denunciations from the time of the Reformation no longer are valid. The ecumenical dialogue has proved the existence of a basic unity, for instance, in the question of justification through faith.[51]

The Pope also stressed, as during his Nordic visit, that Lutherans and Catholics continue to share together a common heritage: "in Sweden Bridget is loved and venerated by Lutherans and Catholics alike. Her life and work thus constitute a shared inheritance; Saint Bridget is, as it were, a fulcrum of unity." Thus, in this case, ecumenical progress on justification is proclaimed in a context in which Lutherans and Catholics are celebrating a renewed awareness of a common spiritual heritage.

---

50. Ecumenical Vespers, October 5, 1991, "The Pope's Homily," pp. 21-22 (emphasis original). Italian original: *Insegnamenti,* XIV, 2 (1991): 747.

51. Ecumenical Vespers, "Archbishop Bertil Werkström's Address," p. 23.

In 1992 a PCPCU-sponsored international commission of Catholic theologians and historians[52] charged with evaluating the 1986 German study, *The Condemnations of the Reformation Era — Do They Still Divide? (Lehrverurteilungen — kirchentrennend? = LK)*, completed its report.[53] Its conclusion concerning justification gave further support for an official reception process on that theme, if not yet on sacraments and ministry, the other subjects *LK* treated. It concluded, after examining *LK*'s analysis of the canons of the Council of Trent on justification:

> in spite of the absence of an extended discussion on the question of law and gospel in relation to these canons, we agree with *LK* that canons 1-32 of the decree on justification do not apply to Lutheran doctrine as determined by the confessional books. This conclusion is supported by recent research and dialogue results that indicate that the doctrine of justification by faith is no longer a church dividing issue. (manuscript, p. 30)

This report was never formally published by PCPCU. Instead, Secretary Bishop Pierre Duprey sent it in January 1993 to Bishop Karl Lehmann and Bishop Eduard Lohse, the co-chairs of the German ecumenical working group which produced *LK*, not as an official response of the Vatican (it had not gone through all the necessary steps), but as a PCPCU contribu-

---

52. The commission consisted of nine theologians and historians, who worked in three teams. A team from the USA worked on justification and consisted of K. McDonnell, OSB (coordinator), C. Peter (replaced after his untimely death by G. Tavard) with some contributions made by R. Trisco; a team in Italy consisting of J. Wicks, SJ (coordinator), and J. M. Millas, SJ, worked on ministry; a German team consisted of H. Wagner (coordinator), H. Jorissen, and K. Ganzer. (None of them had taken part in the working group that produced *LK*.) Two PCPCU staff assisted: H.-A. Raem and J. A. Radano. Raem coordinated the project. The coordinators and staff met in Rome in January 1991 to clarify the process and responsibilities of each subgroup, after which each national subgroup did its own work, each developing an approximately fifteen-page evaluation of its assigned part of *LK* during the year. In January 1992, the three subgroups met together in Rome to discuss the work of each, and to put the three parts together into one report. The finished report was given to the PCPCU in November 1992.

53. *LK* issued from a national study group, but from the beginning, at the request of the German Bishops' Conference, a PCPCU staff member (Msgr. Dr. Alois Klein) participated in the work of the joint ecumenical commission that produced it. It was thus appropriate for the PCPCU, which normally only requests evaluations of reports of international dialogues in which it participates, to initiate an evaluation of this text.

tion to the continuing work of that ecumenical group. He asked them "to consider whether the Ecumenical Study group sees itself to be in the position to deal with the areas so far unresolved in a further phase of study."[54] Though never formally published, it had wide circulation and is listed in the *Joint Declaration on the Doctrine of Justification* among its "Resources."

In 1993, in an address to the Bishops' Conference of the Evangelical Lutheran Church of America (ELCA), Bishop Pierre Duprey presented this commission's evaluation of the German condemnations study, which affirmed Catholic readiness for an official response process on justification. He added his personal agreement with that report's conclusions (see below, chapter 10).

54. "The Condemnations of the 16th Century on Justification — Do They Still Apply Today?" Essay by Pierre Duprey, Vatican City, with response by Harding Meyer, Strasbourg, in: *Occasional Papers Contributing to 1997 Decisions* (Chicago: Department for Ecumenical Affairs, ELCA, 1995), pp. 3ff.

Towards a Joint Declaration on the Doctrine of Justification, 1993-1998

Another important step by the LWF and the Catholic Church toward a mutual commitment concerning the doctrine of justification materialized when the third phase of international Lutheran-Catholic dialogue completed its work in autumn, 1993. Its report, *Church and Justification: Understanding the Church in the Light of the Doctrine of Justification,* was published in 1994. While the co-sponsors were reflecting together on the notion of reception, and had questions about each other's approach to receiving dialogue reports, they continued to make reception of their dialogue results a priority. Thus they published, in 1995, a series of Bible studies relating to the themes of *Church and Justification* in order to foster reflection on it in congregations and parishes.[1] At this time the decision to seek a joint declaration was taking shape.

The Decision to Seek a Joint Declaration

An ELCA Initiative with Catholic Support, 1993

The Evangelical Lutheran Church in America came into existence in 1988 with a union of three Lutheran churches. Having altogether more than five

---

1. "Proposals for Ecumenical Bible Study and Discussion Between Roman Catholic and Lutheran Congregations and Parishes" (issued by the Lutheran World Federation and the Pontifical Council for Promoting Christian Unity, Geneva/Rome, 1995), *IS* 89 (1995): 100-110.

million members, it was then the second largest LWF member church. From the beginning it gave strong priority to ecumenical matters, including fostering contacts with church centers not only in the USA, but also in Europe and elsewhere.[2] Bishop Duprey's 1993 address to the ELCA Bishops' Conference was also significant because it gave critical support to an initial step, taken by the ELCA, towards the decision to seek an official response process on justification.

The ELCA Council in 1991 had officially affirmed the 1985 statement *Justification by Faith* to which its predecessor bodies had contributed. In 1989 the USA Conference of Catholic Bishops had also given a positive evaluation of that report. In light of these and other factors, in 1992 the ELCA began to explore a way of responding to the growing consensus on justification, and to the claim of the German study that the sixteenth-century condemnations on justification did not apply to the partner today. A series of meetings took place in 1992 and early 1993 involving both the ELCA and the LWF, as well as Lutherans and Catholics.[3] Since theologians were suggesting that certain sixteenth-century condemnations need not apply to churches today, and were not church-dividing, it was becoming clear that official responses by the churches to dialogue results on these questions were needed. In this context the ELCA Department for Ecumenical Affairs raised the question of "whether it would be possible for this church alone, or with other Lutheran churches and the Roman Catholic Church, to declare in 1997, the 450th anniversary of the Decree on Justification of the Council of Trent, that the mutual condemnations between Lutherans and Roman Catholics on *justification* do not apply today."[4] Investigating this possibility, the Department invited Bishop Pierre Duprey to address the ELCA Conference of Bishops in February 1993 on the topic "The Condemnations of the 16th Century on Justification — Do They Still

---

2. Dr. William G. Rusch, Director of its Department of Ecumenical Affairs from 1988 to 1995, had held a similar position in the Lutheran Church in America, one of the predecessor churches that also had a strong ecumenical policy.

3. William G. Rusch, "The History and Methodology of the *Joint Declaration on the Doctrine of Justification:* A Case Study in Ecumenical Reception," *Agapé. Études en l'honneur de Msgr. Pierre Duprey M.Afr.* Sous la Direction de Jean-Marie Roger Tillard, OP (Chambésy-Genève: Centre Orthodoxe du Patriarchat Oecuménique, 2000), pp. 175-76.

4. William G. Rusch, Director of Department for Ecumenical Affairs, Preface to *Occasional Papers Contributing to 1997 Decisions* (Chicago: Department for Ecumenical Affairs, ELCA, 1995), p. i (emphasis original).

Apply Today?" and Professor Harding Meyer of the Strasbourg Institute to provide a response to Bishop Duprey's presentation.[5]

Duprey and Meyer approached the question in different ways. Bishop Duprey's presentation was designed to respond directly to the question given to him with the invitation, i.e., "what it could mean for the Roman Catholic Church if Lutherans would say by 1997 that the faith, which Lutherans profess today regarding justification, is not what was condemned by the Council of Trent 450 years ago."[6] He encouraged the ELCA to go ahead, saying that this "would be an ecumenical step forward." Putting the proposed ELCA action in historical perspective, he cited, in support, John Paul II's homily of October 5, 1991 (mentioned above), that the Reformation "began from the doctrine of justification and that it [i.e., the different interpretations of the doctrine of justification] destroyed the unity of Christians of the West. A common understanding of justification — and we think we are very close to this goal — will, we are sure, help us to resolve the other controversies directly or indirectly linked to it" (p. 1). Even though this step itself would not bring full fellowship, Duprey said, it would mean "that our relationship gets a new quality" (p. 2). He emphasized the principle of reciprocity, saying that two things are now called for: "first, both sides need to declare the extent to which the results of *The Condemnations of the Reformation Era: Do They Still Divide?* are acceptable for them; second, this needs to be followed by a broad reception of these acceptable results . . ." (p. 3).

He identified with the PCPCU commission's agreement with *LK:* "that the canons 1-32 of the decree on justification do not apply to the Lutheran doctrine as determined by the confessional writings" (p. 6). He again encouraged the ELCA because, although it has been repeatedly stated since the Malta Report that "a far-reaching consensus is developing" on justification, and the German study concluded that the mutual sixteenth-century condemnations on justification "no longer apply to our partners today in any sense that could divide the churches," there are still theologians who have put the far-reaching consensus into question. A clarification has to be stated. "Therefore any steps which might be taken by the ELCA in support of this far-reaching consensus, will have an important ec-

---

5. Rusch, Preface to *Occasional Papers Contributing to 1997 Decisions,* p. ii.

6. Duprey's essay in *Occasional Papers Contributing to 1997 Decisions,* pp. 1-8, here p. 1. Further references to this address will be cited in the text.

umenical significance" (p. 7). He noted that what is called for is not complete identity. But rather "official recognition that both sides agree in the essential contents of the doctrine of justification," and the "official recognition that one side does not affirm what the other is denying and that the other does not deny what the other is affirming." He suggested a program for the "1997 project" expressed in three questions: (1) whether Lutherans could declare that Lutheran condemnations on justification and its consequences do not apply to the partner of today, and (2) whether Lutherans could declare that, on the basis of the German study, they no longer feel condemned by the propositions of the Council of Trent. Positive answers to these questions would be steps toward a healing of memory. Reciprocal questions would be directed by Lutherans towards Catholics. Such a purification of memory would be the necessary precondition for a further and decisive step, leading to the question: (3) "To what extent is it possible for you to express together with us the main contents of the doctrine of justification in an affirmative way?" (p. 7).

Responding to Duprey, Dr. Harding Meyer[7] first expressed strong concurrence with what Duprey had said about "the great ecumenical significance" of a Lutheran declaration on the inapplicability of the sixteenth-century condemnations against Catholic teaching on justification. Second, he underlined "the extraordinary importance" of the fact that the PCPCU commissioned evaluation of the German condemnations study "concurs with" *LK,* affirming that canons 1-32 of Trent's decree on justification do not apply to Lutheran doctrine as determined by the confessional writings (p. 9). Third, concerning Duprey's three questions to the ELCA, Meyer urged that any declaration on justification and related condemnations should keep together and integrate the elements of all three. Like Duprey, Meyer encouraged the ELCA to go ahead with its project, because ongoing debate among theologians now required authoritative decisions to be made. His argument was that two great Protestant church bodies in Germany (the United Lutheran Church in Germany-VELKD, and the Arnoldshain Conference, on behalf of the United Evangelical Churches) had responded affirmatively to the condemnations study, as had the

---

7. Harding Meyer, "A Response to the Paper of Bishop Pierre Duprey on 'The Condemnations of the 16th Century on Justification — Do They Still Apply Today?," *Occasional Papers Contributing to 1997 Decisions,* pp. 9-12. Further references to this address will be cited in the text.

PCPCU commission. But because each made the response separately from the partner, these responses were "conditional," awaiting the affirmation of the partner, and thus matters remained unresolved. He emphasized that only "a theological intervention of the churches themselves" could resolve the matter by affirming unambiguously that the results of the study are now the actual teaching of the churches (p. 10). Thus the project being considered by the ELCA was both necessary and urgent (p. 11).

Asking whether a "unilateral" action of the ELCA (without involving the Roman Catholic Church, and the whole Lutheran Communion, the LWF) would be feasible and legitimate, Meyer suggested that the structural asymmetry between the Catholic Church and the Lutheran world family (cf. *Strategies for Reception*) would make a (more preferable) reciprocal and worldwide Lutheran–Roman Catholic declaration unlikely for the time being. The ELCA action would thus be possible and legitimate for three reasons. First, it would be a theological declaration, not an act establishing Catholic and Lutheran church fellowship which, from the Roman Catholic perspective, would need "to involve the Roman Catholic Church as a whole," and from the Lutheran perspective "might impinge upon the worldwide fellowship or Communion of Lutheran churches." Second, while ecclesially "unilateral," it would, nevertheless, theologically involve the Roman Catholic Church because the USA Lutheran-Catholic report on justification was favorably received by the U.S. Conference of Catholic Bishops, and the German study was evaluated positively by the PCPCU. Third, other Lutheran churches or the LWF could not argue against such a theological declaration of the ELCA since a declaration on the inapplicability of doctrinal condemnations contained in the Lutheran confessions does not touch those confessions as such, nor jeopardize the commitment to the confessions on which the Lutheran Communion rests (p. 11). Thus a possibly unilateral declaration by the ELCA on the condemnations concerning justification would be both legitimate and feasible (p. 12).

He concluded presuming that in keeping with its policy statement on "ecumenism," the ELCA would inform the LWF and its member churches of this action, consider their comments and responses, "and appeal to them to join its action or to undertake a similar one" (p. 12).

Another development favorable to the ELCA action, besides Duprey's and Meyer's encouragement, was the creation, in February 1993, of a U.S. Lutheran–Roman Catholic Joint Coordinating Committee to pursue the feasibility of a joint declaration on the condemnations concerning justification and to authorize the next phase of U.S. Lutheran–Roman Catholic dialogue. In this positive framework, the U.S. National Committee of the LWF (a group identical with the governing body of the ELCA's Department for Ecumenical Affairs) voted, in March 1993, to seek the advice of the LWF on the possibility that the ELCA would declare "the condemnations related to justification not applicable to the contemporary Roman Catholic Church," and communicated this to General Secretary Gunnar Stålsett in late March 1993.[8]

LWF/PCPCU 1993 Decision to Seek a Declaration in 1997

The LWF Council responded to the ELCA at its June 1993 meeting in Kristiansand, Norway, by taking it a step further, making it a matter for the whole LWF. On recommendation of its Standing Committee for Ecumenical Affairs, the LWF established a process to consider "lifting" (declaring that they do not apply to the present partner) the sixteenth-century Lutheran-Catholic condemnations on justification.[9]

The process included three parts: first, sharing texts and information about this recommendation with LWF member churches; second, requesting them to study and comment on the specific proposal to lift the condemnations on justification in order to help shape a consensus to be declared by the Lutheran World Federation Assembly; and third, a commitment to see the LWF as the summarizer of this process and as the place for a culminating affirmation by the global Lutheran communion, and to pursue this process "in the closest possible collaboration with the Roman Catholic Church" (Ecumenical Resolutions, LWF Council, Kristiansand, 28 June 1993).[10]

When approached, "in response to the LWF, the PCPCU declared itself

8. Michael Root and William G. Rusch, "Can the Sixteenth-Century Condemnations on Justification Be Declared Nonapplicable? An Introduction," *Justification by Faith: Do the Sixteenth-Century Condemnations Still Apply?* ed. Karl Lehmann, Michael Root, and William G. Rusch (New York: Continuum, 1997), p. 13.

9. Root and Rusch, "Can the Sixteenth-Century Condemnations on Justification Be Declared Nonapplicable?," p. 14. Cf. "Go-Aheads for Process to Lift Condemnations: Consultation with Adventists," *LWI* (July 8, 1993): 4; and "LWF Member Churches Called to Consider Whether to Take Global Doctrinal Positions," *LWI* (June 24, 1993): 4-5.

10. The second and third parts of the resolution address the gap in the Lutheran response process identified in *Strategies for Reception.*

ready to work toward the possible declaration concerning the inapplicability today of the condemnations in question," setting together the target date of 1997, "the 450th anniversary of the Roman Catholic condemnations of Lutheran teaching on justification by the Council of Trent."[11] By the end of 1993, the LWF and the PCPCU appointed a small joint task force[12] to work on a first draft, whose members had participated in dialogues producing key reports on justification.[13] The task force reported to the LWF-PCPCU joint staff group, with each side in consultation with its appropriate authorities, which took responsibility for guiding the drafting process over the next several years.[14]

From the Lutheran side, the initial emphasis for a joint declaration on justification was on lifting the condemnations of the past. But it became clear that to do so it was necessary to formulate a common understanding on justification in order to have a clear basis on which to declare that the condemnations on that doctrine do not apply to the partner's teaching today.[15] And there were already dialogue reports contributing to both aspects.

---

11. The history of the events and details, described in the last four paragraphs leading to the LWF/PCPCU decision to work toward a declaration in 1997, follows the account described by Michael Root and William G. Rusch, "Can the Sixteenth-Century Condemnations on Justification Be Declared Nonapplicable?," pp. 13-14.

12. *Catholics:* L. Ullrich, G. Tavard, and PCPCU staff person H.-A. Raem; *Lutherans:* H. Meyer, J. Reumann, and LWF staff person E. Brand.

13. 1972 Malta Report (Meyer), 1985 USA *Justification by Faith* (Reumann, Tavard); 1986 *Lehrverurteilungen — kirchentrennend?* (Meyer); 1988 draft text "Ascertaining the 'Far-Reaching Consensus on Justification'" (Brand, Meyer, Ullrich); 1992 PCPCU evaluation of *Lehrverurteilungen — kirchentrennend?* (Raem, Tavard); 1993 *Church and Justification* (Brand, Meyer, Raem, Ullrich).

14. In May 1993, as the third phase of international dialogue was coming to a close, and just before the joint decision was made to seek a joint declaration on justification, a small PCPCU/LWF planning committee met to determine issues to be taken up in a fourth phase of dialogue (*Lutherans:* G. Stålsett, H. Meyer, E. Brand; *Catholics:* Bishop P. Duprey, L. Ullrich, J. Radano, H.-A. Raem). A proposal was considered that included a series of projects on church-dividing issues that could be taken up in the dialogue and brought to closure by finding sufficient consensus to enable further concrete steps toward unity. A "project justification" was one of these. But by 1994 it was clear that the project of seeking a joint declaration on justification would be handled by the separate task force, and not by the international dialogue.

15. Cf. Sven Oppegaard, "A History of the 'Joint Declaration,'" *LWI* (October 31, 1999): 9.

Drafting a Joint Declaration on Justification, 1994-1997

The drafting began in the midst of a basically positive atmosphere that fostered hope for a successful conclusion to this project.[16] At its first meeting, March 1-5, 1994, in Geneva, the LWF-PCPCU task force produced an initial draft of a joint declaration on justification.[17] The drafters' purpose had not been to develop a new treatment of the issues concerning justification, as they had available to them the results of international and national Lutheran-Catholic dialogues, and other sources.[18] At the same time, as one member of the later expanded drafting team gave witness, "the inner dynamic of drafting such a document did lead at times to insights that express our churches' teaching with nuances that go beyond the preceding dialogues."[19] This draft was sent to various experts on each side, and examined by the LWF Standing Committee on Ecumenical Affairs in June 1994. Taking into account the reactions received, a second draft was prepared in September 1994. The joint staff meeting of the LWF and PCPCU approved it for submission to the churches,

16. CDF Prefect Cardinal Ratzinger added to this positive atmosphere during a meeting in 1994 with representatives of the ELCA, even before work on the joint declaration had begun, by expressing the view that a Lutheran-Catholic consensus on justification is possible (according to H.-A. Raem, "Katholische und lutherische Lehrverurteilungen — weiterhin kirchentrennend?," *Una Sancta* 49 [1994]: 306, cited by Pawel Holc, *Un ampio consenso sulla dottrina della giustificazione: Studio sul dialogo teologico cattolico-luterano* [Roma: Editrice Pontificia Università Gregoriana, 1999], pp. 322-23, note 20).

17. Root and Rusch, "Can the Sixteenth-Century Condemnations on Justification Be Declared Nonapplicable?," p. 14. The chief drafters were Harding Meyer (Strasbourg) and Lothar Ullrich (Erfurt). See Jared Wicks, "Joint Declaration on the Doctrine of Justification: The Remote and Immediate Background," *Justification and Sanctification in the Traditions of the Reformation,* ed. Milan Opočenský and Páraic Réamonn (Geneva: World Alliance of Reformed Churches, 1999), p. 130, note 2.

Dr. Heinz-Albert Raem was the PCPCU staff person who coordinated the Catholic participation in the drafting meetings and took part in all of them from 1994 to 1997, working closely with Dr. Eugene Brand of the LWF. Dr. Raem died in March 1997, not long after the last drafting meeting.

18. In his letter dated October 13, 1993, inviting George Tavard and Lothar Ullrich to participate in the task force, PCPCU Secretary Bishop Pierre Duprey mentioned the pertinent dialogue reports the task force could draw on, including the Malta Report, *Church and Justification,* "Ascertaining the Far-Reaching Consensus on Justification" (manuscript) *Justification by Faith, Lehrverurteilungen — kirchentrennend?*, the PCPCU evaluation of *Lehrverurteilungen — kirchentrennend?* He also mentioned the 1990 Christological agreement between the Catholic Church and the Malankara Orthodox Syrian Church (PCPCU Archive).

19. Wicks, "Joint Declaration on the Doctrine of Justification," p. 130.

and each side sent it out early in 1995 for study and reaction by its respective constituency, requesting responses by early 1996.[20] It was also discussed during the annual LWF-PCPCU joint staff meetings.

The process of study within the Catholic Church included two aspects. One involved study of the draft in Rome, by a joint subcommission of the Congregation for the Doctrine of the Faith and the Pontifical Council for Promoting Christian Unity.[21] There was close collaboration between these two offices in this response process. The other aspect involved consultation about the draft by the PCPCU with a number of Catholic episcopal conferences, particularly those with large numbers of Lutherans in their area.

By 1996, critical comments on the draft had come from the joint CDF-PCPCU subcommission and a number of ecumenical secretariats of Catholic episcopal conferences, as well as from thirty-eight LWF churches. Taking these into account, a larger fourteen-member LWF-PCPCU drafting committee, meeting June 2-8, 1996, produced a revised version.[22] As each side again consulted within its constituency about this newer text, it became clear that the original goal of completing the text, and having official responses to it by 1997, was no longer feasible.

Another drafting meeting took place January 16-18, 1997, to introduce further revisions based on comments coming, on the Catholic side, from the Congregation for the Doctrine of the Faith, and from a Lutheran consultation brought together in December 1996 by Bishop H. Hirschler in Hanover, Germany, and from further insights from the eleven participants in that meeting.[23] The joint LWF-PCPCU annual staff meeting, in February 1997, agreed that this revised text was no longer a draft proposal, but rather the completed version that would be submitted for study aimed at

20. Oppegaard, "A History of the 'Joint Declaration,'" p. 10. Oppegaard outlines especially the Lutheran process.

21. It first met November 6-7, 1995. The three PCPCU appointees were Bishop Paul-Werner Scheele, Professor Lothar Ullrich, and staff person Dr. Heinz-Albert Raem.

22. Its members, who met in Würzburg, Germany, included: *Lutherans:* T. Dieter, M. Root, and H. Meyer, Strasbourg; E. Brand, Geneva, LWF, E. Huovinen, Helsinki, M. Piske, Brazil, J. Reumann, Philadelphia, D. Wendebourg, Göttingen; *Catholics:* K. Becker, Rome, CDF, J. Fitzmyer, Washington, DC, H. A. Raem, Rome-PCPCU, P. W. Scheele, Würzburg, L. Ullrich, Erfurt, J. Wicks, Rome. See Wicks, *Justification and Sanctification,* p. 130, note 2.

The close collaboration between the PCPCU and the CDF on this project is reflected also by the presence of a CDF consultor on the Catholic team.

23. Wicks, "Joint Declaration on the Doctrine of Justification," p. 130, note 2. It also met in Würzburg.

official adoption, to the Catholic Church and to the LWF member churches around the world. They did so not without some uneasiness as to whether the process would be successful.[24] The responses of both partners would come in June 1998.

Some Key Features of the
Joint Declaration on the Doctrine of Justification

The *Joint Declaration* is a concise presentation consisting of forty-four paragraphs. The heart of the common understanding on justification is stated in no. 15:

> In faith we together hold the conviction that justification is the work of the triune God. The Father sent his Son into the world to save sinners. The foundation and presupposition of justification is the incarnation, death, and resurrection of Christ. Justification thus means that Christ himself is our righteousness, in which we share through the Holy Spirit in accord with the will of the Father. Together we confess: By grace alone, in faith in Christ's saving work and not because of any merit on our part, we are accepted by God and receive the Holy Spirit, who renews our hearts while equipping and calling us to good works.

The achievement of the *JD* is expressed especially in nos. 40 and 41. First, that the understanding of justification found therein "shows that a consensus in basic truths of the doctrine of justification exists between Lutherans and Catholics" (no. 40). It has been described as a "differentiated consensus."[25] It is a consensus in basic truths, not *the* basic truths. There

24. Present at the February 15, 1997, joint staff meeting in Geneva were, *for the LWF:* General Secretary Ishmael Noko, Michael Root, Theo Dieter; *for PCPCU:* Cardinal Cassidy, Bishop Duprey, Bishop Périsset, Heinz-Albert Raem, John A. Radano. Each side described for the other some of the internal process by which the text was approved for this decisive stage. Dr. Noko indicated that the LWF Executive Committee asked if there was a guarantee from the Roman Catholic Church that the text would go through its response process successfully. Each side desired to have some guarantee from the other that the text would pass through this final process successfully.

25. For an explanation of "differentiated consensus" see Harding Meyer, "Ecumenical Consensus," *Gregorianum* 77, no. 2 (1996): 213-25, and "Consensus in the Doctrine of Justification," *Ecumenical Trends* (December 1997): 5/165-8/168.

are remaining differences of language, theological elaboration, and emphasis in the understanding of justification described in paragraphs 19-39, but these are acceptable because the Lutheran and the Catholic explications of justification "are in their difference open to one another and do not destroy the consensus regarding the basic truths" (no. 40). And this means that the doctrinal condemnations of the sixteenth century concerning the doctrine of justification "appear in a new light: The teaching of the Lutheran churches presented in this Declaration does not fall under the condemnations of the Council of Trent. The condemnations in the Lutheran Confessions do not apply to the teaching of the Roman Catholic Church presented in this Declaration" (no. 41).

Rather than condemning each other, Lutherans and Catholics can now confess together basic truths of the doctrine of justification. In the language of the Declaration:

> We confess together that all persons depend completely on the saving grace of God for their salvation. (no. 19)

> We confess together that God forgives sin by grace and at the same time frees human beings from sin's enslaving power and imparts the gift of new life in Christ. (no. 22)

> We confess together that sinners are justified by faith in the saving action of God in Christ. By the action of the Holy Spirit in baptism, they are granted the gift of Salvation, which lays the basis of the whole Christian life. (no. 25)

> We confess together that in baptism the Holy Spirit unites one with Christ, justifies and truly renews the person. (no. 28)

> We confess together that persons are justified by faith in the gospel "apart from the works prescribed by the law" (Rom. 3:28). (no. 31)

> We confess that the faithful can rely on the mercy and promises of God. In spite of their own weakness and the manifold threats to their faith, on the strength of Christ's death and resurrection, they can build on the effective promise of God's grace in Word and Sacrament and so be sure of this grace. (no. 34)

> We confess together that good works — a Christian life lived in faith, hope and love — follow justification and are its fruits. When the justi-

fied live in Christ and act in the grace they receive, they bring forth, in biblical terms, good fruit. . . . Thus both Jesus and the apostolic Scriptures admonish Christians to bring forth the works of love. (no. 37)

At the same time the declaration made clear that this agreement was only one step toward visible unity. A number of other issues needed to be resolved before unity could be achieved. (cf. no. 43)

Pope John Paul II's Support During the Drafting Process: Statements 1995-1997

During the years in which this process of drafting and redrafting a common statement on justification was taking place, Pope John Paul made statements in 1995, 1996, and 1997, more explicit each year, alluding to that process and expressing hope and support for its successful completion.

In March 1995, when the second draft of a proposal for a joint declaration had been sent out for study, the Pope said to participants in a conference on Catholic-Lutheran relations held at the International Bridgettine Center in Farfa, Italy, that "a very fundamental stage of dialogue was reached when the doctrine of justification became the central issue, and we must look forward with confidence to the document on which Lutherans and Catholics are now hard at work and which aims at expressing a common understanding of this central theme of our faith."[26]

In December 1995, John Paul spoke to a visiting ELCA delegation of the importance of the present moment, that "a very significant stage in Lutheran-Catholic dialogue was reached when it became possible to consider the doctrine of justification." It must be our shared prayer, he continued, "that a common understanding of this central theme of our faith will be attained."[27]

More forcefully in 1996, during his third pastoral visit to Germany,[28] just weeks after a further revised version of the joint declaration project had been completed, the Pope recalled with satisfaction, in two addresses in

---

26. "To Catholic-Lutheran Dialogue Conference, March 14, 1995," *IS* 90 (1995): 128.

27. "To Delegation of the Evangelical Lutheran Church in America, December 11, 1995," *IS* 92 (1996): 98.

28. "Pope John Paul II's Third Pastoral Visit to Germany, June 21-23, 1996," *IS* 93 (1996): 154-58.

Paderborn, that after his first visit to Germany in 1980, a mixed ecumenical commission proposed a study of the Catholic Church's sixteenth-century doctrinal condemnations and those of the Lutheran confessional writings. This study, he said when meeting representatives of the Evangelical Church of Germany (EKD) and of a working group of Christian churches, "has worked out a variety of agreements and rapprochements in essential questions of faith."[29] "Thanks to this research," he asserted in his homily in an ecumenical service, "many of the controversies at that time appear today in a new light. Differences which previous generations believed to be irreconcilable have been overcome."[30] And specifically in regard to justification, he affirmed that:

> In the doctrine of justification a broad-reaching rapprochement has been achieved. Whenever one looks at the various consensus statements on the doctrine of justification, there is an ever stronger impression that in the important basic questions of the understanding of the message of justification there is fundamental agreement.[31]

Continuing, the Pope also pointed to questions still to be resolved, but raised the issue of what weight these differences have:

> However, not all the differences have been overcome, but now we can ask more precisely what weight the remaining differences have. Although the theological relationship between the Lutheran understanding of justification and the Catholic doctrine on baptism and the Church needs further discussion, one can still hope that we will reach agreement on that question which was at the heart of the theological controversies of the 16th century.[32]

In 1997, after a third and final version of the *Joint Declaration* had been offered as the final text of the agreement to the Catholic Church and the Lutheran churches for official response and was still being evaluated, the

---

29. "Address to Ecumenical leaders, June 22, 1996," *IS* 93 (1996): 155. German original: *Insegnamenti*, XIX, 1 (1996): 1564.

30. "Address During Ecumenical Service, June 22, 1996," *IS* 93 (1996): 158. German original: *Insegnamenti*, XIX, 1 (1996): 1573.

31. "Address to Ecumenical Leaders, June 22, 1996," p. 155. German original: *Insegnamenti*, XIX, 1, (1996): 1564.

32. "Address to Ecumenical Leaders, June 22, 1996," p. 155.

Pope again offered his support. In a message to the LWF's Ninth General Assembly in Hong Kong, 1997, reiterating what he had said in Germany the year before, that "in the doctrine of justification a broad-reaching rapprochement has been achieved," he added:

> Years of research and dialogue have in fact brought us to the point in which we are able to consider officially a proposal for a joint declaration on the doctrine of justification. The process of discernment of this important text is not yet complete in either of our communities, but both Catholics and Lutherans can undoubtedly see this moment as one of grace and can say with the Psalmist: "I will give thanks to the Lord with my whole heart; . . . I will sing praise to your name, O most high." (Ps 9:1-2)[33]

The Holy Father emphasized a spiritual motivation for working to bring the process to a successful achievement: "we need to keep before us the Lord's prayer for his disciples: 'that they may all be one' (Jn 17:21). This has to be our motivation. Because it is the will of Christ that we should seek unity, there can be no turning back on the path of ecumenism."[34]

The Pope's message to the Assembly was welcomed. But this was a critical moment for LWF member churches in the official response process regarding the *Joint Declaration,* and they had many questions and concerns about its reception also within the Catholic Church (and vice-versa). Thus, one Assembly plenary session was dedicated to the *Joint Declaration,* and the LWF General Secretary Noko invited Cardinal Cassidy to give one of several major addresses at the session. After an introduction to the meaning and evolution of the *JD* by Bishop Christoph Stier, Chair of the Standing Committee for Ecumenical Affairs, Cardinal Cassidy addressed the pastoral implications of the *JD,* and ELCA President Dr. H. George Anderson spoke of the meaning of justification today. Cardinal Cassidy spelled out in considerable detail ways in which the implications of the agreement on justification could be brought into the life of the Catholic Church, including opportunities for Lutheran-Catholic cooperation. He also mentioned some of the limitations that would still exist, since the acceptance of the *Joint Declaration* would not bring the two partners into full

---

33. "To Dr. Gottfried Brakemeier, President, Lutheran World Federation," *IS* 95 (1997): 98.

34. "To Dr. Gottfried Brakemeier, President, Lutheran World Federation," p. 98.

communion.[35] Both the Pope's message and the Cardinal's address were strong indications of the desire within the Catholic Church that the *JD* be officially, mutually approved. The Assembly, for its part, expressed "thanks for three decades of Lutheran–Roman Catholic dialogue which has resulted in growing doctrinal convergence and ever deepening spiritual communion," expressed its "gratitude for the completion of the Joint Declaration," and, in this resolution, gave an important responsibility to the LWF Council, namely, to discuss carefully the responses of the member churches to the *JD*, "and to determine whether a consensus among the member churches can be declared." If a *magnus consensus* was not clearly achieved, it should consult the member churches.[36]

---

35. Edward Idris Cardinal Cassidy, "Pastoral Consequences of the Joint Declaration on the Doctrine of Justification," *"In Christ — Called to Witness," Official Report of the Ninth Assembly of the Lutheran World Federation, Hong Kong, 8-16 July 1997* (Geneva: Lutheran World Federation, 1977), pp. 102-6, and *IS* 95 (1997): 99-101.

36. "Resolutions: Joint Declaration on the Doctrine of Justification," Official Report of the Ninth Assembly of the Lutheran World Federation, Hong Kong, 8-16 July 1997 (Geneva: Lutheran World Federation, 1997), p. 62.

CHAPTER 11

Official Responses to the Joint Declaration,
June 1998

From February 1997 to June 1998, while the proposed text for a joint declaration was being examined by the two communions, the PCPCU and the
LWF kept in close contact, especially through the joint staff meetings.[1]
They informed one another of the progress in their respective reception
processes, including specifically those aspects of the proposal which their
constituencies found difficult.[2] One of the issues discussed at the joint

1. Joint staff meetings were held January 30-31, 1998, in Geneva, and May 26-27, 1998, in
Rome. PCPCU representatives: Cardinal Cassidy, Bishop Duprey, John Radano; for the
LWF: Ishmael Noko, Sven Oppegaard (Assistant General Secretary for Ecumenical Affairs),
Michael Root, Theo Dieter, both of the Strasbourg Institute. They also used other occasions
to speak together, such as the annual meeting of the conference of Secretaries of Christian
World Communions in October 1997, at which the LWF's Noko and the PCPCU's Duprey,
each with a staff member, were present. Cardinal Cassidy and Bishop Duprey, and Dr. Noko
and Sven Oppegaard also had an intense private conversation at the 1998 Anglican Lambeth
conference at which they were guests.

2. For Lutherans, one concern was the question in No. 18 of the *JD* proposal concerning
justification as "an indispensable criterion," serving "to orient all the teaching and practice
of our churches to Christ." Lutherans emphasize the unique significance of this criterion
without denying the interrelation and significance of all truths of faith. Catholics are
"bound by several criteria," while not denying the "special function of the message of justification." For Catholics, one concern was the Lutheran position found in No. 29: "at the same
time righteous and sinner." Some had difficulty in seeing how it could be considered fully
compatible with the Catholic position in No. 30, and questioned whether there was agreement on this point.

Avery Dulles, SJ, a participant in the Lutheran-Catholic national dialogue in the USA

staff meeting of January 30-31, 1998, for example, concerned the different reception processes for the *JD* within the two communions. The LWF Council planned to make a final decision on approval of the *JD*, based on its member churches' responses, at its Council meeting, June 8-17, 1998, in Geneva. The Catholic reply was also expected in early summer.[3] They also began to consider ways in which they could cooperate, once approval of the *JD* took place, in press coverage and on other issues related to the celebration and signing of the *JD*.

An Intense Debate in Germany

During this same period an intense debate over the *Joint Declaration* continued in Germany, before the official responses were made public in June 1998, but after as well. Over 140 Protestant university professors signed a statement published January 29, 1998, in the daily *Frankfurter Allgemeine Zeitung*, urging Lutheran church leaders in Germany to reject the *Joint Declaration* in its present form, claiming that there exists no consensus on basic truths of the doctrine of justification.[4]

Both Protestants and Catholics in turn challenged the university professors. The (Bensheim) Institute for Interconfessional Research of the Protestant Church in Germany (EKD) refuted this claim, as well as the professors' view that the *JD* is a component within a Roman Catholic program aiming at integrating Protestant clergy into the structure of the Roman Catholic hierarchy. It urged that Protestant synods and church leaders can agree to the *JD* as a first step toward a greater ecumenical fellowship.[5] Bishop Horst Hirschler of Hanover, Presiding Bishop of the United Evangelical Lutheran Church of Germany (VELKD), in a letter February 5, 1998, to the 140 professors, criticized them for, among other things, not mentioning that their critique include points that have long been formulated and included in the recommendations for decision given to the Lutheran churches, which proposed to the churches that they give a

---

for many years, expressed serious criticism of some important aspects of the *JD*. See, for example, his "Two Languages of Salvation: The Lutheran-Catholic Joint Declaration," *First Things* 98 (December 1999): 25-30.

3. "LWF and Vatican Staff Hold Annual Session," *LWI* (February 5, 1998): 3.

4. "Controversy over Joint Declaration Continues in Germany," *LWI* (February 5, 1998): 5.

5. "Controversy over Joint Declaration Continues in Germany," p. 5.

qualified "yes" to the *JD* while clearly identifying the critical points.[6] Catholic Professor Gerhard Ludwig Müller objected that the Protestant theologians had attempted to guarantee confessional identity merely by resorting to old confessional formulae while failing to take account of the changed historical situation and the ecumenical process during this century. Bishop Jean-Claude Périsset, Associate Secretary of the Pontifical Council for Promoting Christian Unity, expressed his conviction that despite the protests, the *JD* would be signed by the LWF and the Catholic Church.[7]

Despite the ongoing debate,[8] the official responses, published in June 1998, showed that both partners were ready for a mutual commitment to the agreements on justification achieved through dialogue. Nonetheless, the responses and questions raised after both responses were published reflected some of the differences in approaches to reception mentioned years before in *Strategies for Reception,* and some of the difficulties about particular formulations in the *JD* which they had reported to each other as the responses were being prepared. The response of each was the first step in the official response process. But since the partners had arrived at their published responses separately, and in different ways, it was still to be ascertained that they understood and confirmed the *JD* in a compatible way, allowing a joint signing.

The LWF Response, June 16, 1998

The LWF gave its official response affirming the *Joint Declaration* when the LWF Council, meeting in Geneva, took an action on June 16, 1998, adopting a recommendation presented in the Report of its Standing Committee for Ecumenical Affairs.[9] That recommendation had two parts. The first, "Background," summarized the development of the *JD* from the beginning

6. "Presiding Bishop Horst Hirschler Defends Joint Declaration," *LWI* (February 19, 1998): 3.

7. Müller and Périsset are both cited in "Roman Catholic Theologians Repudiate Criticism of Joint Declaration," *LWI* (March 10, 1998): 7.

8. Articles in the *Frankfurter Allgemeine Zeitung* fueled the debate over a period of time. See André Birmelé, *La Communion Écclésiale* (Paris: Éditions du Cerf; Genève: Labor et Fides, 2000), III "La Déclaration Commune," pp. 115-16.

9. "Response of the Lutheran World Federation," *LWI* (June 23, 1998): 15-22, *IS* 98 (1998): 90-93.

of the official Lutheran-Catholic dialogue to the recent point in which a joint declaration on justification could be undertaken, and described the nature of the *JD*, and the consensus in basic truths of the doctrine of justification that it affirms. The "Background" makes clear that this does not mark the end of Lutheran-Catholic dialogue on justification, because of "certain topics . . . found especially difficult . . . even by some churches which have affirmed the 'Joint Declaration' and will need . . . continued discussion between Lutherans and Catholics." The most significant difficulties are "related to the status of the doctrine of justification as criterion (no. 18), concupiscence and sin in the justified (nos. 28-30), and the relation of good works to the preservation of grace (no. 38)." Nonetheless, the recommendation pointed out that the *Joint Declaration* sets forth what may be called a differentiated consensus, one that is sufficient for a specific purpose, and thus compatible with remaining differences in that these differences "are no longer the occasion for doctrinal condemnations."

The second part, "Recommendation," includes two sections. The first, "Premises," outlines the response process within the LWF, including the number of churches affirming the *JD*.[10] The "Premises" concluded with an important statement describing the location of authority in this process, namely that "an action of this type by the Council on behalf of the LWF is a concluding moment. . . . Specifically, the Lutheran affirmation of the 'Joint Declaration' is a result of a process involving both the action of the affirming churches and the action of the LWF Council" (no. 32).

The second part of the Recommendation was an "Affirmation." Among several recommendations offered for affirmation on the basis of the premises was:

> that, on the basis of the positive responses of the said majority, the agreements regarding the doctrine of justification as presented in the "Joint Declaration" be affirmed, and that, on the basis of these agreements, the doctrinal condemnations in the Lutheran confessional writ-

10. By June 8, 1998, it states, eighty-six LWF member churches had responded to the General Secretary's letter of February 1997, which asked if they could affirm the conclusions of the *Joint Declaration*. Seventy-nine member churches (= 78.5 percent of the LWF constituency) of the eighty-six that had responded up till then, "have affirmed the differentiated consensus claimed by the 'Joint Declaration' (no. 29). An even greater number have affirmed that the condemnations in the Lutheran confessions do not apply to the teaching of the Roman Catholic Church presented in the 'Joint Declaration'" (no. 30).

ings regarding justification be declared not to apply to the teaching of the Roman Catholic Church as presented in the "Joint Declaration." (no. 37)

Another recommendation referred to the next aspect of the reception process, the joint action of both partners. It requested that, once the Roman Catholic response had been published, steps be taken in coordination with the Roman Catholic Church to determine "how the 'Joint Declaration' might most appropriately be jointly confirmed by the Lutheran World Federation and the Roman Catholic Church" (no. 41).

The Council voted unanimously to approve these recommendations. Thereby, the LWF officially accepted the *Joint Declaration,* which the great majority of LWF member churches had affirmed.

After its publication, neither the PCPCU nor other offices of the Holy See made requests for clarification of any aspect of this official Lutheran response to the *JD.*

Response of the Catholic Church, June 25, 1998

The response of the Catholic Church, published on June 25, 1998, was introduced at a press conference by Cardinal Cassidy. The Cardinal's introduction,[11] though not part of the response itself, briefly gave some historical background, traced the Lutheran-Catholic dialogue, international and national, over the decades, and described the evolution of the *Joint Declaration,* and some features of its content. He affirmed that the *JD* is an important step forward, saying too that it also has limits, since it does not claim to resolve all the issues that Lutherans and Catholics need to face and resolve. The Cardinal concluded with a strong statement: "that the consensus reached on the doctrine of justification, despite its limitations, virtually resolves a long disputed question at the end of the twentieth century, and on the eve of the new millennium. . . . It will be an encouragement to the whole ecumenical movement."

The response, issued in the form of an explanatory Note, prepared by

---

11. "Presentation of the Roman Catholic Response to the Vatican *Sala Stampa* of His Eminence Edward Idris Cardinal Cassidy President of the Pontifical Council for Promoting Christian Unity, 25 June 1998," *IS* 98 (1998): 95-97.

common agreement between the Congregation for the Doctrine of the Faith and the Pontifical Council for Promoting Christian Unity, included three headings: "Declaration," "Clarifications," and "Prospects for Future Work."[12] LWF leaders would raise serious questions for clarification concerning this Catholic response.

The "Declaration" affirmed the *JD*'s statement that "a high degree of agreement" (*JD* 4) has been reached, and that there is "a consensus in basic truths of the doctrine of justification" (*JD* 5). But it also indicated that on some points "the positions are, in fact, still divergent." The Catholic Church, it pledged, intends to contribute to overcoming "the divergencies that still exist" by listing points that still constitute an obstacle to agreement between the Catholic Church and the LWF on all the fundamental truths concerning justification.

This it did in the section called "Clarifications." To briefly mention some of its concerns, it raised problems with section 4.4's treatment of "The Justified as Sinner." The title, it said, is already a cause for perplexity from a Catholic point of view. Since, from a Catholic perspective, everything that is really sin is taken away in baptism, the formula "at the same time righteous and sinner" as it is explained at the beginning in no. 29 is not acceptable, and does not seem compatible with the renewal and sanctification of the interior man of which the Council of Trent speaks. It remains difficult to see, in the current state of the presentation in the *Joint Declaration,* how we can say that this doctrine on *"simul iustus et peccator"* is not touched by the anathemas of the Tridentine decree on original sin and justification. Concerning no. 18 the response would have liked more clarity on the way the message of justification is integrated into the fundamental criterion of the *"regula fidei."* In no. 21, it would have liked more clarification on the way Lutherans understand the compatibility of full personal involvement in faith, and the reception "mere passive" of justification, in order to determine more exactly the degree of consensus with Catholic doctrine.

The response addressed the condemnations of the sixteenth century in this way. "If," it said, "it is true that in those truths on which a consensus has been reached the condemnations of the Council of Trent no longer apply, the divergencies on other points must, on the contrary be overcome

---

12. "Response of the Catholic Church to the Joint Declaration of the Catholic Church and the Lutheran World Federation on the Doctrine of Justification," *IS* 98 (1998): 93-95.

before we can affirm, as is done generically in no. 41, that these points no longer incur the condemnations of the Council of Trent. That applies in the first place to the doctrine on 'simul iustus et peccator.'" Mentioning these and some other points, the Clarifications ended by raising a question that had been raised when an LWF delegation came to Rome in 1992 (see Chapter 9). It spoke of "the different character of the two signatories of this Joint Declaration." Referring to the LWF process of arriving at its formal decision about the declaration, through consultation of the Synods, it stated that there still remains "the question of the real authority of such a synodal consensus, today and also tomorrow, in the life and doctrine of the Lutheran community."

The third section, "Prospects for the Future," expressed the hope that "this important step forward towards agreement in the doctrine on justification may be followed by further studies that will make possible a satisfactory clarification of the divergencies that still exist."

Pope John Paul II's Statement
After the Catholic Response, June 28, 1998

As he had done at every other stage of the way, Pope John Paul gave his support at this stage of official response as well. Before praying the Angelus on Sunday, June 28, 1998, he referred to the *Joint Declaration,* saying that "we can now rejoice at an important ecumenical achievement." Although the declaration does not solve all the problems concerning the teaching of the doctrine of justification, "it expresses," he said, referring to the response of the Catholic Church, "*a consensus in basic truths of the doctrine of justification*" (emphasis his). He expressed the hope that this progress "will encourage and strengthen the declared goal for which Lutherans and Catholics are striving: the achievement of full visible unity." He thanked all Catholics and Lutherans "who have contributed to this important advance."[13]

---

13. "Pope John Paul II's Reflection," *IS* 98 (1998): 100, and *L'Osservatore Romano* (Weekly Edition in English), July 1, 1998. Italian original: *Insegnamenti,* XXI, 1 (1998): 1517.

Determining a Common Understanding
of the Responses, 1998-1999

The publication of the LWF's and the Catholic Church's official responses completed a critical stage of the response process. But Lutheran reactions to the Catholic response signaled that another critical stage had begun, namely, that of ascertaining whether the two separate responses understood the *Joint Declaration* in the same way, enabling the two partners to sign the declaration together as an expression of their common mind. Strong Lutheran reactions, and calls for clarification, initially put this in doubt. In the months that followed, starting in July 1998, significant Catholic authorities did in fact clarify the meaning of the response, and a way was found by June 1999 for the LWF and the Catholic Church to express together, in writing, their common understanding of the achievement of the *Joint Declaration*.

The Concerns of Lutherans and Others, 1998

Lutheran requests for clarifications of the Catholic response came immediately. Reactions in the Lutheran world "ranged from amazement, to anger, to disappointment. Saner voices urged patience and conversation with Vatican officials to determine what the actual situation was."[14] On June 25, the day the response was released, LWF General Secretary Dr. Ishmael Noko issued a statement raising a number of questions. He first directly addressed the Catholic response's question about the "real authority" of the LWF process in achieving its response, saying that "[t]he authority of the LWF to speak in such a matter is based on its ability, affirmed in its constitution, to represent the churches in such matters as the churches assign to it," and describing in this connection other key aspects of their process. Furthermore, he said, the Catholic response seen as a whole "raises fundamental questions for our understanding of the official position adopted by the Roman Catholic Church to the agreements formulated in

---

14. William G. Rusch, "The History and Methodology of the *Joint Declaration on the Doctrine of Justification*: A Case Study in Ecumenical Reception," *Agapé. Études en l'honneur de Msgr. Pierre Duprey M.Afr.* Sous la Direction de Jean-Marie Roger Tillard, OP (Chambésy-Genève: Centre Orthodoxe du Patriarchat Oecuménique, 2000), p. 179.

the 'Joint Declaration.'" While the LWF has declared on the basis of the *Joint Declaration* that the doctrinal condemnations in the Lutheran confessional writings do not apply to Roman Catholic teaching regarding justification as presented in the *Joint Declaration,* in the Catholic reply, "reservations are made on essential points, whereby the basis becomes unclear for jointly declaring that the mutual condemnations from the time of the Reformation no longer apply." He expressed hope that clarification on these essential points might be reached in the time to come so that "the full intention of the 'Joint Declaration' might be accomplished."[15]

Other Lutheran leaders who supported the process leading to the *Joint Declaration* reacted with great dismay, both in Germany[16] and the USA,[17] though there were also prominent Lutheran leaders who saw the response in more positive terms.[18] LWF President Bishop Christian Krause called for a careful unhurried examination of the Vatican's response, affirming that only such an analysis would show whether ecumenism had suffered a setback.[19]

Some Lutheran *and* Catholic members of the international Lutheran-

---

15. "Reflection of Dr. Ishmael Noko, LWF General Secretary, June 25, 1998," *IS* 98 (1998): 97-98, taken from *Lutheran World Information,* July 9, 1998, pp. 7-8.

16. For example, Dr. Harding Meyer wrote to Cardinal Cassidy on June 27, 1998, expressing his great disappointment. Also, *LWI* (July 9, 1998): 9, indicated that Bishop Horst Hirschler, presiding bishop of the United Evangelical Lutheran Church of Germany (VELKD) and bishop of the Evangelical Lutheran Church of Hanover, was "taken aback by Vatican response." The Bensheim Institute criticized the response as giving a clear "yes" and a clear "no" to the *JD*. From *Lutheran World Information,* July 9, 1998, p. 10.

17. Robert W. Jenson, a Lutheran participant in the third phase of the international Lutheran-Catholic dialogue, stated that while the major Lutheran churches "singly and in concert, have now declared the condemnations inactive . . . the Vatican has after all refused." "This outcome has surprised almost everybody, and some it has not only surprised but traumatized, like the German Lutheran bishops who rammed the Declaration through against vehement protest from many publicly influential members of their church." See "On the Vatican's 'Official Response' to the Joint Declaration on Justification," in "Symposium on the Vatican's Official Response to the Joint Declaration on Justification," *Pro Ecclesia* (Fall 1998): 401, 402.

18. ELCA President Dr. H. George Anderson underlined that the Vatican admits there is a "consensus on basic truths of the doctrine of justification." Both the LWF and the Vatican responses agreed that the work must continue. "Presiding Bishop H. George Anderson Satisfied with Consensus," *LWI* (July 9, 1998): 9.

19. "Vatican's Response to Joint Declaration to Be Carefully Examined," *LWI* (July 9, 1998): 9.

Catholic dialogue, whose next meeting was scheduled for August 28–September 3, 1998, in Opole, Poland, also found difficulty with the Catholic response.[20] Catholic leaders such as Cardinals Ratzinger and Cassidy had already begun to respond to the criticisms directed to the response, and to reassure Lutherans that the Catholic Church had accepted the *JD* (see next paragraphs), even before this session of the dialogue met. But the outcome of their efforts was still unclear, and whether a joint signing of the *JD* would take place was still in question. At its meeting, therefore, some members of the dialogue commission had harsh criticism for the response, and wondered whether it was worthwhile to continue the dialogue. After that meeting several Catholic dialogue members expressed directly to Rome their deep concerns about the Catholic response, and the way it was seen by their Lutheran counterparts.[21] Other interested Catholics expressed their concerns as well.[22]

20. Even before the dialogue meeting in Opole, the Catholic Co-Chairman, Bishop Walter Kasper of Rottenburg-Stuttgart, hearing the very strong reactions in Germany to the Catholic response, and questions being raised that tended to put the dialogue itself in danger, wrote to Cardinal Cassidy on July 23, 1998, asking if a high representative of the PCPCU, even the Cardinal himself, could attend that meeting, to answer the serious questions he anticipated would be raised by dialogue members, and thus help restore the confidence in the dialogue process that had been put into question. The Cardinal, however, was not able to come.

21. Jared Wicks, SJ, wrote to Cardinal Cassidy on September 4, 1998, indicating that there were four hours of discussion at Opole relating to the present problematic on the *JD*, the Catholic response of June 25, and the more recent interventions and clarifications. He underscored that the discussion was quite incisive in criticizing the Catholic response as ambiguous in its content, mentioning in this regard three Catholics and three Lutherans. He said that there was a tone of disappointment, disillusionment, and pessimism about the present state of L-RC relations on the world level. He mentioned that one evening, when the commission was hosted for supper at the University of Opole, one of the speakers, a Polish Lutheran Bishop, expressed the view that while the LWF adhered to the *JD*, the Catholic Church declined to do so. Wicks commented that time will tell whether the ninety or so Lutheran churches adhering to the *JD* agree with that reading of the situation, "or will accept the interpretive helps offered by Cardinal Ratzinger and yourself." (Letter of Father Wicks cited with permission.)

As to the "interpretive helps," the dialogue members knew of Ratzinger's letter of July 14, 1998, and Cassidy's letter of July 30, 1998, to Dr. Noko mentioned below. But there was still a sense that further clarification of points in the Catholic response might still be needed. Cf. also note 30 for another significant step taken after this meeting.

22. Richard John Neuhaus, "Setback in Rome," *First Things*, October 1998, pp. 80-82.

Reassurances by Catholic Leaders, June 1998–January 1999

In the months that followed the publication of the Catholic response, key Catholic leaders, including Vatican officials such as Cardinals Cassidy and Ratzinger, and Bishop Pierre Duprey, stated publicly and consistently that the Catholic response to the *JD* indeed confirmed that a consensus on justification had been reached. Also, on the release of the response, June 25, Bishop Karl Lehmann, President of the German Bishops' Conference and co-editor of *LK*, stated that the core of the Catholic response "corresponds to the Lutheran statement that a consensus has been reached on basic truths of the doctrine on justification. It is an important step," he continued, "that both partners officially affirm this substantial agreement which has been in preparation for decades through many theological studies. This is a long hoped for, and now binding step."[23] Cardinal Ratzinger, in a letter to the *Frankfurter Allgemeine Zeitung (FAZ)*, July 14, 1998, addressed Lutheran concerns, writing that the official response should be read on two levels, one being the declaration on which both churches agree, the other the clarifications, which were designed for internal discussions by the churches.[24]

Cardinal Cassidy, in a lengthy letter dated July 30, 1998, to Dr. Ishmael Noko, with which he formally sent the official Catholic response to the LWF, offered some reflections "which seem necessary in view of certain misreadings of the Catholic response that have appeared."[25] Citing and continuing in the line of Cardinal Ratzinger's letter to *FAZ* just mentioned,

23. "No reason for disappointment or resignation, Comments of Bishop Karl Lehmann and Cardinal Joseph Ratzinger," *LWI* (July 9, 1998): 11. The same issue, on the same page, under the title "Cardinal Ratzinger welcomes qualified consensus on basic truths," summarized a report in the Catholic news agency (KNA-OKI) that even on June 18, Cardinal Ratzinger spoke of the *Joint Declaration* as an "event of the century," referred to its theological substance as basically "positive," stated that the Roman Catholic side affirms and welcomes the qualified consensus reached on basic truths, and "left no doubt that the moment had come for an official and public signing."

24. Though a letter to a secular newspaper, and not a formal statement issued by the CDF, this was a key intervention in clarifying the meaning of the response, as noted by theologians, both Lutheran (cf. Rusch, "The History and Methodology of the *Joint Declaration*, p. 179) and Catholic (J. Augustine DiNoia, OP, "A Gift of God's Spirit of Wisdom: The Official Catholic Response to the Joint Declaration on Justification," *Pro Ecclesia* [Fall 1998]: 416).

25. "Letter of Cardinal Cassidy to LWF, July 30, 1998," *IS* 98 (1998): 98-100.

Cardinal Cassidy said that "[l]ittle attention seems to have been paid to the very important distinction . . . between the Declaration and the Clarifications. . . ." Only the Declaration "is to be considered strictly as a response to the question raised in the Joint Declaration, and this response is clear and unequivocal: *'there is a consensus in basic truths of the doctrine of justification'*" (emphasis original). The Clarifications have "a completely different value" with respect to the Declaration. They could have been presented as "explanations" since they deal with some of the questions considered in the *Joint Declaration*. The latter, and the LWF resolution in response to the *Joint Declaration*, both state that dialogue needs to continue with respect to certain questions. The Vatican response "goes a little further and indicates those points requiring some further dialogue." He judged that there seems to have been a very "one-sided reading" of the second part by "some Lutheran commentators" who have spoken of "the many reservations" made in the Catholic response. In fact, the Cardinal said, "there are no 'reservations' and just a very *few* clarifications" (emphasis original), and then presented some reflections on the points at issue.

The most prominent concern was the question of the "justified as sinner." Discussing the Lutheran position as presented in the *JD* (no. 29) in light of Catholic teaching and what is said elsewhere in the *JD* (no. 15), the Cardinal made clear that the problem "comes from *a presentation of doctrine* that seems to contradict itself" (emphasis original). The Catholic response "does not state that the relative condemnation of Trent remains, but that it is difficult to see how in the present presentation the doctrine on *'simul iustus et peccator' is not touched* by the anathemas of the Tridentine decree on original sin and justification" (emphasis original). He asked, could this not be resolved by "a Lutheran presentation that explains the unusual use of sin in this context, by which that word loses its normal character of being a *willed and voluntary* opposition to God? In this case, there would be no real problem and the question of the condemnation would no longer exist" (emphasis original).

Cardinal Cassidy addressed other issues as well. He concluded by reiterating that the Catholic Church accepted without reservation the *Joint Declaration*'s conclusion that "a consensus on basic truths of the doctrine of justification has been reached," that the Clarifications do not negate that consensus, and that the Catholic Church would have no difficulty in affirming and signing the *Joint Declaration*. He noted the slight difference between the LWF and Catholic responses in the treatment of no. 41, concerning the condemnations. The LWF response asks for further study on some points but declares that the condemnations in the Lutheran confessions do not apply to the teaching of the Roman Catholic Church presented in this declaration. The Catholic response states that where a consensus has been reached, namely on fundamental truths of the doctrine of justification, the condemnations of the Council of Trent no longer apply. Furthermore, "the Catholic response does *not* state that any condemnation of the Council of Trent still applies to the teaching of the Lutheran Churches as presented in the Joint Declaration" (emphasis original). Still, with the current state of the presentation of *"simul iustus et peccator"* the Catholic Church hesitates, without further study and clarification, to affirm categorically that it no longer incurs the condemnation.

Concerning Lutheran reaction to the Catholic response's question about the authority possessed by the LWF, the Cardinal said that there was no intention of calling into question the authority of the Lutheran consensus. But even with the overwhelming approval that the *JD* received from the Lutheran Synods, "there still remain important differences concerning the understanding by the two partners of authority in the Church which leave unanswered certain questions," and thus it was felt necessary to indicate this as a matter for further study in the ongoing dialogue.

Lutheran World Information (September 14, 1998) published Cardinal Cassidy's letter of July 30. The same issue (p. 3) published excerpts of a letter with which General Secretary Noko had sent Cardinal Cassidy's letter to the LWF Executive Committee in preparation for its meeting in November 1998, and to member churches. Dr. Noko's comments illustrated that the Cardinal's letter had helped to clarify the meaning and intent of the Catholic response, but that the LWF was not yet ready to go further. The letter, Noko said, "does not alter what is stated in the Roman Catholic Church's official response," but it opens up "a new perspective on how to read, understand and interpret this response." It is "clear that the distinction now claimed between the nature of the two parts of the Roman Catholic response constitutes a new emphasis. If we had had this distinction from the outset, some of the debates that have taken place, owing to the lack of clarity regarding the character of the Roman Catholic response, could have been avoided." The issues raised in the Clarifications would not have been understood as formal reservations to the agreements expressed in the *JD* but as "specifications of issues requiring further clarification" as we proceed. Nonetheless, whether or not these "recent elucidations from the Vatican" provide the necessary clarifications to work out a joint confirmation of the *Declaration* remains a "moot point for the LWF Executive Committee in November." Thus for the time being, pending a decision by the Executive Committee, there are "no plans for a joint confirmation."

PCPCU Secretary Bishop Pierre Duprey also affirmed without hesitation the Catholic response's acceptance of the agreements of the *JD*. Addressing an ecumenical forum in January 1999, in New York City,[26] he said that the *Joint Declaration* ". . . has now been officially accepted by the Lutheran World Federation and the Catholic Church." More forcefully, "Because of their acceptance of the *Joint Declaration* this is now an ecclesial agreement which has ecclesial consequences." He mentioned also that it has been deemed necessary "to add clarifications in order 'to further substantiate the consensus reached in the *Joint Declaration*.'"[27] He explained this and the intense debate over the Catholic response, saying that all of this shows how difficult it is to discern what is essential to the common statement of faith in the different approaches coming from different theological traditions. He recalled a classical distinction expressed by Pope John XXIII in his opening address for the Second Vatican Council, that "the substance of the ancient doctrine of the deposit of faith is one thing, and the way in which it is presented is another." The differentiated consensus claimed for the *JD* "is perhaps the furthest realization of this effort of discernment." It is normal "that, on either side, there are some who are tempted to judge that this discernment has been carried too far; that understanding and respect for different approaches, different theological traditions, has meant that certain aspects of faith have been forgotten or, at the least, have not been given sufficient importance." Different aspects of a given truth, for example, that *"the justified also are continuously exposed to the power of sin still pressing its attack,"* will be differently felt within a different theological view.[28]

---

26. Organized at St. Peter's Lutheran Church, January 15, 1999, by the pastor, Revd. Amandus J. Derr, with the assistance of Mr. Robert Busch and Dr. William Rusch, former director of the ELCA's Department of Ecumenical Relations and at this time director of the Commission on Faith and Order of the National Council of Churches of Christ in the USA. Among others participating were Dr. Harding Meyer, one of the drafters of the *JD*.

27. Pierre Duprey, "The Ecumenical Dialogue: What Has Been Achieved and Prospects for the Future," *Lutheran Forum* (Spring 1999): 30, 32.

28. Duprey, "The Ecumenical Dialogue," pp. 32, 33 (emphasis original).

The Need for Additional Clarifications:
Steps Taken in October-November 1998

Catholic officials consistently affirmed that the Catholic response accepted the agreements of the *JD.* Nonetheless, the intense discussion over the response soon made clear to both Lutherans and Catholics that if the LWF and the Catholic Church were to take the next step in the response process together, that is, on the basis of the two responses, to confirm their agreement by signing together the *Joint Declaration,* some additional step and/ or clarification was needed.[29] It had to be evident that they understood the agreements in the *JD* in the same way. Finding a way of making this clear soon became the shared concern of the LWF and the PCPCU. Each began to consider some statement or "protocol" that could accompany the signing of the *JD,* and explain that the signatories had the same understanding of its content, and "elucidations," which would explain the precise meaning of the *JD*'s presentation of those issues that the responses said needed further clarification. Important steps on these matters were taken during October and November 1998.

On the Catholic side, leaders in Rome took steps in early October to envision the content of a "protocol."[30] At least two preliminary versions

29. While LWF President Bishop Christian Krause, in his initial reaction to the Vatican response, called for a careful examination of it to see if there was an ecumenical setback, he also began to envision the need for some kind of "bridge" to make the planned joint signing possible (*LWI* [July 9, 1998]: 9). Dr. Harding Meyer, in a letter to Cardinal Cassidy of 27 June 1998, expressing his disappointment with the Catholic response, thought that an additional necessary step to get out of the difficult situation would be a pronouncement of the Holy Father affirming the consensus reached on the substance of faith with regard to justification, while acknowledging also the need for further common investigation on the level of theological expressions and traditional theological formulae. He indicated that he had also written directly to the Holy Father on June 26 in this same sense, and asked the Cardinal to speak directly to the Holy Father, advocating these concerns (letter cited with permission of Dr. Meyer). The Cardinal responded to Meyer on July 27, making some of the clarifications found in his letter of July 30 to Dr. Ishmael Noko, cited above.

30. Concerns expressed by both sides in the 1998 session of the international Lutheran-Catholic dialogue, mentioned above, led to an initiative, described in July 2005 by Cardinal Walter Kasper, now President of the PCPCU, in a note to the author. "During the Plenary session in Opole (Poland) of the Lutheran-Catholic Commission for Unity, strong critique was expressed from both sides, so that the continuation of the dialogue seemed to be in danger. Bishop Kasper in agreement with Bishop Nossol, member of this commission, decided therefore to write a confidential letter to Pope John Paul II. On occasion of the next feria

of a "protocol" began to emerge.[31] Initial steps were also taken to envision clarifications or "elucidations" on particular issues.[32] In taking these steps, they were convinced that they also had the support of the Pope to resolve the difficulties. On the occasion of a Vatican press conference, October 15, 1998, CDF Prefect Cardinal Ratzinger responded to an *Ecumenical News International (ENI)* question about the *Joint Declaration,* suggesting that the two communions could elaborate a "supplementary" statement that could deal with some of the outstanding issues. "In order to resolve the misunderstandings," he was quoted as saying, "we are considering a possible plan which of course would have to be worked out in greater detail. A supplementary declaration could be attached to the joint declaration enabling us to go beyond the problems which have arisen since June." Cardinal Ratzinger did not elaborate on the possible content of a "supplementary" statement, but stressed the importance of the consensus already reached by the two communions, and "pointed out that the LWF, as well as the Vatican, had raised points which needed further study."[33]

The PCPCU and LWF both had important internal meetings in No-

---

quarta (the Wednesday meetings) of the CDF, Cardinal Ratzinger asked Bishop Kasper to prepare a draft for a clarification. Bishop Kasper immediately informed the PCPCU and sent his draft at the same time to Cardinal Ratzinger and to Cardinal Cassidy. In this way the process was anew opened."

31. Bishop Kasper had visited Cardinal Cassidy at the PCPCU on October 7, 1998, to discuss the content of a "protocol." After this meeting, Cardinal Cassidy also worked out a version of a "protocol," a statement that could be made at the time of the signing, which could explain that the signatories had a common understanding of the *JD*. The Cardinal faxed his version to Bishop Kasper on October 8 as suggestions, but urged Bishop Kasper to develop the draft protocol according to his own insights, which he did. This process was still developing, so that Cardinal Cassidy was able to bring two possible examples of a protocol for discussion with LWF leaders at a meeting on October 26 (cf. note 30).

32. Jared Wicks, SJ, a member of the International Lutheran-Catholic Commission on Unity, contributed reflections on the notion of "simul iustus et peccator" to the PCPCU in October 1998. For his perspectives see his essay "Living and Praying as *simul iustus et peccator,*" *Gregorianum* 70 (1989): 512-48.

Catholic reflection on this was also published independently by Professor Heinz Schütte in *KNA* (1998): 8-10. His involvement in the Regensburg meeting in November 1998, which made a significant contribution towards finding a solution to the stalemate, is seen below.

33. "Ratzinger Suggests Solution to Difficulties over Lutheran Agreement" (*ENI*-98-0476), *ENI News Service,* October 20, 1998.

vember 1998, which would take up these questions.[34] In October, therefore, they kept in close contact with each other, particularly at a meeting on October 26, keeping in mind especially the possible supplementary documents just mentioned.[35] As a result of their consultations, the possible shape of a common draft of a "protocol" or "official common statement" was emerging by the end of October.

Besides the LWF and PCPCU collaboration, an informal, though very significant initiative on November 4, 1998, assisted the process in going an important step further. Bishop Johannes Hanselmann, former LWF President (1987-90), contacted Cardinal Ratzinger, asking if they could discuss the situation, and look toward a solution to the stalemate threatening the signing. They met in Regensburg, Germany, where, assisted by theologians Joachim Track[36] and Heinz Schütte, they developed a draft text of elucidations[37] on some of the disputed themes raised by the Catholic response, which might accompany the joint signing of the *JD*.[38] The contents of the text had the potential to lead the process out of a seeming

34. The LWF Executive Committee would meet November 13-14. The PCPCU and CDF would have an important interdicasterial meeting on November 6th.

35. LWF General Secretary Dr. Ishmael Noko and Revd. Sven Oppegaard met at the PCPCU on October 26, 1998, with Cardinal Edward Cassidy and Msgr. John Radano and discussed the content of a possible protocol to accompany the signing of the *JD*, a theme that the meetings in November would take up.

36. According to Professor Track, Bishop Hanselmann, urged at a meeting of retired bishops of the VELKD to use his good relations with Cardinal Ratzinger to ask for a meeting, consulted Track. They both agreed that Hanselmann should do that, and that they should also invite Professor Schütte. Cardinal Ratzinger agreed, and Professor Track informed the LWF President and General Secretary about it (response of Track to the author's question about the origin of the meeting, on the occasion of the LWF-PCPCU joint staff meeting, November 6-7, 2005, Rome).

37. The process used in the meeting, according to Track, was that Bishop Hanselmann, Schütte, and Track first worked on a common draft, based on a proposal of Schütte and rooted in his comments on the "Note" of Rome (published in *KNA*), and on Track's internal paper on the "Note" of Rome written for the LWF. With this prepared common draft, they then came to the discussion with Cardinal Ratzinger. In the meeting with the Cardinal they used that common draft as the basic text for developing the "Regensburg Text" (response of Joachim Track to the author's question about the process in that meeting, on the occasion of the LWF-PCPCU joint staff meeting, November 6-7, 2005, Rome).

38. A story about this private meeting was reported later in *Sonntagsblatt, Evangelische Wochenzeitung für Bayern,* Sonntag, 6 Juni 1999, Nr. 23-25. Track also referred to this meeting in his address at a ceremony in Augsburg, October 30, 1999, the day before the signing of the *JD*, in paying tribute to Bishop Hanselmann, who died early in 1999. See *IS* 103 (2000): 12.

stalemate, but it posed some challenges.[39] Both the LWF and the PCPCU studied this text and even revised it somewhat over the next few days. This draft, along with other materials, was found useful by both the LWF[40] and, in Rome, by the CDF and PCPCU, as the two communions continued in the months ahead to construct a supplementary statement of clarification that would not go beyond the agreements reached in the *JD* itself, would make clear that there was a common understanding of the *JD*, and therefore enable a joint signing to go ahead.[41] Thus, even by mid-November

39. According to LWF official Sven Oppegaard, the LWF was faced with a dual challenge. First, sending a new theological text to LWF member churches for approval could seem to put in doubt the decision already taken by the LWF Council based on the support for the *Joint Declaration* of the vast majority of the member churches. These churches would also ask how their responses to the new text would relate to the responses they had already officially submitted. Second, it was clear that the Regensburg text itself required further work that would need to be carried out carefully with the PCPCU.

To face these challenges, Dr. Ishmael Noko called together a small group of consultants, including Professor Joachim Track in Geneva, on November 10, 1998. It seemed obvious that a new theological text could only be affirmed if it was clear that it did not go beyond the agreements reached and stated in the *JD* itself. The text would need to be worked on in order to avoid any doubt on that point. Concerning the formal difficulty related to an affirmation of a new theological text, Dr. Noko proposed that the formal joint endorsement of the *JD* should be carried out by means of a very short text, to which an explanatory theological text could be attached. The LWF Executive Committee meeting shortly afterwards supported this approach. The PCPCU also approved this procedure, and the work would then be continuing to edit what would become later the "Official Common Statement" by which the *JD* would be signed, and the explanatory "Annex" (Oppegaard's note to the author dated October 10, 2005).

40. The LWF Executive Committee, meeting November 13-14, 1998, emphasized again that a joint signing "can take place only if there is a common understanding of what is being signed." Having discussed the question of whether, "in light of the responses given in June, a brief supplementary statement might be agreed on, substantiating how the joint declaration might be jointly signed without reservations," it requested the General Secretary to consult further, "together with the Roman Catholic Church." It would act on the outcome of this further consultation. "Statement on the Process of the Joint Declaration on Justification," *LWI* (November 23, 1998): 4. Cf. "Further Consultation Proposed on Joint Declaration Between Catholics and Lutheran World Federation," same issue, pp. 3-4.

41. A publication of some of Cardinal Ratzinger's writings entitled *Pilgrim Fellowship of Faith: The Church as Communion,* ed. Stephan Otto Horn and Vinzenz Pfnür (San Francisco: Ignatius Press, 2005), presented by the Cardinal's former students on the occasion of his 75th birthday, includes a 1993 exchange of letters between Bishop Hanselmann and Cardinal Ratzinger concerning the 1992 CDF communication "On Some Aspects of the Church Understood as Communion." The "Introduction" to the volume, putting all its contents in perspective, recalls that the two at one point were bishops of their respective communities in

1998, there were initial drafts of what eventually became the "official common statement" and of an "annex," the two documents which, when completed in Spring 1999, would achieve this purpose.

At one point, despite the Catholic reassurances, and the mutual efforts to find a process that would satisfy both sides as to the common understanding of the *Joint Declaration,* some 243 Protestant theologians in Germany signed a statement expressing their hesitations as to whether consensus was achieved.

The "Official Common Statement" and "Annex," May 1999

It became public in May 1999 that the second step in the official response process, a mutual confirmation of a common understanding of the *Joint Declaration,* could now take place. On May 27, Dr. Ishmael Noko announced that he had received a letter that day from Cardinal Cassidy confirming that the Holy See was ready to sign the *Joint Declaration.* Months of discussion to clarify particular issues of concern to both, had led to two documents which, the Cardinal wrote, were now approved by the Holy See: an "Official Common Statement" with an "Annex," which together expressed the necessary elucidations on those issues, and clarified the basis for a joint signing. Announcing this, Noko stressed a point made very clear in the "Official Common Statement" which, for many, the Catholic response of June 1998 had not made clear: "Now it can be declared without reservation," he said, "that the doctrinal condemnations which were set forth mutually by the Lutheran and Catholic sides at the time of the Reformation, do not apply to the teaching on justification by the two parties expressed in the *Joint Declaration.*" The Cardinal, expressing gratitude to the LWF for the "superb cooperation" over the lengthy process required to reach this conclusion, wrote that he was "authorized . . . to sign the 'Official Common Statement' together with the Joint Declaration . . . at a place and on a date to be jointly agreed on."[42]

Bavaria. Without mentioning this Regensburg meeting, it comments that ". . . it is not least thanks to the good relationship between the Bishop of Munich and the Provincial Bishop of the Evangelical Lutheran Church in Bavaria, Johannes Hanselmann . . . that the *Joint Declaration on the Doctrine of Justification* was adopted ecclesially along with the *Official Common Statement,*" pp. 14-15.

42. "LWF, Roman Catholics Ready to Sign 'Joint Declaration,'" *LWI* (May/June 1999): 9-10.

Joint Announcement on June 11, 1999, of the Place and Date of Signing

At a joint press conference in Geneva on June 11, 1999, Cardinal Cassidy and Dr. Noko spoke more about these two documents and announced together that the Catholic Church and the Lutheran World Federation would sign the *Joint Declaration* on October 31, 1999, in Augsburg, Federal Republic of Germany.[43] Dr. Noko presented the "Official Common Statement" and the "Annex" which were to be used in the signing, and commented on the significance of the date chosen. Since October 31 is annually celebrated as "Reformation Day" in various Protestant churches, its choice for the signing "underlines the understanding of the Reformation itself as a movement not aimed at creating division within the church of Christ, but aimed at reforming the one church in certain areas." Cardinal Cassidy described the *Joint Declaration* itself "as one of the greatest acquisitions of the ecumenical movement."[44]

Cardinal Cassidy stated that these two texts "have been approved by the Pontifical Council for Promoting Christian Unity and by the Congregation for the Doctrine of Faith. His Holiness Pope John Paul II has been informed accordingly and has given his blessing for the signing of the *Joint Declaration on the Doctrine of Justification* together with the *Official Common Statement* with its attached *Annex* on the date and in the place to be decided by the two partners."[45]

Cassidy and Noko made clear that these two documents do not go beyond the *JD*, but rather "further substantiate the consensus reached in the *Joint Declaration*" (Cassidy, *IS*) and reflect "the significance of the 'Joint Declaration' itself . . . affirmed by a resolution of the LWF Council in June 1998" (Noko, *LWI*). The function of the "Official Common Statement," Cassidy stated, is that it explains "clearly and unequivocally just what the two part-

43. "Signing of 'Joint Declaration' Significant for Ecumenical Movement," *LWI* (May/ June 1999): 13.

44. "Signing of 'Joint Declaration' Significant for Ecumenical Movement," pp. 14, 15. The "Official Common Statement" and "Annex" were also published in this same issue of *LWI*, pp. 16-18. Cf. also Introduction, note 1, p. xxii. Further references to this *LWI* story will be made in the text (as Noko, *LWI*).

45. "Statement of Edward Idris Cardinal Cassidy at Press Conference, Geneva, July 11, 1999," *IS* 103 (2000): 3-4. Further references to this statement will be made in the text (as Cassidy, *IS*).

ners understand by their act of signing the *Joint Declaration*," namely, they "declare *together*" (emphasis original) that a consensus has been reached in basic truths of the doctrine of justification as set forth in the *Joint Declaration*, and on the basis of this consensus "they declare together" that the teaching of the Lutheran churches and of the Roman Catholic Church presented in the *JD* does not fall under the condemnations of the Council of Trent, on the one side, and of the Lutheran confessions, on the other. The "Statement" also sets out future work that the partners intend to pursue, e.g., "continued and deepened study of the biblical foundations of the doctrine of justification" and issues mentioned in *JD* (no. 43), as well as continuing their ecumenical efforts to interpret the message of justification in language relevant for human beings today. The function of the "Annex" is that, in reference to the questions raised by the responses, it "takes up those questions that were causing some uncertainty on the part of one or other of two partners and *without altering the Joint Declaration* removes that uncertainty . . . to the satisfaction of both partners" (Cassidy, *IS*, emphasis original).[46]

On July 2, 1999, Dr. Noko wrote to Cardinal Cassidy to inform him that the LWF Council, meeting June 22-29, "gave its full support of the procedure and the agreements reached regarding the joint confirmation of the *Joint Declaration*" and "endorsed the plans made for a signing celebration in Augsburg on 31 October 1999."[47] A joint staff meeting on September 14 clarified the various aspects of the plans for the celebration that would take place over three days, 29-31 October.[48]

46. The "Annex" elucidates questions related to the presentation in the *JD* concerning "*simul iustus et peccator*" and the concept of "concupiscence"; the tension between justification "by grace alone," by faith alone, and "God's will and express command that believers should do good works which the Holy Spirit works in them"; the specific meaning of the doctrine of justification as an "indispensable criterion" within the overall context of the Church's fundamental Trinitarian confession of faith; and states that "notwithstanding different conceptions of authority in the church, each partner respects the other partner's ordered process of reaching doctrinal decisions."

47. Noko's letter reprinted in *IS* 103 (2000): 4.

48. PCPCU participants at the joint staff meeting were Cardinal Cassidy, Bishop Walter Kasper, who had been appointed PCPCU Secretary in March 1999, Msgr. John A. Radano, and Revd. Dr. Matthias Türk who joined the PCPCU staff in early 1999.

Preparations for the signing celebration were organized by Catholics and Lutherans in Augsburg in cooperation with the LWF and the PCPCU. The LWF communications department initiated, among other things, plans for a video of the events. Dr. Türk and Revd. Sven Oppegaard were liaisons for PCPCU and LWF respectively, for overseeing the development of these preparations.

CHAPTER 12

The Signing of the Joint Declaration on the Doctrine of Justification, Augsburg, Germany, October 31, 1999

Authorities of the Catholic Church and the Lutheran World Federation signed the *Joint Declaration on the Doctrine of Justification* on October 31, 1999, in Augsburg, Germany, at the culmination of three days of prayer, ceremonies, and speeches.[1]

Three Days of Celebration, October 29-31

Programs organized by Augsburg's churches during the month of October helped create a festive atmosphere in preparation for that last weekend. These included weekly sessions entitled "Talking About Justification" held over the four weeks of October, each in a different church in the city. There were also special lectures on October 18, 20, and 29 addressing pertinent ecumenical issues. On October 20, for example, Prof. Dr. Günther Wenz, (Lutheran member of the fourth phase of international Lutheran-Catholic dialogue) and Professor Dr. Otto Herman Pesch (Catholic theologian whose pioneering research showing points of contact between Aquinas

---

1. See "Events in Augsburg October 29-31, 1999," *IS* 103 (2000): 6-35 (hereafter "Events" plus page). These pages include two of the main addresses at the press conference (October 29), eight addresses at the City Hall ceremony (October 30), the vespers service including two homilies (October 30), the two ecumenical prayer services, including the two addresses at each related to the signing ceremony (October 31), and the papal statement at the time of the signing (October 31) and several others following it.

and Luther had contributed to convergences that paved the way for the *Joint Declaration*) discussed the "Meaning and Limits of the Joint Declaration on the Doctrine of Justification."

The joyful atmosphere was enhanced during the weekend of October 29-31, as the main celebrations (see below) were accompanied by a variety of other programs that added to the festive atmosphere already permeating the city. Some events featured music, dance, and other expressions of art. Others offered opportunities for explicit Christian witness, such as the meeting on October 30 entitled "Am I Really of Value?" and held at the Evangelical Lutheran Church of St. Ulrich. At this, well-known speakers such as Chiara Lubich, founder of the Focolare Movement, and Professor Andrea Riccardi, founder of the St. Egidio Community, were invited to give witness to the faith. In the evening of the same day, an Ecumenical Youth Prayer service took place in the same church, reflecting the fact that the organizers of these celebrative events tried to involve youth as much as possible.

For the weekend of the signing, the PCPCU and the LWF had each invited many guests, including a number of those who had participated over the years in the dialogues whose reports contributed to the consensus on basic truths of justification now being celebrated in the *Joint Declaration*. Representatives of other Christian communions with which the LWF and the PCPCU were in dialogue were there as well.

The events directly associated with the signing began with a press conference on Friday, October 29th, involving PCPCU President Edward Idris Cardinal Cassidy and Secretary Bishop Walter Kasper, and LWF President Bishop Christian Krause and General Secretary Revd. Dr. Ishmael Noko, as well as leaders of the Catholic and Lutheran churches in Germany.[2] This gave opportunities to put the *JD* in historical and theological perspective. A festive ceremony the next morning, October 30th, in the "Golden Hall" of Augsburg's City Hall, sponsored by the city of Augsburg in collaboration with the LWF and the PCPCU, provided these opportunities as well.

---

2. *Catholics:* Bishop Paul Werner Scheele (Bishop of Würzburg, Chairman of the Ecumenical Commission of the German Bishops' Conference, and a participant in the joint team that drafted the *JD*), Bishop Victor Joseph Dammertz, OSB (Bishop of Augsburg); *Lutherans:* Oberkirchenrat Dr. Ernst Öffner (Evangelical Lutheran Regional Bishop for Augsburg and Schwaben), Friedrich-Otto Scharbau (President of the Lutheran Church Office of the United Evangelical Lutheran Church of Germany). Only the statements of Cardinal Cassidy and Dr. Noko are referred to below.

Praise and thanksgiving were themes of an ecumenical vespers service at the Basilica of Sts. Ulrich and Alfa in the evening of the same day. The historic signing took place on the morning of October 31st in the context of an ecumenical service of the Word in two churches. After the first part, or "Statio," in the Cathedral of the Catholic Diocese of Augsburg, the participants set out in procession through the streets of Augsburg singing hymns of praise and thanksgiving, arriving at St. Anna Lutheran Church, where, in the midst of prayerful celebration, the signing of the *Joint Declaration* took place.

Press Conference, October 29

The Historic Achievement for Lutherans and Catholics

During these days of celebration, a number of addresses spoke of the historical achievement represented in the signing of the *JD*. At the press conference on October 29, Cardinal Cassidy spoke of the "very historic event that we are about to celebrate here . . . when you think that for more than 400, almost 500 years, there has been a barrier between the Lutheran and the Catholic world, which could not be overcome. . . ." Through dialogue in these past thirty-five years, "the barrier has been removed on these fundamental understandings of the truth of justification, which was at the very heart of the Reformation."[3] Dr. Noko said that it was appropriate that the city of Augsburg should witness this event, "having witnessed the failure of efforts in 1530 to reconcile the disputing parties and to prevent a split in the church." Through the *Joint Declaration*, "the Roman Catholic Church and the Lutheran World Federation, as historical opponents on this very central issue, are together witnessing to the gospel message which is God's living gift itself." The *Joint Declaration* represents an important contribution to the establishment of a culture of peace. It "carries a special message of peace for Europe, in view of the tensions regarding European 'integration' both then (under the Holy Roman Empire) and now (through the European Union) . . . [but also] for the whole world." The division resulting from the Reformation "became the focal point for wars and political and economic tensions throughout the subsequent centu-

---

3. "Statement of H. E. Edward Idris Cardinal Cassidy," "Events," p. 6.

ries," divisions and conflicts exported and multiplied throughout the world. "The *Joint Declaration* helps to draw a line under this painful history, as well as under the doctrinal anathemas regarding justification. Wherever Lutherans and Roman Catholics live together, let the world know that they are not opponents, but sisters and brothers in the one church of Jesus Christ and in the world."[4]

And in light of the turning point in history fast approaching, a new millennium and century, Cardinal Cassidy also indicated that the signing was a source of great joy to Pope John Paul II, who understood it as a response to the hope that separated Christians could arrive at the Great Jubilee 2000 "if not fully united at least much closer to the unity to which our Lord Jesus Christ calls us."[5]

Celebration at Augsburg City Hall, October 30

History was a major focus also in the celebration at City Hall the next morning, October 30, hosted by the Lord Mayor of Augsburg, Dr. Peter Menacher. In his words of gratitude to the city, LWF President Bishop Christian Krause said that "[f]or the first time in the history of the Lutheran churches, representatives of this world communion are gathering with those of the Roman Catholic Church in the country of the Reformation before Reformation Day in this historical place of Augsburg, in order to set an important ecumenical sign and to build a bridge in the very place where it once was broken down. Thus — we hope — a new joint Augsburg *Profession* follows the Augsburg *Confession*" (emphasis original).[6]

Lord Mayor Menacher, himself a historian, gave a lengthy reflection on the *JD*'s place in history.[7] Illustrating "the intricate involvement of Christian history and secular history," of which the history of Augsburg is concrete evidence, he put the *Joint Declaration* in broader historical perspective in two different ways. First, in terms of its place within the last millennium. The citizens of Augsburg, he said, will remember this historic event easily "in the following context: 955: The Battle of Lechfeld (with

4. "Statement of Revd. Dr. Ishmael Noko," "Events," p. 7.
5. "Statement of H. E. Edward Idris Cardinal Cassidy," "Events," p. 7.
6. "Expression of Thanks by Bishop Christian Krause," "Events," p. 18.
7. Dr. Peter Menacher, "Augsburg, the City of Ecumenism Welcomes Its Guests," "Events," pp. 8-10.

Bishop Ulrich); 1555: The Peace of Augsburg; 1999: The Joint Declaration of Justification (with many bishops and guests from all over the world). Second, in reference to the centuries from the Reformation until the present, he cited this event as the last of a series of thirteen dates in Augsburg's history. To mention five: 1518: Cardinal Cajetan and Dr. Martin Luther "stand facing each other in the Fugger palace. There is no common declaration." 1530: the chancellor of Saxony publicly reads the Augsburg Confession to Karl V. The "Confessio Augustana" becomes a "household word." 1555: The Peace of Augsburg is decided at the Imperial diet. Its rule of thumb, "Cuius regio, eius religio," leads to an attempted one-sided assumption of power, and does not last long. 1648: The Peace of Westphalia brings about parity; "an interesting model of 'Augsburg parity' is established . . . an attempt to achieve a balance." And more recently, 1987: Pope John Paul II visiting Augsburg states at an ecumenical service in St. Ulrich Basilica that the church schism resulting from the Reformation "did not penetrate the common roots," and then asks, in the Augsburg Cathedral, "Why keep going our separate ways, when we could walk together now?" "A partial answer" to this question, said the mayor, can be found in 1999, "in this city of ecumenism."

The JD's *Wider Ecumenical Meaning*

Besides these historical perspectives, other addresses at City Hall celebrated the event with reflections on the wider meaning of the *JD,* beyond its significance for the two signing communions. Bishop Krause expressed the conviction that the LWF signs the "Official Common Statement" also on behalf of "our sisters and brothers in some other Protestant churches who have backed us in this entire process of the *Joint Declaration*," and also recognizes "our fellowship with the Evangelical Church of Germany (EKD) as well as globally with the World Council of Churches. . . . Together we hope that this step will lead to a more profound and solid fellowship between the Roman Catholic and the Protestant churches."[8] Cardinal Cassidy, picking up a point also raised by Dr. Noko, said that this step is of interest to other Christian communities, but also "a step forward in the search for greater unity here in Europe and for all humankind." That no

8. "Expression of Thanks by Bishop Christian Krause," "Events," pp. 18-19.

important move for unity is without meaning also for others besides those directly involved "seems especially the case when such a step is made here in Europe, which has suffered so much as a result of religious divisions and . . . has taken those divisions into other continents," adding to the difficulties of those nations "to overcome their internal divisions and contribute to the unity of all peoples."[9] WCC General Secretary Dr. Konrad Raiser witnessed that it is good when "those who try today to live in the spirit of the gospel can . . . look over the shoulder of those who will be signing the *Joint Declaration*. . . . They can and should hold us and the participating churches" to the *JD*'s commitments. The issue is not only about annulling sixteenth-century doctrinal condemnations, "but also about the commitment to proclaim the gospel together as the message of the grace of God which liberates because it is unmerited." The public can expect that the consequences of what is signed tomorrow will become evident "in the demeanour of the churches" in their dealings with each other, and "their cooperation in shaping a humane culture."[10]

Some Perspectives on Theology and Dialogue

Some theological perspectives on this achievement were offered at the City Hall celebration by Professor Joachim Track, Chair, LWF Program Committee for Theology and Studies, and Bishop Karl Lehmann of Mainz, President of the German Bishops' Conference.

Bishop Lehmann highlighted the importance of theological dialogue, and the difficulties of reception of dialogue results.[11] The intense forty years of patient theological dialogue that led to the *JD*, show that there is "no alternative to carefully working through the fundamental differences which led to the separation in the 16th century." But the achievement proves "that sound theological research will make itself heard eventually."

He referred to the difficulties of reception, of the patience required to allow consensus-building documents to have an impact on the life of the church. It takes a long time "for the hundreds of years of attitudes and be-

---

9. "Word of Gratitude to the Lord Mayor by Edward Idris Cardinal Cassidy," "Events," p. 18.

10. "Greetings from Konrad Raiser," "Events," pp. 17-18.

11. Bishop Prof. Dr. Karl Lehmann, "Basic Agreement Reached," "Events," pp. 14-17.

haviour to be removed and for a new language, sometimes alien to all concerned, to prove itself." Even the theologians were taken by surprise in a sense by the *Joint Declaration,* "because it is evident that relatively little attention has been paid in many parts to the internal trends and numerous proofs provided by decades of ecumenical work. Official ecumenism had not correctly assessed the tempo, breadth and depth of the necessary reception."

Commenting on the consensus process represented by the *Joint Declaration,* Lehmann suggested that some were perhaps disappointed. They may have expected a "more comprehensive consensus to be reached," or understood consensus as "an unrestricted agreement on all aspects of an issue," or have definitions of consensus characterized by a "logical trend towards uniformity" that requires removing every difference concerning justification. But in both churches, classical theology has always distinguished between what is required and not required for consensus, e.g., Vatican II's teaching on the "hierarchy of truths" in Catholic doctrine, which "vary in their relation to the fundamental Christian faith" (*UR* 11). Thus, despite their differences, "the Christian Churches are able to be one in the fundamentals of their faith." He illustrated this by two further examples from the discussion on the 450th anniversary of the Augsburg Confession. In 1980 John Paul II said "that 'major pillars of the bridge have been saved from the storm of time,' and that we have rediscovered 'how broad and strong are the common foundations of our Christian faith.'" Cardinal Willebrands had said on the same occasion, "that the rift of that time did not go down to the shared roots, and what unites us is much greater and deeper than what separates us."

Lehmann referred also to two characteristics of the *JD.* First, it involves a "differentiated consensus." This is intended to mean that the agreement needed for the community of churches is certainly achieved in the contentious problems, but that the type of agreement needs to be given more concrete form, because a stage of consensus, once achieved, is still not unity. Second, the agreement reached concerned consensus in "basic truths." Agreement on this is still not full consensus, as in the development of the whole doctrine of justification, but there is agreement with regard to the fundamentals and the convictions on which they are based. If there are still differences, this commonality will not be simply rendered null and void. Thus it is consensus in "basic truths, not *the* basic truths." "There could well be, therefore, other basic truths with regard to which no consensus has [yet] been reached." Realizing this reduces the difficulties faced.

The *Joint Declaration* "does not cover all that either church teaches about Justification" (no. 5), but does show "that the remaining differences in its explication are no longer the occasion for doctrinal condemnations" (no. 5). Thus, questions remain within the doctrine of justification, and the "extent of the differences in such a 'differentiated consensus' must certainly be clarified."

Lehmann suggested that it would be inappropriate to move ahead immediately to different topics. Among other things, he had in mind the 243 critical signatures by university lecturers who "jeopardise our claim to have reached a 'consensus in basic truths.'" In light of their hesitation, "the further discussion of the statements themselves must be strongly encouraged." He concluded by saying that eventually the *Joint Declaration* could also give impetus to further ecumenical work on the topics that remain open in the area of the sacraments, the church, and the question of the offices, given that the corresponding condemnations are still largely undealt with.

Professor Dr. Joachim Track[12] put the *Joint Declaration* in the larger context of the new ecumenical consciousness that has arisen in the past century, bringing Christians together. He affirmed that the *JD* is already changing the relationship between the Roman Catholic Church and the Lutheran churches, and that it is a decisive step toward recognition of one another as churches, and "toward realisation of the Christian churches' common responsibility for witness and service to the world."

Track briefly traced the steps during the twentieth century that led to the *JD*. Efforts to bring about agreement on the doctrine of justification began in the first half of our century and took on new intensity around Vatican II; research on Luther and Thomas contributed, as did efforts toward an agreement on the Confessio Augustana as an ecumenical document; two fundamentally important documents for the *Joint Declaration* are *The Condemnations of the Reformation Era — Do They Still Divide?* and *Justification by Faith.*

He paid tribute to many who brought the *Joint Declaration* into existence, singling out first, those who developed the initial draft of a declaration: Harding Meyer, John Reumann, Eugene Brand, Lothar Ullrich, George Tavard, and Heinz-Albert Raem; second, the negotiations between the Pon-

---

12. Prof. Dr. Joachim Track, "The Significance of the *Joint Declaration on the Doctrine of Justification* for Future Relations Between the Roman Catholic Church and the Lutheran Churches," "Events," pp. 11-14.

tifical Council for Promoting Christian Unity led by Cardinal Cassidy and the Lutheran World Federation staff led by General Secretary Noko; and third, "the initiative of . . . the late Bishop Hanselmann, which made possible the conversation at Regensburg with Cardinal Ratzinger and our colleague Schütte." He described the *JD* as a "shaper of the future" because "it was developed in a common dialogue in which each side gained in understanding of its own and of the other's doctrine and shared with the other in speaking about both. In this way, despite all remaining differences in concepts of the Church and areas of unreadiness for mutual recognition as churches, recognition of one another, in church teachings and as churches, did take place." He praised the quality of dialogue that allowed the partners in every difficulty, especially following the "Response of the Catholic Church," to look for a solution together rather than break off the process.

Track emphasized that efforts toward ecumenical understanding have spiritual and ethical dimensions. Therefore in debate concerning consensus on the doctrine of justification there is more at stake, namely our fundamental way of dealing with others and with ourselves — our understanding of salvation and how it is communicated. Since Christians are defined by the truth of justification, and even the trust in this truth is not at our disposal, we have the freedom to see the historical character of the concrete statements about this truth, and to handle them in faithfulness to their acknowledged truth and in openness to new understanding. Understanding and agreement on these matters take place "in the prayer for the Holy Spirit to be present in us and in the community of believers."

The achievement of the *Joint Declaration* on this issue which no other doctrine may contradict, and which points the entire teaching and practice of the Church toward Christ, gives hope as we seek to resolve remaining issues such as achieving a common agreement on the Church and its ministry.

Ecumenical Vespers, Basilica of Sts. Ulrich and Alfa, October 30[13]

The signing of the *Joint Declaration* took place in an atmosphere of formal ecumenical prayer services within which some of the essential theological meaning of the *Joint Declaration* was called to mind. These began with an

---

13. The service and the homilies given during the service are found in "Events," pp. 19-24.

ecumenical vespers on Saturday evening, October 30, at the Catholic Basilica of Sts. Ulrich and Alfa, and continued on Sunday morning with services in the Cathedral of the Catholic Diocese of Augsburg and in the Lutheran Church of St. Anna.

A primary theme of the vespers service on October 30 was the celebration of Jesus Christ as the light of the world, a theme reflecting well the Christological foundation of the *JD* (cf. nos. 5, 15). The opening hymn was a third-century Greek hymn, "A Song of the Light," whose opening words are: "Jesus Christ is the light of the world." Next, a prayer of thanksgiving included the petition: "Enlighten our darkness by the light of your Christ; May his Word be a lamp to our feet and a light to our path." The Word was presented in two Scripture readings, first, Ezekiel 11:17-20, followed by a responsory including the prayer "Your Word is light and truth, it enlightens all my ways." The second reading, from Colossians 1:13-20, was followed by a responsory: "Lord, your Word is a lamp to my feet and a light to my path." Homilies were given by PCPCU Secretary Bishop Walter Kasper (on Ezekiel) and by LWF General Secretary Revd. Dr. Ishmael Noko (on Colossians). Both homilies celebrated, with different emphases, the saving grace of God for salvation which the *JD* enables Lutherans and Catholics to confess together before the world.

Reflecting on Ezekiel's words, "I gather you," "I assemble you," Kasper preached that a fundamental characteristic of the Old and New Testaments is that God assembles his people. Jesus prayed that "all may be one." Thus the lack of unity among Christians is "in contradiction to the gospel," it is "truly sin," and a scandal to the world.

Bishop Kasper raised the question that if we ask, "How can we create unity?" the prophet's words might suggest that we cannot "make" the unity of the Church. "God alone is able to save us; He is the only one who gathers us through His Holy Spirit. This is His gift, His saving grace. There applies the principle: 'sola gratia' [cf. *JD* 15] for the individual person and for the Church." Scripture describes this gift of what God's grace achieves with many words and images: life, reconciliation, salvation, liberation, and not least, the justification of the sinner. "That means: God gives us a new heart. He is the one who makes us justified. He transforms us and makes us a new creation." And "this is the good news to which we now — fortunately — can bear common witness before the world. We can now testify in common: a new beginning is possible, and that means hope. . . . We can live in hope, because we are permitted to live in grace."

At the same time, this gospel of grace "does not discharge us from our responsibility. Whoever plays off the formula 'sola gratia — grace alone' against acting has misunderstood it. The prophet speaks of the new heart, 'so that they may walk in my commandments, and keep my judgments and fulfil them.' These judgments are summarized in the commandment of love. As new human beings we may and can live from grace.

"The gospel of the gracious God and of the gracious human being is not a message . . . only for the 16th century. It is a message that today's world needs. With this good news we go together into the new century and the new millennium."

Dr. Noko's homily, a reflection on Colossians 1:13-20, highlighted justification as forgiveness of sins [cf. *JD* 22] and the implications this has for the justified forgiving one another. Paul writes to the church in Colosse reminding them that prior to baptism they had been enslaved to sin, and lived in the dark shadows of doubt, pain, despair, and hatred. But being transferred from the kingdom of darkness to the kingdom of Christ means that we are transferred from condemnation to forgiveness. Through Christ "we are redeemed from the power of sin, we are declared just in the eyes of God." God's message of forgiveness and renewal "takes place when the gospel of forgiveness of sins, and the faith which embraces this forgiveness, moves and encourages us to acknowledge and mutually forgive where we have failed one another." The "highest point of my discipleship is reached," he said, not just in giving to the poor and homeless, or having knowledge of the gospel "in order to teach in tongues of men and angels," but rather "when I, through God's grace, identify with the deepest needs of my fellow human beings, namely by the forgiveness of sins and release from guilt."

Applying this more directly to the *Joint Declaration,* if we are co-sharers in the forgiveness of God, "it is only natural that we endeavor in the spirit of reconciliation to overcome the doctrinal anathemas that separate us from the gift of unity." Seen from the perspective of God's gracious forgiveness, "the affirmation of the *Joint Declaration on the Doctrine of Justification* by signatures is an attempt to appropriate God's forgiveness into the life of the churches. If God has indeed forgiven us in Christ then the next natural step can only be that we find responsible ways of overcoming remaining anathemas."

Signing Ceremony, the Cathedral and St. Anna's Church, Sunday Morning, October 31, 1999

The signing ceremony took place on Sunday morning, October 31st, in the context of an ecumenical worship service in two different churches, with a procession in pilgrimage from one church to the other.

The "Statio" in the Cathedral[14]

The starting point, or "Statio," began at 9:30 in the Cathedral of the Catholic Diocese of Augsburg. This service emphasized repentance and thanksgiving, a spiritual preparation for the great event of reconciliation that the signing of the *JD* would encompass.

At the beginning, Bishop Dr. Viktor Joseph Dammertz, Bishop of Augsburg and Oberkirchenrat Dr. Ernst Öffner, Regional Dean of the Evangelical Church of Augsburg and Schwaben, welcomed the faithful and their guests. Their greetings helped put in perspective the events that unfolded. Bishop Dammertz explained the appropriateness of beginning the ceremony at the Cathedral, since a number of significant events reflecting the conflicts of the sixteenth century took place near it: "Only a few meters away, a plaque reminds us of an incident . . . in October 1518, when Martin Luther put up on the Cathedral's portal a bill protesting against the opening of the trial of heretics in Rome. And on the western side of the Cathedral we can read an inscription on a plaque: 'Here was situated the Bishop's palace . . . in whose chapter hall, on June 25th, 1530, the *Confessio Augustana* was proclaimed.' Finally, the Cathedral's pulpit reminds us of the Jesuit Petrus Canisius, the most important exponent of Catholic reform and renewal of the church in Germany. Here . . . [he] worked from 1559 to 1566 as a cathedral preacher who was firmly resolved to defend the Catholic doctrine against the teachings of Luther and his preachers."

His explanation helped clarify why this service began with a "Liturgy of Repentance." This included four prayers praising God for what he has done for us in the redeeming work of Jesus Christ, each ending in a statement of confession, followed by the singing of the Kyrie Eleison. Thus:

---

14. The essential aspects of the ceremony and addresses given at the Cathedral are found in "Events," pp. 25-27.

"We confess now together how difficult it is for us to learn from Jesus and how unwillingly we follow him," "We confess that in our lives we have not always chosen the way of unity," "We confess that in our lives we have not always chosen the way of the Cross," "We confess that in our lives we have not always chosen the way of love." This liturgy of repentance closed with words of forgiveness, a prayer of thanksgiving, and the singing of a Gloria.

Oberkirchenrat Öffner's greeting helped orient the participants to the next stage of the celebration: "The worship service begins here in the Cathedral. It continues by the common road through the city and then finally reaches the signing ceremony in St. Anna." In the long road behind us the Augsburg Confession in 1530 attempted in vain to bridge the gap and from then on the dividing lines became more important than the agreements in faith that were still present. This worship service makes it clear that the road continues. We want to walk "from the Catholic Cathedral to the Evangelical Church of St. Anna . . . in the street, publicly. Because we are convinced that the Gospel of Jesus Christ, the message of the justification of the sinner, is relevant and seeks to become public. We believe this together."

At the conclusion of the "Statio" the procession, including the church leaders, the Mayor, the faithful, left the cathedral and went through the streets of Augsburg to St. Anna's Church.

St. Anna's Church[15]

The service continued in St. Anna's Church and began with a hymn of praise, and a petition to Jesus Christ, the "sure foundation on which your Church has been built," to bring about the unity of his church. Scripture readings were from 1 Corinthians 3:10-11 after which Cardinal Cassidy preached, and the Gospel of John 3:16-18 after which Bishop Krause preached.

A "Remembrance of Holy Baptism" came next. After proclaiming that "[w]e are baptized in the name of the Father, and of the Son, and of the Holy Spirit," the congregation confessed the common Christian faith in the words of the Apostles' Creed, which, as the service booklet explained, "in the Western church tradition has been confessed at baptism since the

---

15. The ceremony in which the signing took place, and the addresses, are found in "Events," pp. 27-33.

time of the ancient church." A hymn completed this portion of the service and led to the signing ceremony.

The "Signing" began with the reading of three full core paragraphs of the *Joint Declaration*, paragraphs "expressing basic truths of our common faith": *JD* 15, 25, and 44. After a hymn, the "Official Common Statement" was read in its entirety and signed. In the "Signing Ceremony" the singing of the Veni Creator asked the grace of the Holy Spirit on what was taking place.

Signatories on behalf of the Catholic Church were Edward Idris Cardinal Cassidy and Bishop Walter Kasper, President and Secretary respectively of the Pontifical Council for Promoting Christian Unity. The signatories on behalf of the Lutheran World Federation were the President, Bishop Christian Krause, the General Secretary, Reverend Dr. Ishmael Noko, and six Vice-Presidents: Dr. Sigrun Møgedal (Treasurer), Ms. Parmata Ishaya (Africa), Reverend Dr. Prasanna Kumari (Asia), Bishop Julius Filo (Europe), President Huberto Kirchheim (Latin America), and Bishop H. George Anderson (North America). During the signing the congregation burst into spontaneous applause.

The peace was given and the Te Deum was sung; there were prayers of intercession, each followed by the Kyrie Eleison, and the Lord's prayer. The dismissal included the hymn "Wie Schön Leuchtet" sung in German and English, and after a prayer praising and thanking God, the final hymn: "Nun Danket Alle Gott." Church bells rang, joyously alerting all that a great event had just taken place.

The Pope's Statement in Rome at the Moment of the Signing, October 31

Virtually at the same time as the signing of the *Joint Declaration* on October 31, Pope John Paul II, before reciting the Angelus prayer at 12:00 noon to a large crowd gathered at St. Peter's Square in Rome, made a statement.[16] He announced the signing, saying that "[i]n Augsburg, Germany, a very important event is taking place at this moment," which he described as a "milestone on the difficult path to re-establishing full unity among

---

16. "The Pope's Statement, October 31, 1999," "Events," p. 34. Italian original: *Insegnamenti*, XXII, 2 (1999): 679-80.

Christians." He referred to its historical meaning, saying that it is "highly significant that it is taking place in the exact city where in 1530 a decisive page in the Lutheran reform was written with the *Augsburg Confession*." The Pope assessed it as "a valuable contribution to the *purification of historical memory* and to our *common witness*" (emphasis original). He also saw it as a sound basis for continuing ecumenical theological research "and for addressing the remaining problems with a better founded hope of resolving them in the future."

The Pope expressed his gratitude to the Lord "for this intermediate goal on our journey," describing this event as "a significant response to the will of Christ, who before his passion prayed to the Father that his disciples would be *one* (cf. Jn 17:11)." He described it, too, in light of the coming Jubilee year, as an "encouraging sign" toward his hopes that Christians can celebrate the Great Jubilee, "if not completely united, at least much closer to overcoming the divisions of the second millennium" (*Tertio millennio adveniente*, no. 34). He thanked all those "who prayed and worked to make this Joint Declaration possible."

The Pope spoke of the *Joint Declaration* at least three more times in the remaining two months of 1999. On November 13 he presided at an ecumenical celebration at St. Peter's Basilica on the occasion of the naming of St. Bridget of Sweden as a Co-Patroness of Europe. Participating with him were the Lutheran archbishops of Uppsala, Sweden, and of Turku, Finland, and the Catholic bishops of Stockholm, Sweden, and of Copenhagen, Denmark. The Royal family of Sweden was present. In his homily, the Pope recalled what he had said concerning a common understanding of justification at a similar service on October 5, 1991, an ecumenical service on the occasion of the 600th anniversary of the canonization of St. Bridget, again, with Lutheran leaders and the Swedish Royal family participating. The common understanding that he had hoped for eight years before, "today, thank God, has become an encouraging reality." He mentioned the solemn signing of the *Joint Declaration* on October 31 as "a milestone on the way to full and visible unity." While "we still have a long way to go . . . we must continue to walk together, supported by Christ. . . ." The *JD* says that the consensus in basic truths of the doctrine of justification "must come to influence the life and teachings of our Churches" (no. 43). And on this path, "we trust in the ceaseless action of the Holy Spirit."[17]

17. "Ecumenical Service in St. Peter's Basilica on the Occasion of St. Bridget of Sweden

On December 9, 1999, the Pope received an LWF delegation led by President Bishop Christian Krause. The signing of the *JD* involved "a subject that for centuries was a sort of symbol of the division between Catholics and Protestants," he said, referring again to the signing as a milestone, and an encouragement to continue theological research and to remove obstacles that still stand in the way of unity. He added a pastoral note that "we must join forces in working together so that the content of the doctrine is translated into the language and life of our contemporaries."[18]

And in his address to Cardinals, Papal Household, and Roman Curia, on December 21, he said that the document on justification, recently signed in Augsburg, "is a great step forward and an encouragement to pursue our dialogue with determination so that Christ's invocation 'Father . . . that they may be one' (Jn 17:11, 21) may be fulfilled."[19]

Being Named a Co-Patroness of Europe," "Events," pp. 34-35. Italian original: *Insegnamenti,* XXII, 2 (1999): 889-90.

18. "To Lutheran World Federation Delegation, December 9, 1999," "Events," p. 35. German original: *Insegnamenti,* XXII, 2 (1999): 1130-31.

19. "To Cardinals, Papal Household and Roman Curia, December 21, 1999," "Events," p. 35. Italian original: *Insegnamenti,* XXII, 2 (1999): 1232-33.

Press conference, October 29, 1999, at Augustanahaus, Augsburg. From left, Rev. Sven Oppegaard of the Lutheran World Federation; Mr. R. Hammerschmidt, Press Secretary, German Bishops' Conference; Bishop Walter Kasper, Secretary, Pontifical Council for Promoting Christian Unity; Cardinal Edward Cassidy, President, PCPCU; Dr. Bishop Christian Krause, President, LWF; Rev. Dr. Ishmael Noko, General Secretary, LWF; and Marc Chambron, Press Secretary, LWF. (Photo JAR)

Press conference. From left, Bishop Walter Kasper, Cardinal Edward Cassidy, Dr. Bishop Christian Krause, and Rev. Dr. Ishmael Noko. (Photo JAR)

Gathered at St. Ulrich Haus before going to ceremonies at Augsburg City Hall, October 30, 1999, are (from left) Msgr. John Radano; Bishop Paul-Werner Scheele, Bishop of Wurzburg; Bishop Walter Kasper; Cardinal Edward Cassidy, President, PCPCU; and Bishop Pierre Duprey, former Secretary, PCPCU. Bishop Paul-Werner Scheele was co-chair of the third phase of the Lutheran-Catholic international dialogue and also participated in the drafting of the *Joint Declaration.* (Photo JAR)

Bishop Krause addressing the civic officials and ecumenical guests at Augsburg City Hall, October 30, 1999. Cardinal Cassidy addressed the assembly as well. (Photo JAR)

Dr. Harding Meyer and Bishop Pierre Duprey at the social event following the ceremony at Augsburg City Hall. Dr. Meyer helped to draft the *Joint Declaration*. Bishop Duprey, while secretary of the PCPCU, strongly supported the development of the declaration. (Photo JAR)

At the Catholic Cathedral in Augsburg, October 31, 1999, from left, Oberkirchenrat Dr. Ernst Öffner, Regional Dean of Augsburg and Schwaben; Dr. Christian Krause; Dr. Ishmael Noko; Bishop Walter Kasper; Cardinal Edward Cassidy; and Bishop Dr. Viktor Josef Dammertz, Bishop of Augsburg. (Photo JAR)

Procession from the Cathedral in Augsburg to St. Anna Lutheran Church, where the signing of the *Joint Declaration* would take place, October 31, 1999. (Photo courtesy of Photo Archive, Lutheran World Federation)

Bishop Krause (left) and Cardinal Cassidy together sign the *Joint Declaration* at St. Anna Lutheran Church as Dr. Noko and Bishop Kasper (far right) await their turns to sign. (Photo by Annette Zoepf, Augsburg)

Dr. Noko and Bishop Kasper sign. (Photo KNA)

CHAPTER 13

Summary and Reflections

The primary achievement reflected in these pages is that in roughly four decades the Catholic Church and the Lutheran World Federation gradually moved away from centuries of mutual isolation, began to develop a new relationship characterized by friendship and the realization that they share significant aspects of the apostolic faith, and reached the point of being able to make a profound mutual commitment. Though they have not reached full visible unity, they have affirmed together, in a binding way, their agreement on basic truths of the doctrine of justification — the doctrine at the heart of the conflict between Martin Luther and the church authorities in the sixteenth century, which led to divisions that still linger. This step removes a significant obstacle in the journey towards visible unity.

The LWF and the Catholic Church each contributed in significant ways to the creation of new relations between them. The Second Vatican Council was the watershed event within which their partnership began and then developed during more than three decades, leading eventually to the *Joint Declaration* in 1999.

The Second Vatican Council:
Context for the Emergence of Lutheran-Catholic Fellowship

Catholic participation in that process leading to the *Joint Declaration* came, in a primary sense, in response to the mandate given by the Second Vatican

Council, which exhorted all the faithful "to participate skillfully in the work of ecumenism" (*UR* 4). The steps taken in that process over several decades reflect the various ecumenical activities described by the Council, though shared in common with other Christians, which foster unity among Christians. These include, for example, dialogue between competent experts from different churches and communities, dialogue that aims at a truer knowledge and just appreciation of the teaching of both communities, cooperation in projects for the common good, and common prayer. The goal of all these activities, in the perspective of the Council, is that all Christians will be gathered into that unity of the one and only church which Christ bestowed on his church from the beginning. This will be achieved "little by little, as the obstacles to perfect ecclesiastical communion are overcome" (*UR* 4). The *Joint Declaration* represents the overcoming of a major obstacle to that unity for which the Council asked Catholics to work.

An ecumenical dynamic was at work in the Second Vatican Council from its beginning. Pope John XXIII's creation of the Secretariat for Promoting Christian Unity in 1960, and his authorization in 1961 to invite other churches and ecclesial communities to delegate observers to the Council, ensured that this would be so. The observers, including the Lutheran observers, had an influence on the shape of the Decree on Ecumenism. The Lutheran observers, like others, were engaged in the Council through contacts of different degrees of intensity and opportunity — with the SPCU, the Council fathers and other theologians, and the Popes. The Lutheran observers were *effective* in several ways. Even while the Council was still in session, some of the observers successfully encouraged the LWF to seek formal dialogue with the Catholic Church. Several of them took part in the new Lutheran-Catholic joint working group, which met in 1965 for the first time and led to the formal dialogue.

Some observers were effective in fostering Lutheran-Catholic relationships after the Council. Some took part in the formal dialogue between the LWF and the Catholic Church that began in 1967, helping to produce several of the reports instrumental in leading to the *Joint Declaration,* and/or in shaping the formulations within the *Joint Declaration.* In this sense, they were part of a process leading directly from the Second Vatican Council to the *Joint Declaration,* even if they did not participate personally in drafting the *JD* in the 1990s. Thus, George Lindbeck and Vilmos Vajta took part in the first phase of international dialogue, as member and consultant respectively, which produced the Malta Report. Lindbeck was co-chairman of the second phase, which produced *All Under One Christ,* and several other reports that received and applied the Malta Report's claim of a "far-reaching consensus" on justification. Vajta was a secretary or staff person or consultant for most of the second-phase documents. Lindbeck had an important role also in the American Lutheran-Catholic dialogue when it produced *Justification by Faith* (1985).

The Emerging Lutheran-Catholic Fellowship: Context for the *Joint Declaration*

In his analysis of the Decree on Ecumenism in 1965, Lutheran observer Edmund Schlink said that the statements of faith formulated in the sixteenth century, and their corresponding anathemas, are "the greatest stumbling-block against reunion." He also observed that the Vatican Council fathers expressly reiterated their acceptance of Trent's dogmatic decisions "together with all its anathemas against the doctrines of the non-Roman communions." He saw that *they* were not going to address these issues. But standing within the Council, at a transition point between the old attitudes and the new, he also commented that "we see today in both Protestant and Roman Catholic theology our task in a reinterpretation of these old dogmatic statements and in explaining them in their historical setting" (*Dialogue on the Way,* p. 203; cf. Chapter 2).

From its beginning, the theological dialogue between Lutherans and Catholics on justification and the related anathemas, as well as other topics over the decades, took place in the larger context of efforts made to move from centuries of mutual isolation and into a new Lutheran and Catholic fellowship. While the Council fathers themselves did not deal with the questions Schlink was concerned with, they did make the decisions that would enable the Catholic Church to move toward new fellowship with the Lutheran family, and to engage in the dialogue that would resolve old disagreements that had resulted in anathemas.

The Lutheran-Catholic joint working group, which first met in 1965, recommended not only dialogue, but also mutual contacts on a variety of levels, in order to shape this new relationship. In the early post-conciliar period, exchanges of correspondence (1967), mutual invitations for observers at meetings (1967), and exchanges of visits by leaders of the LWF and PCPCU (the first in 1969), began at virtually the same time as the international dialogue (1967). The narrative above gives details of a variety of other contacts that took place over the decades that followed. As part of the broader effort to create a new relationship, the dialogue produced the theological and historical rationale for proceeding towards a common agreement on justification. A further development in this relationship, the decision in 1988 to have joint LWF-PCPCU staff meetings, provided a common instrument to monitor and to some degree guide the joint declaration project that began in 1993. A close working relationship between them helped weather some ecumenical storms in the years 1994-99 when the historic event requiring mutual commitment was taking shape.

Authorities of the Holy See and the *Joint Declaration*

The highest authorities of the Holy See were involved over the decades in contacts with the Lutheran family, helping to bring about a new relationship between Lutherans and Catholics. The highest authorities of the Holy See were involved in the major steps leading to the mutual acceptance of the *Joint Declaration on the Doctrine of Justification*. On the Catholic side, the initiatives and decisions of the several Popes were crucial in this regard. So too were the contributions of the heads of some offices of the Roman Curia.

Luther had opposed the papacy because he considered it one of the "main obstacles to achieving the practical effects of the doctrine of justification: protecting the honor of Christ as the sole mediator and providing consolation for burdened consciences."[1] But three Popes involved with the Second Vatican Council each contributed in significant and forceful ways to the steps taken by the Holy See to establish and deepen new relations, including dialogue, with the Lutheran World Federation. These new relationships provided the context that encouraged dialogue to resolve differences on justification, which led in 1999 to the signing of the *Joint Declaration on the Doctrine of Justification*. One of these Popes accompanied the *Joint Declaration* process in the 1990s with continuing encouragement at every step of the way.

Pope John XXIII opened that ecumenical journey for Catholics by taking concrete steps to ensure that pastoral concern for Christian unity was on the agenda of the Second Vatican Council, initially by creating the Sec-

---

1. Scott H. Hendrix, *Luther and the Papacy: Stages in Reformation Conflict* (Philadelphia: Fortress Press, 1981), p. 149.

retariat for Promoting Christian Unity in 1960 to serve the Council, and authorizing invitations to Lutheran (and other) observers to attend it. The presence and participation of the Lutheran observers at the Council also constituted the first steps toward overcoming centuries of mutual isolation between Lutherans and Catholics.

Pope Paul VI broadened that journey for Catholics, by introducing a deeper spiritual basis for the relationships with other Christians. His public call for mutual forgiveness during the Council in 1963 had a significant impact, first of all on the observers. But the LWF Fifth Assembly (Evian, 1970) also remembered "with gratitude" Paul VI's plea for forgiveness. And acknowledging that the judgment of the Reformers upon the Catholic Church and its theology "was not entirely free of polemical distortions, which in part have been perpetuated to the present day," that Assembly in turn expressed its own sorrow for the offense and misunderstanding these polemic elements have caused their Roman Catholic friends.[2] Paul VI showed, even during the Council, deep respect for the Christian heritage of communities separated from the Catholic Church, by encouraging Lutheran-Catholic dialogue, encouraging mutual contacts, and also meeting with official delegations of the LWF.

John Paul II, who had participated in Vatican II, continued to support these activities, but broadened even more, and deepened, Catholic participation in the ecumenical journey taken by Lutherans and Catholics toward reconciliation. He also met Lutheran leaders at national and local, as well as international levels. He showed respect for the Lutheran heritage, using significant anniversaries of the Augsburg Confession and of Luther to underscore the degree of common faith and common Christian heritage shared now by Lutherans and Catholics, even though they still had differences in faith to resolve. Most significantly, John Paul accompanied Catholic participation in the evolution of the *Joint Declaration on the Doctrine of Justification*. He called for response to Lutheran-Catholic dialogue reports, he expressed support for the process leading to the *JD* at different stages of its development, and he acknowledged the historic development that had taken place when the official Catholic response to the *JD*, the publication of which he approved, was published. He approved the steps in clarifying the common meaning of the Lutheran and Catholic official responses to

2. Evian's statement is cited in *Facing Unity* (no. 52) to illustrate a profound change of attitude on the part of Lutheran churches vis-à-vis the Catholic Church.

the declaration. He authorized Cardinal Cassidy and Bishop Kasper to sign the *JD* on behalf of the Catholic Church in Augsburg in 1999, and within minutes of the joint signing there, announced in Rome that this joint signing was taking place, speaking of it as a milestone in Lutheran-Catholic relations. He continued to praise this event in the following years.

If Luther, in the sixteenth century, charged the papacy with being an obstacle to the reception of the effects of justification, three Popes in the twentieth century helped pave the way to Lutheran-Catholic reconciliation on the doctrine of justification. In the *Joint Declaration on the Doctrine of Justification,* Lutherans and Catholics confess together that "[b]y grace alone, in faith in Christ's saving work and not because of any merit on our part, we are accepted by God and receive the Holy Spirit . . ." (no. 15). They confess together that "the faithful can rely on the mercy and promises of God. In spite of their own weakness . . . on the strength of Christ's death and resurrection they can build on the effective promise of God's grace in Word and Sacrament and so be sure of this grace" (no. 34).

Leaders of some offices of the Roman Curia also contributed in significant ways to steps leading to the *Joint Declaration.* Without claiming an exhaustive account, we can illustrate by pointing to some. First of all, to Cardinal Presidents of the Secretariat (Pontifical Council) for Promoting Christian Unity. Cardinal Bea (President 1960-68), besides leading the SPCU in helping to bring the observers into the life of the Council, also presided as a joint working group was created and met in 1965, the first structure mutually created by the LWF and the Catholic Church for planning and implementing steps toward a new relationship between these two families. Bea presided as the official international dialogue began in 1967.

Cardinal Willebrands (President 1969-89), one of the Catholic pioneers in ecumenism, made a formidable and positive impact on the growing Lutheran-Catholic relationship. In his address to the LWF Assembly at Evian, 1970, Willebrands encouraged dialogue on justification, stating that issues such as justification, controversial in the past, were now barely felt as controversial, and that extensive misunderstandings on both sides had previously made factual discussion impossible. His cautious but positive interpretation of Luther in this same groundbreaking address, suggesting that the Second Vatican Council had implemented requests which were first expressed by Martin Luther, among others, was cited in the 1983 dialogue text, *Martin Luther — Witness to Jesus Christ* (no. 23), as expressing the new attitude toward Luther in the Catholic Church. Another statement in the same address, that "Luther's concept of faith, if we take it in its fullest sense, surely means nothing other than what we in the Catholic Church term love," was referred to in the 1986 German study *The Condemnations of the Reformation Era — Do They Still Divide?* (p. 52) when illustrating convergence on a critical point regarding justification, namely that Protestant doctrine understands substantially under the one word "faith" what Catholic doctrine (following 1 Cor. 13:13) sums up in the triad of "faith, hope, and love." Willebrands continued on different occasions in the 1980s to convey the new Catholic attitudes about Luther. In a variety of ways during his twenty-year period as PCPCU President, Willebrands fostered the mutual trust between Lutherans and Catholics and gave the encouragement they needed to eventually take steps toward mutual commitment, as they did with the *Joint Declaration.*

During his term as PCPCU President (1989-2001), Edward Idris Cardinal Cassidy built on the new relations between Lutherans and Catholics that had developed since Vatican II, and continued to contribute to deepening the fellowship with the LWF during the 1990s. He participated from the beginning of his presidency, for example, in the annual joint staff meetings that had begun in 1988. In the 1990s, when the development of the *JD* began to take shape, he, along with the PCPCU staff, worked in close cooperation with the LWF to foster this development. This historic effort was difficult at times, since, as the *JD* was evolving, both sides felt pressures from their own constituencies, even if in different ways, and therefore from each other. But through cooperation that was enabled by a deep partnership, the *Joint Declaration* was signed. Cardinal Cassidy gave strong leadership from the Catholic side during this time, including the period in 1998-99, when, because of reactions to the Catholic response, a solution had to be found to ensure that a joint signing would take place.

The Catholic response to the *JD* was the result of collaboration between the PCPCU and the Congregation for the Doctrine of the Faith. When reactions to the Catholic response threatened in 1998 to prevent the signing of the *JD*, CDF Prefect Cardinal Joseph Ratzinger (the future Pope Benedict XVI) made statements interpreting the Catholic response to indicate that it affirmed a basic consensus on justification. He also joined Lutheran Bishop (and former LWF President) Hanselmann in an informal, but important, consultation in Regensburg, Germany, which proposed a draft project of elucidations for study by both sides, a significant contribution toward resolving difficulties that threatened the signing.

Bishop Pierre Duprey, SPCU/PCPCU staff person 1963-99, and Secretary 1983 to March 1999, participated in that part of the second phase of the Lutheran-Catholic international dialogue which developed the reports *Ministry in the Church* (1981), *Martin Luther — Witness to Jesus Christ* (1983), and *Facing Unity* (1985), and in the LWF-PCPCU joint staff meetings 1988-98. He, along with Dr. Harding Meyer, as speakers at an ELCA bishops' meeting in 1993, encouraged a possible ELCA initiative of declaring unilaterally, in light of the various studies already completed, that the sixteenth-century condemnations on justification no longer apply to the partner today. The LWF took up this initiative as its own project, and then in partnership with the PCPCU, began a mutual process leading eventually to the *Joint Declaration*.

Dialogue and Reception

Dialogue: From the Malta Report (1972) to the Joint Declaration (1999)

One reason for the successful achievement of the *Joint Declaration* was the intense and consistent way in which formal Lutheran-Catholic dialogue, building on previous work done by scholars, focused on the issue of justification. This intense focus involved several aspects.

First, there was consistency within the international dialogue itself as it dealt with justification. The claim made in the report of the first phase of international Lutheran-Catholic dialogue (the Malta Report), that a "far-reaching consensus" was developing on justification, was initially received by the second phase of dialogue. Four of its six reports made some application of the far-reaching consensus to particular questions, e.g., to illustrating the importance of justification to the growing common mind on basic doctrinal truths that point to Jesus Christ *(All Under One Christ)*, to the common view of the message, the saving act of God in Christ, to be proclaimed by ministers *(Ministry in the Church)*, to the growing common appreciation of Luther's basic concerns *(Martin Luther — Witness to Jesus Christ)*, and to the basic agreement in faith required to achieve church fellowship *(Facing Unity)*. The report of the third phase, *Church and Justification*, illustrated that consensus on justification is compatible with a broad variety of ecclesiological themes. Furthermore, *All Under One Christ* and *Martin Luther — Witness to Jesus Christ*, statements occasioned by im-

portant anniversaries, also brought the search for consensus on justification into the realm of seeking common perspectives on important aspects
of the Lutheran heritage. This, in turn, contributed to fostering a healing
of memory between Lutherans and Catholics, basic in working together to
achieve visible unity. Pope John Paul II's constructive statements on the
Augsburg Confession and on Luther during this period were also helpful
in creating a positive atmosphere for seeking mutual commitment to a
common understanding on justification.

Second, there was serious interaction and mutual exchange between
the international and some national Lutheran-Catholic dialogues in such a
way that their dialogue projects on justification, each of independent origin, eventually and clearly fed into one common process. The international and the national dialogues influenced one another. Thus, the international Malta Report in 1972 claimed that a "far-reaching consensus" is
developing on the doctrine of justification. The USA Lutheran-Catholic
dialogue, accepting this challenge, began in 1978 to test this claim, looking
for greater clarity than had been achieved in official discussions up till
then. Specifically it sought to indicate how the historic disagreements in
the interpretation of the doctrine of justification have developed, and to
what extent they could now be overcome. Its findings were published in
1985 *(Justification by Faith)*. An ecumenical working group in Germany,
beginning in 1981, explored the mutual condemnations of the sixteenth
century including those on justification. Showing coherence between these
national dialogues, the German report, *The Condemnations of the Reformation Era — Do They Still Divide?* (original German publication in 1986),
affirms the need to adhere to the Christological foundation expressed in
Justification by Faith (citing, on p. 36, paragraph 156 of the latter's common
statement) if the barricades on justification were to be torn down. The report claimed that the old condemnations on justification do not apply to
the partner today. Then, the third phase of international Lutheran-
Catholic dialogue, beginning in 1986, also felt itself compelled, in light of
the work done up to that time, to test the claim of a "far-reaching consensus" on justification. It built a "platform statement" on justification, rely-
ing heavily on the comprehensive American statement *Justification by
Faith* and on the justification chapter of *The Condemnations of the Reformation Era — Do They Still Divide?* Seeing that a consensus on justification could be claimed, it made its particular contribution by testing that
consensus against a broad range of ecclesiological themes, showing in its

1994 report, *Church and Justification: Understanding the Church in the Light of the Doctrine of Justification,* that they are not in contradiction. At the completion of the latter, the drafting of the *Joint Declaration* began, with the drafters now having the resources they needed for formulating the declaration.

Third, there was some continuity of theological expertise in the process leading from the Malta Report to the *Joint Declaration.* Just as some Vatican II observers helped produce several of the reports used as resources for the *JD*, other theologians, instrumental in fashioning the Malta Report, continued in the theological process that led directly to the *JD*.[3] Other scholars on both sides, if they had not contributed to the Malta Report, contributed to other key studies that helped to fashion the *JD*, and either signed[4] or helped to draft it.[5]

---

3. Walter Kasper contributed to the Malta Report and also signed the *Joint Declaration,* as an official representative of the Catholic Church. He was among the theologians in Germany who, in the 1970s, studied the question as to whether the Catholic Church could recognize the Augsburg Confession as expressing the fundamental Catholic faith, which paved the way for the common statement *All Under One Christ* (1980). He contributed also to the German study on the condemnations, as a member of its Ministry working group. Harding Meyer, besides contributing to the Malta Report and the drafting of the *JD*, participated in the first three phases of international Lutheran-Catholic dialogue, the ecumenical studies on the Augsburg Confession in the 1970s in Germany, and the ecumenical working group in Germany that produced *The Condemnations of the Reformation Era — Do They Still Divide?* (in the Ministry working group). He participated in the *ad hoc* LWF/PCPCU working group that produced *Strategies for Reception* and, with Bishop Pierre Duprey, participated in the program that encouraged the ELCA initiative in 1993 towards declaring unilaterally the sixteenth-century condemnations to no longer apply to the partner (an initiative which the LWF accepted as its own, and in mutual agreement with the PCPCU, began the joint process that led directly to the *JD*). Joseph Fitzmyer, SJ, besides contributing to the Malta Report, and to a 1996 *JD* drafting session, also contributed to *Justification by Faith.* Bishop Hans Martensen, before contributing to the Malta Report, had participated in the joint working group which in 1965-66 had prepared for the international dialogue. He then participated in the first three phases of the international dialogue up to the completion of *Church and Justification* (1994).

4. H. George Anderson (Lutheran) contributed to the USA report *Justification by Faith,* and was one of the LWF Vice-Presidents who signed the *Joint Declaration.*

5. John Reumann (Lutheran) contributed to *Justification by Faith* and took part in the drafting of the *JD*. George Tavard (Catholic) worked on *Justification by Faith* and on the PCPCU response to the Condemnations study, and took part in the first drafting meeting for the *JD*.

The Continuing Attention to Reception
and the Continuing Problem of Reception

Their many contacts and engagements during and after Vatican II enabled the LWF and the Catholic Church to begin to receive one another as brothers and sisters in Christ. From four centuries of mutual rejection since the Reformation, the LWF and the Catholic Church have taken significant steps in recent decades toward mutual respect and friendship, acknowledging that they share important aspects of the apostolic faith. In short, they have moved toward a level of mutual reception anchored in a mutual commitment to an understanding especially of a central aspect of faith — justification — which once divided them. At the same time, they clearly understand that the way toward visible unity and full communion requires the resolution of other significant issues.

The LWF and the PCPCU did not neglect the specific question of the reception of dialogue reports. Mutual steps toward reception were taken shortly after the publication of the Malta Report in 1972. Some reports of the second phase of international dialogue published in the 1980s requested reception, and also practiced it to some degree by receiving and applying in different ways the Malta Report's claim of a "far-reaching consensus" developing on justification. In Catholic circles John Paul II encouraged reception of dialogue results. Cardinal Willebrands discussed the meaning and importance of reception in Catholic settings in the 1970s, and, in significant Lutheran assemblies in the 1980s, described a Catholic understanding of reception. Looking toward official response to dialogue results, the LWF and the PCPCU together published a position paper on reception *(Strategies for Reception)* in 1991.

But reception continued to be a challenge and a problem up to and beyond the publication of the official responses to the *Joint Declaration*. *Strategies for Reception* already suggested difficulties that might be encountered in an official response process as it pointed to the different approaches to reception by the Lutheran World Federation and the Catholic Church. In 1992 each side also raised questions about the other's capacity for reception.

From 1994 to 1997, when the *JD* was being drafted, in order to foster the reception of the declaration and work toward official responses, the LWF and the PCPCU each took steps to see that their respective authorities and constituencies had an opportunity to study initial drafts and to comment on them. Their comments and concerns were seriously taken into account as revised drafts were produced. In shaping the final proposal of the *JD*, produced in 1997, and sent out to the churches early that year for final decision, the Lutheran and Catholic drafting committee had incorporated these various concerns into the final text in the best way possible.

Nonetheless, the difficulties involved in reception were seen in the hesitations about this final version, reflected in the intense debate among Protestant theologians in Germany both before and after the official LWF response was published, and in what appeared to some to be certain hesitations in the official Catholic response, even though it affirmed the *Joint Declaration*'s statement that a high degree of agreement had been reached, and that there is "a consensus in basic truths of the doctrine of justification" (Declaration). Bishop Karl Lehmann's observations (Augsburg City Hall, October 30, 1999) seem useful both to explain those hesitations, and as an alert for future efforts of reception. It takes a long time, he said, "for hundreds of years of attitudes and behaviour to be removed and for a new language, sometimes alien to all concerned, to prove itself." Even the theologians, he said, have been awakened by the *Joint Declaration* "because it is evident that relatively little attention has been paid in many parts to the internal trends and numerous proofs provided by decades of ecumenical work. Official ecumenism had not correctly assessed the tempo, breadth and depth of the necessary reception."

An Achievement for the Ecumenical Movement

The *Joint Declaration* is the most significant achievement thus far of the partnership between the Catholic Church and the Lutheran World Federation, and evidence that the degree of fellowship they share is now deep enough to make a mutual binding commitment to an agreement when it is patiently and properly prepared. Because it illustrates that even a very central issue over which divisions took place in the sixteenth century can be resolved, it gives hope that other dividing issues can be resolved as well. For this reason, the achievement of the *Joint Declaration on the Doctrine of Justification* remains one of the most important developments of the modern ecumenical movement.

The Holy See and Reception of the Joint Declaration, 2000-2006

This study has followed events to the end of the twentieth century with the signing in 1999 of the *Joint Declaration on the Doctrine of Justification*. But it is useful to illustrate, even briefly, some ways in which the Holy See continued to receive the *JD* in the early years of the twenty-first century, the period from 2000 to 2006. Another major development took place in 2006 when the World Methodist Council and its member churches affirmed their fundamental doctrinal agreement with the *Joint Declaration* and officially associated themselves with it.

Continuing Papal Affirmation

During this period, Pope John Paul II and then Pope Benedict XVI continued to affirm the *Joint Declaration* as a milestone in the ecumenical movement.

John Paul II mentioned the *JD* a number of times during his remaining five years of life, often adding other comments supporting efforts for Christian unity. On January 28, 2000, speaking to a plenary meeting of the Congregation for the Doctrine of the Faith (CDF) about the Church's commitment to the restoration of unity, he recalled CDF's contribution to the *Joint Declaration*. "Together with the Pontifical Council for Promoting Christian Unity, you helped to reach the agreement on fundamental truths of the doctrine of justification that was signed on 31 October last year in

Augsburg. Trusting in the help of divine grace," he said, "let us go forward on this journey, even if there are difficulties."[1]

In October 2000, reminding the German ambassador to the Holy See that the Reformation had begun in Germany, the Pope said that he was "pleased to recall the solemn signing of the *Joint Declaration* by representatives of the Catholic Church and the Lutheran World Federation, which took place almost a year ago in Augsburg." He repeated what he said that day: "I see it as a 'milestone on the difficult path to re-establishing full unity among Christians' and . . . a sound basis for further theological research in the ecumenical field and for addressing the remaining problems with a better founded hope of resolving them . . ." (Angelus, 31 October 1999).[2]

In April 2001, addressing German Catholic and Protestant theologians, led by Cardinal Karl Lehmann and Bishop Hartmut Löwe, John Paul again described the *JD* as "a milestone in the ecumenical process."[3] In November 2002, he assured the Lutheran Bishop of Nidaros, Norway, that "[w]e are committed to moving further ahead on the path to reconciliation," and that the *Joint Declaration* "paves the way for more extensive common witness. It brings us a step closer to the full visible unity which is the goal of our dialogue." He prayed that the Lord help us treasure what has been achieved so far, and "sustain us in our efforts to hasten its development into ever broader cooperation."[4]

Three times in 2003, he affirmed that the *Joint Declaration* represents a new level of relationship between Lutherans and Catholics. In January, he described the present time as "a new ecumenical moment in which we can acknowledge a real, if still incomplete, communion," and the *Joint Declaration* is "a concrete sign of this new situation as a 'brotherhood rediscovered.'"[5] In March, he told a visiting ELCA delegation that recently, "we have come to appreciate more deeply the fellowship existing between Lutherans and Catholics, which led to the *Joint Declaration on the Doctrine of*

1. "Address to Congregation for Doctrine of the Faith, January 28, 2000," *IS* 105 (2000): 158. Italian original: *Insegnamenti*, XXIII, 1 (2000): 132.

2. "To Ambassador of Federal Republic of Germany, October 19, 2000," *IS* 106 (2001): 20. German original: *Insegnamenti*, XXIII, 2 (2000): 657.

3. "To Catholic and Evangelical Theologians from Germany, April 3, 2001," *IS* 107 (2001): 58. German original: *Insegnamenti*, XXIV, 1 (2001): 654.

4. "Visit of a Delegation from the Lutheran Diocese of Nidaros (Trondheim), Norway, November 16, 2002," *IS* 111 (2002): 218.

5. "To Ecumenical Delegation from Finland, January 20, 2003," *IS* 112 (2003): 25.

Justification. . . . In that document we are challenged to build on what has already been achieved, fostering more extensively at the local level a *spirituality of communion* marked by prayer and shared witness to the Gospel."[6] In April, he said to the Catholic Bishops' Conference of Scandinavia that the awareness of the common history shared by Christians has given rise to a "rediscovered brotherhood" from which "spring many of the fruits of ecumenical dialogue" such as "joint statements (not least of which is the *Joint Declaration on the Doctrine of Justification*)."[7]

In 2004, addressing a Finnish Lutheran and Catholic delegation that visits Rome in January to celebrate Finland's patron saint, St. Henrik, the Pope expressed his gratitude for ecumenical progress made between Catholics and Lutherans "in the five years since the signing of the *Joint Declaration on the Doctrine of Justification.* A promising sign of this progress on our path to full and visible unity," he said, "has been the establishment of a new dialogue group between Lutherans and Catholics in Finland and Sweden."[8]

John Paul made one of his last statements on ecumenism in January 2005, a few months before his death, to the Finnish Lutheran-Catholic delegation visiting that year. He continued to single out the importance of the *Joint Declaration* in fostering ecumenical progress: "Over the years our dialogue has been strengthened by mutual visits, shared prayers and, *in a particular way,* by the Joint Declaration on Justification."[9]

Both during his last years,[10] and also at his death,[11] several Lutheran

6. "To the Delegation of the Evangelical Lutheran Church in America, March 24, 2003," *IS* 112 (2003): 26.

7. "To Bishops' Conference of Scandinavia, April 5, 2003," *IS* 114 (2003): 161.

8. "Visit of the Delegation from Finland, January 19, 2004," *IS* 115 (2004): 10.

9. "To an Ecumenical Delegation from Finland, January 15, 2005," *IS* 118 (2005): 2 (emphasis mine).

10. Two Lutheran signatories of the *JD* paid tribute to John Paul II. Bishop H. George Anderson, at the end of his term as ELCA Presiding Bishop in 2001, brought to Rome a tribute to Pope John Paul, expressing the ELCA's gratitude to him, for his "untiring efforts to reconcile historic differences between many Christian traditions" and "particularly . . . for the development of the *Joint Declaration on the Doctrine of Justification*" ("Message of the ELCA Presiding Bishop Anderson to Pope John Paul II, September 20, 2001," *IS* 108 [2001]: 163). At the end of his term as LWF President, in 2003, Bishop Christian Krause visited the Pope and expressed gratitude "for all you have contributed to the growth of ecumenical relations between Lutherans and Roman Catholics . . ." recalling especially the *Joint Declaration* ("Visit to Rome of Bishop Dr. Christian Krause, President of the LWF, April 11, 2003," *IS* 113 [2003]: 73).

11. At his death, LWF President Bishop Mark Hanson and General Secretary Dr. Ishmael Noko both paid tribute to the Pope's ecumenical leadership, noting especially the

leaders made public tributes to John Paul II expressing gratitude for his consistent continual support of the *Joint Declaration.*

Pope John Paul II died on April 2, 2005, and Cardinal Joseph Ratzinger was elected Pope on April 19, 2005, taking the name Benedict XVI. He immediately made strong statements about his ecumenical commitment, in his first address as Pope on April 20, speaking to the Cardinals who elected him,[12] and to ecumenical representatives the day after his inauguration.[13]

During 2005-06, Benedict spoke of the *Joint Declaration* on a number of occasions, affirming its achievement. Two references called attention to his own contribution to the *JD's* evolution. Pope Benedict's first visit to Germany in August 2005, to the World Youth Day in Cologne, also included an ecumenical meeting. He recalled, then, Pope John Paul II's first visit to Germany in 1980 (while Ratzinger/Benedict was Archbishop of Munich), when a decisive step towards the *Joint Declaration* was initiated.

> I would like to mention the re-examination of the mutual condemnations, called for by John Paul II during his first visit to Germany. I recall with some nostalgia that first visit. I was able to be present when we were together at Mainz in a fairly small and authentic fraternal circle. Some questions were put to the Pope and he described a broad theological vision in which reciprocity was amply treated.
>
> That colloquium gave rise to an episcopal, that is, a Church commission, under ecclesial responsibility. Finally, with the contribution of theologians it led to the important *Joint Declaration on the Doctrine of*

---

achievement of the *Joint Declaration* during his pontificate (*IS* 118 [2005]: 14 and 13 respectively). The President and the General Secretary of the World Alliance of Reformed Churches, Revd. Dr. Clifton Kirkpatrick and Revd. Dr. Setri Nyomi in their tribute also mentioned the Lutheran-Catholic *Joint Declaration* as among the achievements that they too were grateful for (*IS* 118 [2005]: 14).

12. "That he takes on as his primary task the duty to work tirelessly to rebuild the full and visible unity of all Christ's followers. This is his ambition, his impelling duty." He "is prepared to do everything in his power to promote the fundamental cause of ecumenism." "Initial Message of Pope Benedict XVI, Wednesday, April 20, 2005," *IS* 118 (2005): 27. Latin original: *Insegnamenti di Benedetto XVI*, I, 2005 (Aprile-Dicembre, Città del Vaticano: Libreria Editrice Vaticana, 2006), p. 5.

13. He assured the ecumenical representatives present for that occasion, that "[i]n the footsteps of my Predecessors, especially Paul VI and John Paul II, I feel strongly the need to reassert the irreversible commitment taken by the Second Vatican Council and pursued in recent years." "Address to Ecumenical Representatives, April 25, 2005," *IS* 118 (2005): 28. French original: *Insegnamenti Benedetto XVI*, I (2005): 28.

Justification (1999) and to an agreement on basic issues that had been a subject of controversy since the 16th century.[14]

He referred here to the joint ecumenical commission set up by the German Episcopal Conference and the Council of the Evangelical Church in Germany and co-chaired by himself when Archbishop of Munich, and Bishop Edward Lohse of Hanover. As a result of its first meeting, May 6-7, 1981, Cardinal Ratzinger and Bishop Lohse wrote to the ecumenical study group of Protestant and Catholic theologians (initiated long before by Bishops Jaeger and Stählin) asking it to study the mutual condemnations of the past, saying that there is a conviction that they no longer apply to our partner today, but this "must be established by the churches in binding form."[15] The group's 1986 report, *The Condemnations of the Reformation Era: Do They Still Divide?*, was one of the important resources used in the development of the *Joint Declaration*.

Furthermore, at Cologne, the Pope suggested a theological issue that could be addressed "following the clarification regarding the Doctrine of Justification." While ecclesiological issues and questions regarding ministry are the main obstacles still to be overcome, "the real question is the presence of the Word in the world." He proposed the need to address the combination of Word, witness, and the rule of faith "and consider it as an ecclesiological matter. . . ."[16]

A year later he mentioned his own participation again, at an ecumenical vespers service in Regensburg, during his pastoral visit to Germany, September 9-14, 2006. Referring to "many memories" his visit there evoked, "Obviously I think in particular of the demanding efforts to reach a consensus on justification. I recall all the stages of that process up to the memorable meeting with the late Bishop Hanselmann here in Regensburg — a meeting that contributed decisively to the achievement of the conclu-

14. "Address at Ecumenical Meeting: Cologne, August 19, 2005," *IS* 119 (2005): 90. German original: *Insegnamenti Benedetto XVI,* I (2005): 440-41. Cf. "Documentation," *The Condemnations of the Reformation Era: Do They Still Divide?* (Minneapolis: Fortress Press, 1989), pp. 168-70.

15. "Letter from the two Chairmen of the Joint Ecumenical Commission to the Chairmen and theological Directors of the Ecumenical Study Group of Protestant and Catholic theologians." Cf. "From the Minutes of the First Meeting of the Joint Ecumenical Commission Held in Munich on 6 and 7 May, 1981." Found in "Documentation," pp. 168-70.

16. "Address at Ecumenical Meeting, Cologne, August 19, 2005," p. 91. German original: *Insegnamenti Benedetto XVI,* I (2005): 441-42.

sion."[17] He then made an important pastoral observation. "The agreement on justification," he said, "remains an important task which — in my view — is not yet fully accomplished," because "in theology, justification is an essential theme, but in the life of the faithful today — it seems to me — it is only dimly present." He continued illustrating the need for a rediscovery of God in our midst.[18]

On other occasions in this period Benedict affirmed the importance of the *Joint Declaration*. To a Lutheran World Federation delegation, on November 7, 2005, the Pope referred to the productive and promising results of many years of Lutheran-Catholic dialogue, affirming that "one of the results of this fruitful dialogue is the *Joint Declaration on Justification*, which constitutes a significant milestone on our common path to full visible unity. This is an important achievement." He urged that, "to build on this accomplishment," the remaining differences "regarding this central question of justification" need to be addressed "together with the ways in which God's grace is communicated in and through the Church."[19] In turn LWF President Hanson also affirmed the signing of the *Joint Declaration* as "a significant milestone," and acknowledged Pope Benedict's role in bringing this about: "We are aware of how you yourself, with the support of Pope John Paul II, actively contributed to the fulfilment of this ecumenical landmark."[20]

Pope Benedict underlined the achievement of the *JD* several times in 2006. He said to a Finnish Lutheran and Catholic delegation, January 19, 2006, that "[t]he present Lutheran-Catholic Dialogue Commission in Finland and Sweden builds upon the substantial accomplishment of the *Joint Declaration on Justification*. In the specific context of the Nordic countries

17. "Ecumenical Vespers at Regensburg, September 12, 2006," *IS* 122 (2006): 49. German original: *Insegnamenti Benedetto XVI*, II, 2 (2006): 269. The decisive importance of their meeting in November 1998 is described in Chapter 11 above.

18. "Because of the dramatic events of our time, the theme of mutual forgiveness is felt with increased urgency, yet there is little perception of our fundamental need of God's forgiveness, of our justification by him. . . . Behind this weakening of the theme of justification and of the forgiveness of sins is ultimately a weakening of our relation with God. In this sense, our first task will perhaps be to rediscover in a new way the living God present in our lives, in our time and in our society." "Ecumenical Vespers at Regensburg, September 12, 2006," p. 49.

19. "Visit to Rome by Representatives of the Lutheran World Federation, November 7-8, 2005," *IS* 120 (2005): 160.

20. "Bishop Hanson's Address," *IS* 120 (2005): 161.

the Commission is continuing to study the achievements and practical implications of the *Joint Declaration*. In this way it seeks to address the still-existing differences between Lutherans and Catholics concerning questions of faith and ecclesial life, while maintaining fervent witness to the truth of the Gospel."[21]

Benedict's pastoral visit to Poland, May 25-28, 2006, included an ecumenical service at the Lutheran Church of the Most Holy Trinity in Warsaw. He recalled John Paul II's words there in 1991, that "[t]he challenge that we face is to overcome the obstacles step by step . . . and to grow together" in unity. "Since that encounter," said Pope Benedict, "much has changed. God has granted us to take many steps toward mutual understanding and rapprochement." Among these ecumenical events was "the signing at Augsburg of the *Joint Declaration on the Doctrine of Justification*."[22]

Speaking to the 2006 PCPCU plenary meeting, concerning "progress in reciprocal knowledge, in overcoming prejudices, in the confirmation of certain convergences . . . ," resulting from dialogues with ecclesial communities of the West, the Pope mentioned "in particular the *Joint Declaration on the Doctrine of Justification* which was achieved in the dialogue with the Lutheran World Federation," and he acknowledged the new and important development in 2006, "that for its own part, the World Methodist Council gave its assent to this Declaration."[23]

Pope Benedict affirmed the importance of the World Methodist Council's official initiative to accept the *Joint Declaration* several times, as will be seen below.

Continuing Affirmation of the *Joint Declaration* by the Pontifical Council for Promoting Christian Unity

During 2000-06, the *Joint Declaration* impacted the ongoing work of the Pontifical Council for Promoting Christian Unity in various ways. The Pontifical Council, both in close contact with the Holy Father (cf. above)

21. "To a Finnish Ecumenical Delegation, January 19, 2006," *IS* 121 (2006): 1.

22. "Ecumenical Meeting; May 25, 2006," *IS* 122 (2006): 42. Polish original: *Insegnamenti Benedetto XVI*, II, 1 (2006): 688-89.

23. Plenary Meeting of the Pontifical Council for Promoting Christian Unity, November 13-18, 2006. "Address of Pope Benedict XVI," *IS* 123 (2006): 97. Italian original: *Insegnamenti Benedetto XVI*, II, 2 (2006): 631-32.

and in its own activities, continued to keep the *JD* high on its agenda, aiming to foster awareness and deeper reception of it in the life of the Catholic Church. The PCPCU did some of this in close partnership with the LWF. The two joined in making efforts to foster the interest of other Christian World Communions in the *Joint Declaration*. The impact of the *JD* was felt by other dialogue partners as well.

The significance of the *JD* was consistently upheld. On the occasion of his retirement as PCPCU President in 2001, Cardinal Cassidy described the signing of the *Joint Declaration* as one of "the great moments" for which to be thankful.[24] In his farewell greeting, then, to Cardinal Cassidy, his successor Cardinal Walter Kasper described the achievement of the *Joint Declaration* as "an almost epoch-making turning point."[25] The *Joint Declaration* has caused many Christians to rejoice, Kasper said on another occasion, because "centuries-old polemics and differences which had divided the churches over a central and fundamental point of her message could be overcome through serious ecumenical dialogue."[26]

Writing in *L'Osservatore Romano* during the 2003 Week of Prayer for Christian Unity, Cardinal Kasper listed the "principal milestones" in ecumenical progress since Vatican II as "the abrogation of the excommunications of 1054 between Rome and Constantinople, the Christological declarations with the Ancient Churches of the East, and the *Joint Declaration on the Doctrine of Justification* with the Lutheran World Federation."[27] Also in 2003, Kasper reviewed accomplishments in dialogue, citing and agreeing with Pope John Paul II's description of the *Joint Declaration* as "a milestone." Responding to critics of the *Joint Declaration,* he spoke of its significance in bringing about "a new and deeper dimension and intensity of relations" with Lutherans, "a dimension we do not have with other Protestant denominations." The deeper relationship "enables us to give common witness to the world about the essence of the Gospel: Jesus Christ and his salvific meaning. This in our mostly secularized world is no small

---

24. "Farewell Tribute to Cardinal Cassidy, June 12, 2001," *IS* 107 (2001). Homily by Edward Idris Cardinal Cassidy, p. 51.

25. "Farewell Greeting to His Eminence Edward Idris Cardinal Cassidy by His Eminence Walter Cardinal Kasper, President, *PCPCU*," *IS* 107 (2001): 53.

26. Plenary Meeting of the Pontifical Council for Promoting Christian Unity, November 12-17, 2001, "Prolusio of Cardinal Walter Kasper," *IS* 109 (2002): 12.

27. Walter Cardinal Kasper, "The Priority of Prayer," *IS* 112 (2003): 8. Italian original in *L'Osservatore Romano,* January 19, 2003.

thing."[28] Cardinal Kasper, referring to the important elements of the true church, such as the proclamation of the Word of God, and baptism, in which the Catholic Church is linked with Reformation communities, asserted that these commonalities "have been extended and intensified" in many dialogue documents such as BEM, ARCIC reports, and others, and "especially the *Joint Declaration on Justification*."[29] He also used the *Joint Declaration* as a reference point in light of which other events are presented. *"After* the *Joint Declaration,"* Cardinal Kasper said, "the dialogues continue to progress, albeit slowly, yet seriously, within the context of positive relations."[30]

The *Joint Declaration* made some impact in regard to the PCPCU's relationship with ecumenical partners, first of all, of course, with the Lutheran World Federation. LWF President Bishop Christian Krause claimed the *Joint Declaration* resulted in a "special link" between the two and that "Roman Catholics and Lutherans in many places around the world now see each other in quite a new way as sisters and brothers in the faith."[31] As if to express that "special link," they acted together on some occasions. On the fifth anniversary of the *Joint Declaration* in 2004 Cardinal Kasper and LWF General Secretary Noko together sent a letter to Catholics and Lutherans reminding their constituencies that, as a result of the *Joint Declaration*, "we can give common witness to the essence of the Gospel," and that in a world of growing secularization how important it was for Christians to "be able to testify together to peace and reconciliation which belong at the heart of the Christian message."[32] They called for celebrations, made suggestions for renewed study around the world of what has been achieved, and reiterated that further work still needed to be done, including reflection on "the significance of the gospel of justification in the life of

---

28. Walter Cardinal Kasper, "The Current Situation in Ecumenical Theology," February 26, 2003, at the "Inauguration of the Tillard Chair of Ecumenical Studies at the Angelicum University," *IS* 114 (2003): 192.

29. "Decree on Ecumenism: Read Anew After Forty Years." Opening address of Cardinal Kasper at the Symposium on the 40th Anniversary of *Unitatis redintegratio*, November 11-13, 2004, *IS* 118 (2005): 36, including note 25.

30. "Introductory Report of the President, Cardinal Walter Kasper" to the PCPCU Plenary, November 3-8, 2003, *IS* 115 (2004): 28 (emphasis mine).

31. "Greetings by Bishop Krause, to Pope John Paul II, April 11, 2003," *IS* 113 (2003): 72.

32. "Fifth Anniversary of the *Joint Declaration on the Doctrine of Justification*. Letter of Cardinal Kasper and Dr. Noko, Geneva and Rome, February 6, 2004," *IS* 115 (2004): 9.

the church." They pointed to significant events during these five years. One very significant initiative mentioned was that:

> In 2001, for the first time, Lutherans and Catholics invited others, Methodist and Reformed, to a consultation on "Unity in Faith — The Joint Declaration on the Doctrine of Justification in a Wider Ecumenical Context." This consultation considered how other Communions could relate to the agreements reached in the *Joint Declaration*. As a result, a theologically substantiated affirmation of the *Joint Declaration* is being prepared by the World Methodist Council.[33]

The letter also mentioned that, in light of concerns expressed by some Lutherans and Reformed in regard to the matter of indulgences in the Jubilee Year 2000, the PCPCU together with the LWF and WARC had organized a symposium in 2001 on the meaning of indulgences today.[34]

During this same period, the Lutheran-Catholic international dialogue continued to mention the *Joint Declaration* in its annual press release after dialogue sessions.[35]

The Baptist World Alliance, too, showed interest. For an informal two-day consultation sponsored by the BWA and PCPCU in Rome, December 2003, the BWA asked that the *Joint Declaration on the Doctrine of Justification* be one of two topics discussed. After a Catholic theologian discussed the background, development, and principal content of the *JD*, two Baptist scholars gave excellent analyses of the *JD*.[36] The BWA, however, took no further step in this regard.

But the World Methodist Council took a decisive step. Cardinal Kasper, in his message to Methodists in 2003 during the ongoing three hundredth anniversary celebrations that year of John Wesley's birth, mentioned specifically how "greatly encouraged" he was by the current initiative of the WMC to associate its member churches with the *Joint Declaration*.[37]

---

33. "Fifth Anniversary of the *Joint Declaration on the Doctrine of Justification*," pp. 9-10. An Anglican observer was also present.

34. "Fifth Anniversary of the *Joint Declaration on the Doctrine of Justification*," p. 10. This was the first time the three communions held a meeting on indulgences.

35. See, for example, press releases of the Lutheran-Catholic Commission of Unity in 2002 (*IS* 110 [2002]: 181); 2004 (*IS* 116 [2004]: 136); and 2005 (*IS* 119 [2005]: 143).

36. "Meeting Sponsored by the Baptist World Alliance and the Pontifical Council for Promoting Christian Unity, December 5-6, 2003," *IS* 114 (2003): 198-99.

37. "Message from Cardinal Walter Kasper on the Occasion of the 225th Anniversary of

World Methodist Council Affirms the *Joint Declaration,* 2006

Formal agreement on this once-divisive Reformation issue spread when the World Methodist Council and its member churches formally affirmed their fundamental doctrinal agreement with the teaching expressed in the *Joint Declaration on the Doctrine of Justification,* thus associating themselves with the Lutheran World Federation and the Catholic Church.[38] This was a major step for the wider ecumenical movement as well.

The WMC began to consider this step already in 1999, resolving to send congratulations to the LWF and the Catholic Church at the signing of the *JD* in Augsburg, and resolving to explore with them the possibility of the WMC becoming officially associated with it. In 2001 the Lutheran World Federation and the Catholic Church invited the WMC into a discussion about this.[39] They accompanied the WMC in the process that led to the WMC's official association with the *Joint Declaration* at its Assembly in 2006. The Assembly affirmed a *Methodist Statement of Association with the Joint Declaration on the Doctrine of Justification,* which declared that the common understanding of justification in the *JD* corresponds to Methodist doctrine. It accepted, furthermore, the Lutheran and Catholic explanations of the crucial issues in the doctrine of justification that had been disputed between them at the time of the Reformation, finding their diverse emphases not sufficient cause for division. And, it also presented Methodist teaching on issues related to justification. An *Official Common Affirmation* was signed by the three partners, with Cardinal Walter Kasper and Cardinal Soo-Luwan Kim signing for the Catholic Church.[40] The *Official Common Affirmation* states that the signing partners of the *Joint Dec-*

Wesley's Chapel and the Ongoing Celebration of the 300th Anniversary of John Wesley's Birth, November 2, 2003," *IS* 114 (2003): 185.

A staff report to the PCPCU plenary of November 3-8, 2003, gave a detailed account of the origin of the WMC initiative, including Methodist participants in the consultation "Unity in Faith" mentioned in Kasper and Noko's letter (which took place in Columbus, Ohio), and content of a draft statement they were preparing. "Methodist-Catholic Relations, 2001-2003," *IS* 115 (2004): 56-59.

38. For the basic documentation on this, see "The Affirmation of the *Joint Declaration on the Doctrine of Justification* by the World Methodist Council, Seoul, South Korea, 23 July 2006," *IS* 122 (2006): 55-60.

39. For a concise description of the steps taken, see Geoffrey Wainwright, "The Methodist Process of Becoming Associated with the Joint Declaration," in *IS* 122 (2006): 55-56.

40. These two statements found in *IS* 122 (2006): 56-58.

laration welcome this action of the World Methodist Council and its member churches and that "the three parties commit themselves to strive together for the deepening of their common understanding of justification in theological study, teaching, and preaching."

There has been papal support for this development. Just as Pope John Paul II accompanied the *Joint Declaration* process in the 1990s with supporting statements (see Chapter 11), so too Pope Benedict XVI has supported this recent process. He told a World Methodist Council delegation in 2005 that "I have been encouraged by the initiative which would bring the member churches of the World Methodist Council into association with the *Joint Declaration on the Doctrine of Justification,* signed by the Catholic Church and the Lutheran World Federation in 1999." He expressed the importance of this step: "Should the World Methodist Council express its intent to associate itself with the *Joint Declaration,* it would assist in contributing to the healing and reconciliation we ardently desire, and would be a significant step towards the stated goal of full visible unity in faith."[41] Soon after the WMC took that step in July 2006, the Pope expressed his approval again. Referring to the *Joint Declaration* in an address in Regensburg, Germany, in September 2006, he stated that "I am pleased to see that . . . the World Methodist Council has adhered to the Declaration."[42] And in November 2006, referring to ecumenical progress in an address to a PCPCU plenary meeting, and singling out "in particular the *Joint Declaration on the Doctrine of Justification,*" he could add now "the fact that for its own part, the World Methodist Council gave its assent to this Declaration."[43]

This brief survey of the first six years after the signing shows that the interest of the Holy See in the *Joint Declaration* remains high, and that significant progress in its reception has been made.

---

41. His address in "Visit to Rome by Representatives of the World Methodist Council, December 4-10, 2005," *IS* 120 (2005): 163.

42. "Ecumenical Vespers in Regensburg, September 12, 2006," *IS* 122 (2006): 49. German original: *Insegnamenti Benedetto XVI,* II, 2 (2006): 269.

43. "Address of Pope Benedict XVI" (November 17), *IS* 123 (2006): 97. Italian original: *Insegnamenti Benedetto XVI,* II, 2 (2006): 631-32.

Index

Aarflot, Andreas, 48, 88, 128

All Under One Christ: Statement on the Augsburg Confession by the Roman Catholic/Lutheran Joint Commission (1980), 57n.6, 58-59, 60, 61, 66, 68n.7, 69n.13, 74, 195, 197n.3

Anderson, H. George (Bishop), 144, 154n.8, 180, 202n.10, 197n.4

Appel, Andre, 36

Arnoldshain Conference, 134

Augsburg Confession, 58-60, 74, 77; mentioned at *Joint Declaration* signing, 171, 173, 178, 179; possible Catholic recognition of, 66-68. *See also* John Paul II: and Augsburg Confession

Baum, William (Msgr.), 25n.33

Bea, Augustin, S.J. (Cardinal), 3, 31, 49, 50, 52, 193; correspondence with LWF President Schiotz, 32-33; new Lutheran-Catholic joint working group, 23, 25; and Vatican II observers, 7, 8, 10, 27-28. *See also* John XXIII: acknowledging the role of Vatican II observers; Secretariat for Promoting Christian Unity (SPCU)

Becker, Karl, S.J., 139n.22

Benedict XVI: affirmation of *Joint Declaration*, 203-6; affirms World Methodist Council association with *Joint Declaration*, 206, 211; recalls Regensburg meeting with Bishop Hanselmann, 204. *See also* Ratzinger, Joseph

Bensheim Institute for Interconfessional Research, 147, 154n.16

Bläser, Peter, M.S.C., 25n.23, 33n.12

Brand, Eugene, 137n.12, 138n.17, 139n.22, 174

Brauer, Jerald C., 5n.12, 25n.33, 32, 50-51n.33

Cassidy, Edward Idris (Cardinal), 125-27, 144, 194, 209; explains official Catholic response to *JD*, 155, 156-58; resolves obstacles to the signing, 161n.31, 164-66; signs the *Joint Declaration* in Augsburg, 168-70, 171, 175, 179-80. *See also Joint Declaration on the Doctrine of Justification*

Church and Justification: Understanding the Church in the Light of the Doc-

Lutheran–Roman Catholic coopera-
tion; Lutheran–Roman Catholic dia-
logue; Reception of dialogue reports;
Second Vatican Council; Secretariat
for Promoting Christian Unity
(SPCU)
Root, Michael, 139n.22
Runcie, Robert (Archbishop), 88, 96
Rusch, William G., 97, 132n.2

Scharbau, Friedrich-Otto, 168n.2
Scheele, Paul Werner (Bishop), 87,
139n.21, 139n.22, 168n.2
Schiotz, Frederick A., 32-33, 49
Schlink, Edmund, 5n.13, 6, 8, 21-23, 26,
190
Schmidt-Clausen, Kurt, 25n.33
Schutte, Heinz, 161n.32, 162n.36, 162n.37,
175
Scripture, ecumenical importance of,
36, 73, 94
Second Vatican Council, 3-28; fostering
Lutheran-Catholic relations, 3, 18-20,
27, 31, 32-37, 188-90, 192; *Humanae
salutis* (papal document convening
Vatican II), 4; Lutheran observers at
the Council, 4, 5n.12, 5n.13; Lutheran
observers' influence on the Council,
8-9, 11-13, 16-18, 27-28, 189; Lutheran
observers' influence on LWF after the
Council, 19-20, 23-24, 32-33, 48-51,
51n.33, 51n.34, 51n.35, 109
Secretariat for Promoting Christian
Unity (SPCU; from 1988 Pontifical
Council; later renamed Pontifical
Council for Promoting Christian
Unity [PCPCU]), 3, 4-5, 7, 31, 191-92;
PCPCU continuing affirmation of
the *Joint Declaration*, 206-9; study
commission on *Lehrverurteilungen
— Kirchentrennend?*, 129n.52-30, 133-
35; subcommission with Congrega-
tion for the Doctrine of the Faith

concerning the *Joint Declaration*, 138-
40. *See also* Holy See
Silen, Sven, 5n.12
Skydsgaard, Kristen, 5n.12, 10, 11, 16n.1,
19-20, 24, 25n.33, 32, 49n.30, 50-51n.33,
51n.35, 117
Staack, Hagen A. K., 5n.12
Stålsett, Gunnar, 88, 89, 96, 114, 123-24,
136
Stier, Christoph (Bishop), 144
Stransky, Thomas F., C.S.P., 7n.26, 8-9,
16-17

Tantur Ecumenical Institute, 10, 49
Tavard, George, 137n.12, 174, 197n.5
Teinonen, Seppo Antero, 5n.12
Telewoda, Susannah, 88
Track, Joachim, 162n.36, 162n.37, 172,
174-75
Trent, Council of, 26, 134, 157-58, 190
Türk, Matthias, 166n.48

Ullrich, Lothar, 137n.12, 138n.17, 139n.21,
139n.22, 174
United Lutheran Church in Germany-
VELKD, 134, 147
U.S. Lutheran–Roman Catholic Coordi-
nating Committee, 135-36

Vajta, Vilmos, 5n.12, 20, 24, 25n.33, 32,
50-51n.33, 51n.34, 51n.35, 189-90
Vatican II. *See* Second Vatican Council
Verschuren, Paul (Bishop), 101
Vikström, John (Archbishop), 86, 101,
128
Volk, Herman (Bishop), 25n.23

Wendebourg, D., 139n.2
Wenz, Günther, 167
Werkström, Bertil (Archbishop), 100,
128, 139n.2
Wicks, Jared, S.J., 139n.22, 155n.21,
161n.32
Willebrands, Johannes (Cardinal), 3, 5,

25n.33, 34, 36, 38-39, 48, 52, 67-68, 114, 125, 193-94; and justification, 39, 48, 52, 98, 193-94; and Luther, 35, 39-40, 59, 70, 72-74, 194; and reception, 43-44, 78, 92-93, 103-7, 198

Witte, Johannes, S.J., 25n.33, 33n.12
World Council of Churches, 3, 4, 17, 23, 171, 172
World Methodist Council (WMC), and the *Joint Declaration,* 200, 209-11